Lecture Notes in Computer Science 2255

Edited by G. Goos, J. Hartmanis, and J. van Leeuwen

W0246063

Springer
Berlin
Heidelberg
New York
Barcelona
Hong Kong
London
Milan
Paris
Tokyo

John Dean   Andrée Gravel (Eds.)

COTS-Based
Software Systems

First International Conference, ICCBSS 2002
Orlando, FL, USA, February 4-6, 2002
Proceedings

Springer

Series Editors

Gerhard Goos, Karlsruhe University, Germany
Juris Hartmanis, Cornell University, NY, USA
Jan van Leeuwen, Utrecht University, The Netherlands

Volume Editors

John Dean
National Research Council Canada, Software Engineering Group
1600 Montreal Road, Ottawa, Ontario, Canada, K1A 0R6
E-mail: John.Dean@nrc.ca
Andrée Gravel
Université du Québec à Hull, Pavillon Lucien Brault
101, rue Saint-Jean-Bosco, Hull, Québec, Canada, J8X 3X7
E-mail: Andree.Gravel@nrc.ca

Cataloging-in-Publication Data applied for

Die Deutsche Bibliothek - CIP-Einheitsaufnahme

COTS based software systems : first international conference ; proceedings /
ICCBSS 2002, Orlando, FL, USA, February 4 - 6, 2002. John Dean ; Andrée
Gravel (ed.). - Berlin ; Heidelberg ; New York ; Barcelona ; Hong Kong ;
London ; Milan ; Paris ; Tokyo : Springer, 2002
   (Lecture notes in computer science ; Vol. 2255)
   ISBN 3-540-43100-4

CR Subject Classification (1998): K.6.3, D.2, J.1

ISSN 0302-9743
ISBN 3-540-43100-4 Springer-Verlag Berlin Heidelberg New York

Springer-Verlag Berlin Heidelberg New York
a member of BertelsmannSpringer Science+Business Media GmbH

http://www.springer.de

© Springer-Verlag Berlin Heidelberg 2002
Printed in Germany

Typesetting: Camera-ready by author, data conversion by PTP-Berlin, Stefan Sossna
Printed on acid-free paper   SPIN: 10846018   06/3142   5 4 3 2 1 0

Foreword

Modern software systems increasingly use commercial-off-the-shelf (COTS) software products as building blocks. In some cases, major software systems are assembled with virtually no custom code in the system.

The use of COTS software products as components offers the promise of rapid delivery to end users, shared development costs with other customers, and an opportunity for expanding mission or business capabilities and performance as improvements are made in the commercial marketplace. Few organizations today can afford the resources and time to replicate market-tested capabilities. Yet, the promise of COTS products is too often not realized in practice. There have been more failures than successes in using COTS software products.

The research and software practitioner communities have been working with COTS-based software systems for a number of years. There is now sufficient documented experience in the community to collect, analyze, and disseminate success stories, common failings, lessons-learned, and research advances. The mounting experience shows that the effective use of COTS software products in major software systems demands new skills, knowledge, and abilities, changed roles and responsibilities, and different techniques and processes.

The International Conference on COTS-Based Software Systems (ICCBSS) focuses on the challenges of building and maintaining systems that incorporate COTS software products. The conference sponsors, the National Research Council Canada, the Software Engineering Institute, and the University of Southern California Center for Software Engineering, aim to bring together managers, developers, maintainers, and researchers to share their expertise and experience. ICCBSS 2002 in Orlando, Florida, USA is the first of an annual series of conferences devoted to the building, fielding, and evolution of COTS-based software systems.

The conference series has made an impressive start. For ICCBSS 2002, papers were submitted from the USA, Canada, Europe, the Middle East, Africa, Australia, and Asia. The standard of the papers was very high, and the program committee found it difficult to reduce the number to fit into the conference schedule. These proceedings provide a broad picture of the state of practice and research in the use of COTS software products.

We look forward to a stimulating first conference, and a successful ICCBSS conference series.

February 2002   Lisa Brownsword

ICCBSS 2002 Organization

Planning Committee

General Chair:	Lisa Brownsword
	Software Engineering Institute
Conference Coordinator:	Barb Hoerr
	Software Engineering Institute
Poster Chair:	Chris Abts
	Center for Software Engineering
Proceedings Chair:	John Dean
	National Research Council Canada
Program Co-chairs:	Scott Hissam
	Software Engineering Institute
	Mark Vigder
	National Research Council Canada
Publicity Chairs:	Terese Fiedler
	Software Engineering Institute
	Fred Long
	The University of Wales, Aberystwyth
	Ed Morris
	Software Engineering Institute

Program Committee

Program Committee Co-chairs:
Scott A. Hissam, Software Engineering Institute
Mark Vigder, National Research Council, Canada

Chris Abts	University of Southern California
David P. Bentley	Colonel, USAF, Material Systems Group
Joe Besselman	Major, USAF,
	Logistics Systems Modernization
Frank Bott	University of Wales, Aberystwyth, UK
Alan Brown	Catapulse, Inc.
Daniel Dumas	IBM Belgium Software Group, Belgium
Anthony N. Earl	Sun Microsystems Inc.
Hakan Erdogmus	National Research Council, Canada
Rose F. Gamble	University of Tulsa
Anatol Kark	National Research Council, Canada
Fred Long	University of Wales, Aberystwyth, UK
Cornelius Ncube	Zayed University, UAE
Patricia Oberndorf	Software Engineering Institute

James R. Odrowski   Sprint PCS
Robert C. Seacord   Software Engineering Institute
Nguyen NQ. THUY   Electricité de France, France
Will Tracz   Lockheed Martin Federal Systems
Jeffrey Voas   Cigital

Keynote Speakers

Dr. Ivar Jacobson
Vice President of e-development
Rational Software Corporation

Dr. Barry Boehm
TRW Professor of Software Engineering
Computer Science Department Director, USC Center for Software Engineering

David Baum
Principal Engineer, Motorola Labs

Mike Moore
Deputy Manager, Science System Development Office, ESDIS Project
NASA Goddard Space Flight Center

Sponsoring Institutions

Software Engineering Institute

The Software Engineering Institute (SEI) provides leadership in advancing the state of software engineering practice. We collaborate with industry, academia, and the government to learn about the best technical and management practices and then use what we learn to benefit the software engineering community.

The institute is based at Carnegie Mellon University and is sponsored by the U.S. Office of the Under Secretary of Defense for Acquisition, Technology, and Logistics [OUSD (AT&L)].

Learn more about the SEI at `http://www.sei.cmu.edu`.

National Research Council Canada

The National Research Council (NRC), Canada's premier science and technology research organization, is a leader in scientific and technical research, the diffusion of technology, and the dissemination of scientific and technical information.

Working in partnership with innovative companies, universities, and research organizations, NRC enhances Canada's social and economic well-being and creates new opportunities for Canadians. Through knowledge, research, and innovation, NRC and its partners are expanding the frontiers of science and technology.

Learn more about the NRC at `http://www.nrc.ca`.

USC Center for Software Engineering and CeBASEC-CSE

The USC Center for Software Engineering (USC-CSE) focuses its research and teaching efforts toward helping industry and government address multiple new challenges of concern to software system procurers, developers, and users. We work in partnership with the members of our Affiliates' Program, which includes some two dozen organizations representing a mix of commercial industry, aerospace, government, nonprofit FFRDCs, and consortia. The Center for Software Engineering is based at the University of Southern California.

Learn more about USC-CSE at `http://sunset.usc.edu`.

Panels

Building Survivable Systems from COTS Components: An Impossible Dream?
Moderator: Nancy Mead, Software Engineering Institute
Panelists: Joe Besselman, USAF; Nancy Mead and Howard Lipson, Software Engineering Institute; and Jeff Voas, Cigital

Much of the literature on COTS-based systems and the license agreements for COTS products concede that such systems are not suitable for critical applications for business, government, and defense. However, COTS-based systems are already being used in domains where significant economic damage and loss of life are possible. Can we ever build such systems so that the risks associated with using COTS components in critical applications are commensurate with those typically taken in other areas of life and commerce? Building survivable systems using COTS components is a daunting task because the design team typically has little or no access to the artifacts of the software engineering process used to create the components. These artifacts are the primary sources from which assurance evidence for a composite system is derived, and lack of direct access to the artifacts greatly increases the risks of building critical applications. The key question to be addressed is this: Can those who acquire, design, implement, operate, maintain, or evolve systems that use COTS components adequately manage the risks of using these components in critical applications? This panel will debate if, when, and how COTS components can be used to build survivable systems and discuss strategies for risk mitigation.

COTS Test Strategy
Moderator: Christina Laiacona, BASF Corporation
Panelists: John Dean, National Research Council; William Perry, Quality Assurance Institute; and Randall Rice, Rice Consulting Services

One of the pressures created by COTS applications is the paradigm shift for new testing strategies. This spirited panel discussion will begin the dialogue on COTS Test Strategy for product evaluation, deployment, and maintenance. The following questions will be addressed during the session:

- What are the testing considerations for a COTS Product Evaluation?
- What are the management processes and people considerations of a testing strategy for COTS applications?
- Are there different approaches to testing COTS applications according to the development risk of the systems' ability to capture, create, store, manage, and archive trustworthy data?
- What are the considerations for surveillance/maintenance of COTS systems in a production environment?

Once Burned - Forever Learned - Vendors Be Warned
Moderator: Will Tracz Ph.D., Lockheed Martin Systems Integration
Panelists: Tom Baker, The Boeing Company; Anthony Earl, Sun Microsystems
Inc.; and Ronald J. Kohl, Titan Systems Company

Some people want COTS-based solutions in the worst way. Unfortunately, as we
all know, sometimes they get what they want (i.e., an unpleasant experience).
COTS venders have a checkered reputation for meeting expectations in terms
of component documentation, functionality, quality, and interoperability. The
less than successful use of COTS components cannot always be blamed on user
inexperience, lack of process, or unrealistic expectations (though all three reasons
are applicable more often than not).

Given the market pressures (and maybe a little economic greed), COTS vendors sometimes deliver products with less than perfect documentation, poorly
understood feature interaction, and insufficiently tested interoperability with all
possible permutations of other components (and versions of those components),
presenting the buyer with an impossible task. Besides most vendors have a vested interest in expanding the scope of their products so as to make obsolete the
need to integrate other vendor components with theirs. Finally, some vendors
have assured their customers that bugs will be fixed in the next release of the
system, for free (which is why there are maintenance fees).

The goal of this panel is to identify, based on personal experience, the gaps
between the marketing hype and actual reality of using COTS components and
to come up with a prioritized list of recommendations for COTS vendors. COTS
components are a means to an end and not necessarily an end in themselves.
The user community will continue to waste resources, duplicating efforts until
these issues are resolved.

Poster Sessions

Title: **"Towards a COTS-Aware Requirements Engineering Process"**
Presenters' Names: Lawrence Chung and Kendra Cooper (University of Texas, Dallas)

Title: **"Software Components – Enabling a Mass Market"**
Presenters' Names: Pearl Brereton, Stephen Linkman, Adel Taweel, and Stuart Thomason (all Keele University, UK); Uwe Anders (Tuev Nord, Germany), Jorgen Boegh (Delta, Denmark), Alberto Pasquini (Enea, Italy), Nigel Thomas (Durham University, UK)

Title: **"Reusing COTS Technology in Embedded Weapons Systems"**
Presenters' Names: Jamie Durbin and James Briggs (Lockheed Martin Co.)

Title: **"The Software Spectrum: A Shopper's Guide to COTS, Open Source and Custom Built Software"**
Presenters' Names: Tricia Oberndorf (SEI) and Ron Kohl (Titan)

Title: **"Extended Component Architecture and Maintenance: A Process for Supporting Component-Based Development"**
Presenters' Names: Gerald Kotonya, Walter Onyino, John Hutchinson, Pete Sawyer (all Lancaster University, UK); Joan Canal Gonfaus, Marcel Ubach Miralda, Francisco Mateo Goma (all CCS, Spain); Domenico Presenza, Luigi Briguglio (all ING, Italy)

Title: **"Layered Architecture for Deployment and Assembly of Commercial Business Components"**
Presenters' Names: Hemant Jain and Tata Professors (University of Wisconsin, Milwaukee)

Title: **"MBASE/CeBASE COTS Integration Framework"**
Presenters' Names: Dan Port and Barry Boehm (University of Southern California)

Title: **"A Software Assurance Paradigm for Commercial Off The Shelf (COTS) Software Products for Mission Critical Systems"**
Presenter's Name: Louis Blazy (NASA)

Title: **"Defining Software Measurements"**
Presenter's Name: Bruce Hofman (Continuous Improvement Methods)

Table of Contents

COTS-Based Systems (CBS) Functional Density – A Heuristic for Better CBS Design

Chris Abts

University of Southern California
Salvatori Hall Room 328
941 W. 37th Place
Los Angeles, CA 90089 USA
cabts@sunset.usc.edu

Abstract. The conventional rationale for using COTS (commercial off-the-shelf) components is that the more a software system is built from COTS products, the lower the cost of initial development. Less understood is that during the long term sustainment phase – from deployment through retirement – the cost of maintenance of a COTS-based system generally increases as the number of COTS products used increases. There exists then a tension between the imperative to maximize the use of COTS components to ease CBS development yet minimize the use of COTS components to ease CBS maintenance. A heuristic called the "CBS Functional Density Rule" is proposed to reconcile these two conflicting views. A corresponding metric for characterizing the "efficiency" of a given CBS design relative to another called the "COTS Functional Density" is then suggested. The paper concludes with suggestions for additional research to further validate the empirical foundations of the proposed heuristic and associated metric.

1   CBS Economics - The Conventional View

In the past decade, the total annual value of dollars spent on software around the globe has continued to skyrocket. In 1993, that number (excluding related software services) was estimated to be minimally some $70 billion [1] – by 2002, that number is predicted to balloon to over $127 billion [2]. If you consider software goods and related software service industries together, the trend is even more dramatic. In 1981, global expenditures for the combination were already at $30 billion – by 1995, they exceeded $400 billion [3]. Looked at another way, in 1970, the average size of a software system was about 25 thousand source lines of code. In 1996, the average size had grown to 1.25 million sloc [4].

During that same period, it is estimated that at most 5% of all software projects worldwide were completed on time and within budget – even worse, upwards of 75% of software projects initiated either were *never* completed, or were completed too late to be of any value [5].

The trend implied by the increasing dollars spent on software coupled with the consistently high rates of software project overruns and cancellations is not encouraging.

J. Dean and A. Gravel (Eds.): ICCBSS 2002, LNCS 2255, pp. 1–9, 2002.
© Springer-Verlag Berlin Heidelberg 2002

The cost of failure is growing, and the likelihood of failure does *not* seem to be diminishing – which truth be told is old news. We're now some *thirty* years into the so-called "software crisis". It seems rather specious at this late date to even be referring to a three-decade-old problem as a "crisis". The condition ailing the "body productive" of the software industry is chronic, not acute, and what we have is a software pathology, not a crisis.

As Brooks predicted fifteen years ago, our rescue from this chronic condition does not lie in a radical dose of a miracle cure [6]. Rather, it will be found in the judicious application of a combination of new approaches and technologies. Used individually, these may offer only incremental improvements in software developer productivity, software quality, and long term system sustainability. When taken together, however, they can offer more than incremental systemic improvements in the way we build software.

One of the most significant approaches widely adopted in the last two decades that absolutely represents a systemic change in the way large software systems are created is the now widespread use of commercial-off-the-shelf (COTS) components as system elements. It is likely that not a single large scale software system on the drawing boards today is being designed without the incorporation of at least one COTS component – and probably several.

[There are many flavors of "off-the-shelf" (OTS) components: COTS (commercial OTS), GOTS (government OTS), ROTS ("research" OTS), GFE (government furnished equipment), NDI (non-developmental item); from a technical point-of-view (barring specific procurement and licensing issues), the term "COTS" generally can be considered to encompass all of these as long as a given item is acquired from a third party or outside organization, was not designed specifically for your use, and you have no control over how that item will evolve in the future. Also, vendors can supply COTS software as either "black box" executables or as "white box" uncompiled source code. For the purposes of this paper, however, with respect to "white box" COTS, if a developer does anything to that code other than compile it unexamined and unchanged into his own code, such an item is considered adapted or reused code rather than a true OTS component and thus lies largely outside the scope of this discussion.]

Contrary to what a few may have once believed, however, when compared to building from scratch, COTS solutions aren't necessarily free.

Less than a decade ago, there was perhaps an overeager hope among some software procurers that the COTS approach to building software systems might indeed be – if not Brooks' magic bullet – then at least a very strong prescriptive for containing the software beast. The closer one got to the executive levels far removed from the nuts-and-bolts grind of getting COTS solutions to work, the stronger this hope seems to have become. Policies were established strongly favoring COTS-based systems over in-house development [7]; contracts were reportedly let mandating required levels of COTS supplied functionality; the prevailing attitude was "the more COTS components the better, since it means the less we have to build ourselves".

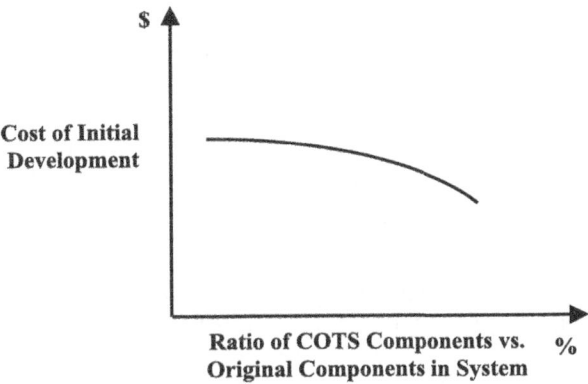

Fig. 1. The conventional view of CBS economics

The flaw in that logic was in not realizing that "not building" did *not* mean "not developing", only developing *differently*. The COTS approach requires effort be spent on tasks different from those that would be encountered if building from scratch, but these new tasks are not necessarily less time consuming. These include assessing and verifying purported capabilities of COTS products via extensive testing (both individually and in combinations of components that must work together), tailoring the components to work in the specific context needed, and creating binding-ware or glue code to plug the components into the overall system. There are also a host of other tasks that must be tackled, including COTS product licensing and vendor management, training of both system developers and end-users, addressing issues of legal liability exposure, etc.

Due to the hard-earned wisdom gained by early adopters of the COTS approach and which is now being shared with others [8,9], it is better understood today that the most frequently encountered scenario when adopting the COTS approach is that effort is time-shifted rather than significantly reduced. That is, initial and prototype systems constructed with COTS elements can often be developed and fielded more quickly than systems built entirely from scratch, but final system testing and post-delivery maintenance and long term sustainment can be highly challenging.

The conventional view of the economic benefits of using the COTS approach to software system development is shown then in Fig. 1. What is missing from this picture is a fully-realized understanding of the significant work that can be required to select, install and configure COTS components that provide the functionality needed, while at the same time providing enough assurances that the components will operate as intended, thus mitigating to an acceptable level your risk of unforeseen project difficulties and possibly even ultimate project failure.

2   CBS Economics - The COTS-LIMO View

There is an alternative view towards the economics of COTS-based software systems to the one discussed above. Anecdotal evidence collected during data collection interviews performed to gather calibration data for the COCOTS [10] COTS integration cost estimation model extension of COCOMO II [11] suggests that generally – though granted not universally – the more COTS software components you include in your overall software system, the shorter the *economic* life will be of that system, particularly if doing present-worth analyses comparing alternative designs using various combinations of COTS components, or when comparing COTS-based designs to simply building the entire system from scratch.

The reason is due to the volatility of COTS components. "Volatility" in this case means the frequency with which vendors release new versions of their products and the significance of the changes in those new versions (i.e., minor upgrades vs. major new releases). When you first deploy your system, you of course have selected a suite of components that will provide the functionality you require while at the same time work in concert with each other. Over time, however, those products will likely evolve in different directions in response to the market place, in some cases even disappearing from the market all together. As a consequence, the ability of these diverging products to continue functioning adequately together if and when you install the newer versions will likely also become more problematic; the more COTS components you have, the more severe the consequences of these increasing incompatibilities will become.

These ideas are expressed in something called the COTS-LIMO (COTS-Life span Model) which can be seen in Fig. 2 [12]. As is seen in the figure, the graph is broken into two regions bisected by the line **n**. As long as the number of COTS components in the system is less than **n**, the increase in experience gained by your system maintainers over time and thus the inherent improvements in their productivity will outpace the increased effort required to maintain the system as the COTS products it contains age and evolve in divergent directions. However, at some number of installed COTS components **n**, the breakeven point is surpassed and no matter how skilled and experienced your maintainers become, the increases in their efficiency at maintaining the system can no longer keep pace with the impact of the increasing incompatibilities arising in the evolving COTS components. At this point you have reached the zone in which the useful life of your system has been shortened considerably and a decision to retire the system will soon have to be made.

The actual value of **n**, the specific shape of the individual contour lines, and the location of the M-R (maintain-retire) line will be highly context sensitive, differing for each software system under review. Also, even though the model as shown uses the raw number of COTS components as the primary decision variable, in fact this is really just a surrogate for some measure of the complexity of the interfaces between the various COTS items in the system. In other words, a CBS with a lot of COTS components but which all have very simple and stable interfaces might still have a longer economic life span than a CBS with fewer COTS components but which all have very complex and volatile interfaces.

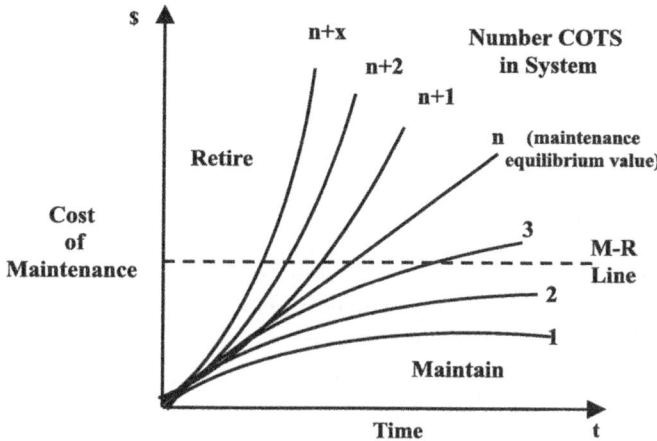

Fig. 2. The COTS-LIMO view of CBS economics

3   CBS Functional Density Rule

So how can these opposing points of view be reconciled? To minimize development costs, the best approach seems to be to maximize your use of COTS components during system design. On the other hand, to minimize maintenance costs, the best approach seems to be to minimize the use of COTS components. What to do?

The answer lies not in increasing the number of COTS components that you use, but rather in increasing the percentage of system functionality that you deliver *via* COTS components. This is a subtle but important change of perspective that suggests the following CBS design rule:

The CBS Functional Density Rule of Thumb:

Maximize the amount of functionality in your system provided by COTS components but using as few COTS components as possible.

This rule may seem obvious in retrospect, almost trivial, but CBS designers are not yet necessarily thinking in these terms – and it still must be applied with caution:

Corollary to the CBS Functional Density Rule:

The absolute number of COTS components in your system should not exceed the maintenance equilibrium value.

(The maintenance equilibrium value is represented by **n** in Fig. 2.)

4   COTS Functional Density Metric

To apply the CBS Functional Density Rule in practical terms, there must be some way to compare one CBS design to another in terms of their relative functional efficiency.

To that end, a simple metric called the *COTS Functional Density* is proposed. To determine the COTS Functional Density (CFD) of a given CBS design, the total functionality represented by the entire software system in terms of standard IFPUG recognized function points [13] must be determined first. Next, those system-wide function points must be divided between system functionality that is to be delivered by code developed in-house and system functionality that is to be delivered by COTS components:

$$System\,Function\,Points = SFP = NCFP + CFP \qquad (1)$$

Where

NCFP = Non COTS Function Points
CFP = COTS Function Points

Then if

NCC = Number of COTS components in the system

Then

$$CFD = CFP/SFP/NCC \qquad (2)$$

CFD represents the percentage of overall system functionality delivered per COTS component. Its range lies from 0 to 1. It is undefined if either SFP or NCC equals zero. The implication is that the larger the CFD, the greater the "efficiency" of a given CBS design, subject to the limitation that NCC must not exceed equilibrium value **n**.

Example 1. Suppose you have a CBS with a total size in function points equal to 2000, with 1400 of those function points being delivered using 30 different COTS components. The COTS Functional Density for this CBS design is thus .023:

$$SFP = 2000 \quad CFP = 1400 \quad NCC = 30$$
$$CFP/SFP = 1400/2000 = .70$$
$$CFD = .70/30 = .023$$

Example 2. Suppose you have a second CBS with a total size in function points also equal to 2000, with 1400 of those function points now being delivered using only 15 different COTS components. The COTS Functional Density for this CBS design is thus .046:

$$SFP = 2000 \quad CFP = 1400 \quad NCC = 15$$
$$CFP/SFP = 1400/2000 = .70$$
$$CFD = .70/30 = .046$$

All other things being equal, CBS #2 is thus a more desirable design than CBS #1, since it offers twice as much overall system functionality per COTS component than does CBS #1.

Example 3. Now suppose you have a third CBS with a total size in function points still equal to 2000, but this time with only 600 function points being delivered via 15 distinct COTS products. The COTS Functional Density for this CBS design is now .020:

$$SFP = 2000 \quad CFP = 600 \quad NCC = 15$$
$$CFP/SFP = 600/2000 = .30$$
$$CFD = .30/15 = .020$$

Based on CFD alone, CBS #1 would seem to be of a more desirable design than CBS #3 (again all other factors being equal), because it has marginally greater COTS Functional Density (.023 vs. .020). Again, CBS #1 offers more overall system functionality per COTS component than does CBS #3. However, CBS #1 does so by using double the number of COTS components as CBS #3. The caution here is that a more "efficient" CBS design is not necessarily a "better" design, if in doubling the number of COTS components CBS #1 has exceeded its COTS maintenance equilibrium threshold value as described in Sect. 2.

However, as long as the equilibrium threshold is not crossed, the suggestion is that a total system life cycle cost profile as illustrated in Fig. 3 may obtain if the CBS Functional Density Rule is obeyed.

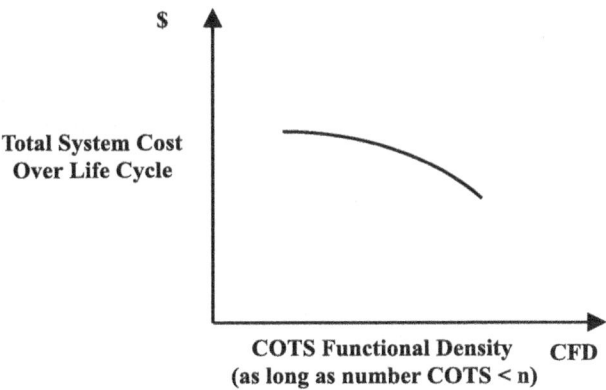

Fig. 3. Potential total life cycle cost profile of a CBS design adhering to the CBS Functional Density Rule

5   Areas for Further Research

Several questions still need to be answered before the CFD metric can really obtain any great utility.

First, the curves in Fig(s). 1, 2 and 3 are based on varying degrees of conjecture and data. Figure 1, for example, is intended to illustrate a *perception* held by people early on regarding the benefits of maximizing the use of COTS components. Figure 2 is based on anecdotal evidence offered during 200+ hours of formal interviews with software managers regarding the still emerging *consequences* of maximizing the use of COTS components. Figure 3 at this stage represents a pure hypothesis. This paper presumes that the perception illustrated in Fig. 1 is false and the anecdotal consensus illustrated in Fig. 2 is true. More empirical data needs to be gathered either supporting or disproving these positions.

Second, there is the issue of whether or not there is true parity between functionality delivered via COTS components and that delivered from scratch, at least as measured by standard function points. The issue is whether it takes the same amount of effort to deliver a COTS function point worth of system functionality as a non-COTS function point worth of functionality. It may be that COTS function points need to be weighted differently from standard function points, and they might even be highly COTS product dependent.

Third, CFD as currently formulated does not consider functional or operational differences between COTS components. Go back to examples 1 and 2. CBS #2 was declared more "efficient" than CBS #1 because it delivered the same number of COTS-based function points as CBS #1 using only half as many COTS products (assuming of course that the maintenance equilibrium value **n** wasn't exceeded). However, if the 1400 COTS-based function points in CBS #1 represent a significantly higher "value added" capability for that system than the value added to CBS #2 by its 1400 COTS-based function points, then CBS #1 might arguably be considered the superior design. Alternate formulations of CFD accounting for such a scenario should be explored. (Consideration of "value added" is essential if designers are to do true economic trade-off studies of the return on marginal dollar investments required between competing CBS designs.)

Fourth, the COTS-LIMO model presumes that it is in fact possible to determine the number of COTS components that exceed the maintenance equilibrium number **n** for a given CBS design. Much work needs yet to be done in this area to validate this assumption.

Fifth, if the above issues can be resolved, the predictive utility of the CFD in terms of helping to characterize CBS designs that are likely to be more successful and cost effective than others needs to be demonstrated on real world industrial projects, the greater in number and variety the better. In other words, empirical data must be gathered either supporting or disputing the curve hypothesized in Fig. 3.

6   Conclusions

This paper has tried to reconcile two conflicting approaches to CBS design: 1) maximize the use of COTS components to ease initial software system development, and 2) minimize the use of COTS components to ease long term system maintenance. The vehicles for reconciliation have been the suggestion of a new heuristic for good CBS design, the *CBS Functional Density Rule*, and the definition of an associated quantitative metric, *COTS Functional Density*. However, much research must still be done to demonstrate genuine applicability of these two ideas.

References

1. Barr, A. and Tessler, S.: An Overview of the Software Industry. Stanford Computer Industry Project, Palo Alto, CA, June (1995),
   `http://www.stanford.edu/group/scip/sirp/swi.overview.html`.
2. 2000-2002 Software Spending Projections. Computer Economics, Inc., Carlsbad, CA, Sept. (2000),
   `http://www.computereconomics.com/content/it/exec000828a.html`.
3. Lateef, A.: Linking Up with the Global Economy: a Case Study of the Bangalore Software Industry. Chapter 2, Sect. 2.3, International Institute for Labour Studies, United Nations International Labour Organization, Geneva, Switzerland, (1997), `http://www.ilo.org/public/english/bureau/inst/papers/1997/dp96/ch2.htm\#2.3`.
4. Maxson, E.: The Software Crisis. Boise State University, Boise, Idaho, May (2001), `http://cispom.boisestate.edu/cis120derickson/webdoc/softcris.htm`.
5. Software, Productivity and Value. The Strong Group, Princeton Junction, NJ, July (2001), `http;//www.stronggroup.com/software.html`.
6. Brooks, F.P., Jr.: No Silver Bullet: Essence and Accidents of Software Engineering. *Computer*, IEEE Computer Society, Washington, D.C., April (1987).
7. Abts, C. and Boehm, B.: COTS Software Integration Cost Modeling Study. USC-CSE tech. Report 98-520, USC Center for Software Engineering, Los Angeles, CA, (1997).
8. Lewis, P., Hyle, P., Parrington, M., Clark, E., Boehm, B., Abts, C. and Manners, B.: Lessons Learned in Developing Commercial-Off-The-Shelf (COTS) Intensive Software Systems. FAA Software Engineering Resource Center, Atlantic City, NJ, October (2000).
9. Albert, C. and Morris, E.: Commercial Item Acquisition: Considerations and Lessons Learned. CMU Software Engineering Institute, Pittsburgh, PA, June (2000).
10. Abts, C., Boehm, B. and Bailey Clark, B.: COCOTS: a COTS software integration cost model. Proceedings ESCOM-SCOPE 2000 Conference, Munich, Germany, (2000).
11. Boehm, B., Abts, C., Brown, A., Chulani, S., Clark, B., Horowitz, E., Madachy, R., Reifer, D. and Steece, B.: Software Cost Estimation with COCOMO II. Prentice Hall PTR, Upper Saddle River, NJ, July (2000).
12. Abts, C.: A Perspective on the Economic Life Span of COTS-based Software Systems: the COTS-LIMO Model. Proceedings of the COTS Software Systems Workshop held in conjunction with ICSE 2000, Limerick, Ireland, May (2000).
13. Garmus, D., and Herron, D.: Measuring the Software Process. Prentice Hall PTR, Upper Saddle River, NJ, (1996).

Meeting the Challenges of Commercial-Off-The-Shelf (COTS) Products: The Information Technology Solutions Evolution Process (ITSEP)

Cecilia Albert and Lisa Brownsword[*]

Software Engineering Institute[**]
4301 Wilson Blvd., Suite 902, Arlington
VA 22203 USA

Abstract. Government and private organizations are escalating their use of commercial off-the-shelf (COTS) products in critical business systems. These organizations find that the traditional development approach rarely works; that is, the process of defining requirements, formulating an architecture, and then trying to find COTS products to meet the specified requirements within the defined architecture. We describe an alternative approach, based on the Rational Unified Process[TM] (RUP)[1], that modifies the acquisition and development processes to more effectively leverage the COTS marketplace through concurrent discovery and negotiation of user needs and business processes, applicable COTS technology and products, the target architecture, and programmatic constraints.

1 Introduction

Building systems from commercial off-the-shelf (COTS) products is an accelerating trend. There is an increasingly vibrant market that delivers COTS software products that provide or support essential business and mission functions. COTS products offer the promise of rapid delivery to the end users, shared development costs with other customers, and an opportunity for expanding mission

---

[*] Colonel David P. Bentley, Director, Business Information SPO, Electronic Systems Command (ESC/MM), USAF, provided the vision, initial funding, and much of the impetus that kept this work moving. Thomas L. Bono and Debora M. Pruitt, The MITRE Corporation, provided a sounding board for the major concepts. Edwin Morris, SEI, developed the COTS marketplace artifacts. David Carney, Tricia Oberndorf, and Pat Place, provided valuable insights into the unique aspects of a process framework for COTS-based systems. John Foreman and Thomas Brandt supported this project as it became more complex than any of us had ever imagined.

[**] Special permission to use the "Meeting the Challenges of Commercial-Off-the-Shelf (COTS) Products: The Information Technology Solutions Evolution Process (ITSEP)" (c) 2001 by Carnegie Mellon University, in *The Proceedings of ICCBSS* is granted by the Software Engineering Institute.

[1] [TM]Rational Unified Process is a trademark of the Rational Software Corporation.

J. Dean and A. Gravel (Eds.): ICCBSS 2002, LNCS 2255, pp. 10–20, 2002.

capabilities and performance as improvements are made in the marketplace. Few organizations today can afford the resources and time to duplicate market-tested capabilities.

But the promise of COTS products is too often not realized in practice. Many organizations find that COTS-based systems are difficult and costly to build, support, and maintain. An important factor in this lack of success is that organizations building COTS-intensive solutions tend either to assume that COTS products can be thrown together or fall back on the traditional development skills and processes with which they are familiar – skills and processes that have been shown not to work in the development and maintenance of a COTS-based system [1].

1.1   Scope of ITSEP

The Information Technology Solutions Evolution Process (ITSEP) integrates COTS lessons learned and disciplined engineering practice to acquire, develop and field COTS-intensive *Solutions*. In ITSEP, a Solution is the integrated assembly of the following:

- one or more pre-existing hardware and software products from the commercial marketplace (i.e., COTS products), the legacy system, in-house reuse libraries, free-ware, shareware, or other reuse products
- any required custom code (including wrappers and "glue")
- appropriate linkage to the broader organization's architecture (e.g., existing systems)
- any necessary end-user business process changes

In ITSEP, Solutions are assumed to be limited to increments of capability that can be delivered in a period of six to twelve months. A typical project consists of a series of increments, where each increment produces a Solution. A more extensive project may consist of multiple increments that are defined and managed concurrently, consecutively, or in some combination of the two. While many of the concepts in ITSEP would apply to managing the relationships across these increments, ITSEP does not attempt to address the additional processes necessary.

1.2   Technical Foundations

ITSEP builds on and integrates the work of many others.

- ITSEP relies heavily on the COTS lessons learned, process, and product evaluation work from the Software Engineering Institute's (SEI) COTS-based systems initiative [2,3,4,5,6].
- The Rational Unified Process (RUP) [7,8] provided a disciplined, risk-based spiral development approach that extends the work of Dr. Barry Boehm [9]. The ITSEP phases, anchor points, and most artifacts, terms and descriptions are from the RUP.

2   ITSEP Objectives

Development and maintenance based on incorporating COTS products is different from typical custom development in that components are not developed to a detailed specification. Instead, the task of building Solutions based on COTS products involves understanding what the products already do and allowing both the characteristics of the products and the motivations of the marketplace (i.e., the factors and forces that motivate the vendors that produce the COTS products) to modify the requirements and end-user business processes, and drive the resulting architecture.

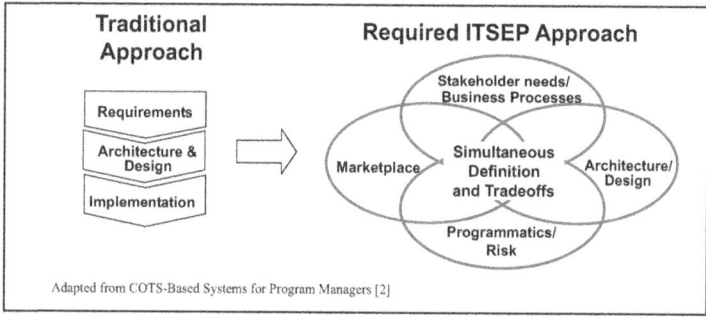

Fig. 1. ITSEP Fundamental Approach

2.1   Simultaneous Definition and Tradeoffs

Key to building Solutions based on COTS products is the need to simultaneously define and tradeoff among four *spheres of influence*, as shown in Fig. 1. The more traditional development approach, shown on the left, consists of defining the requirements, then formulating an architecture to meet those requirements, and only then looking for products that fit into that architecture. Acceptable COTS products are seldom available. Instead, as shown on the right, the two traditional engineering spheres of influence, stakeholder needs/business processes and architecture/design, now consist of understanding the end-user business processes and the organization's tolerance for changing those processes to accommodate COTS products, eliciting a minimum number of "must have" requirements through a process that challenges the significance of each stated stakeholder need, and deriving an architecture and design that will evolve to accommodate technology and product changes. These spheres must be defined simultaneously with the sphere that monitors and evaluates the offerings from the marketplace and a sphere that includes management of the project, planning and implementation of any needed end-user business process changes, and continuous refinement of the project cost, schedule, and risk. An emphasis on balance between the four spheres is critical to ITSEP and must continue throughout the life of a project.

2.2   Iteratively Converging Decisions

In order to maintain balance between the four spheres, ITSEP must create an environment that supports the iterative definition of the four spheres over time while systematically reducing the trade space within each. This allows a decision in one sphere to influence, and be influenced by, decisions in the other spheres. Initially, as shown at the left of Fig. 2, the trade space may be large. There is flexibility for making tradeoffs between the stakeholder needs and end-user business processes, the architecture and design, the offerings of marketplace, and the associated programmatics and risk. As ITSEP drives toward a refined understanding of the Solution, the trade space shrinks. The four spheres increasingly overlap as fewer decisions remain in any single sphere that can be made without significant impact to the others.

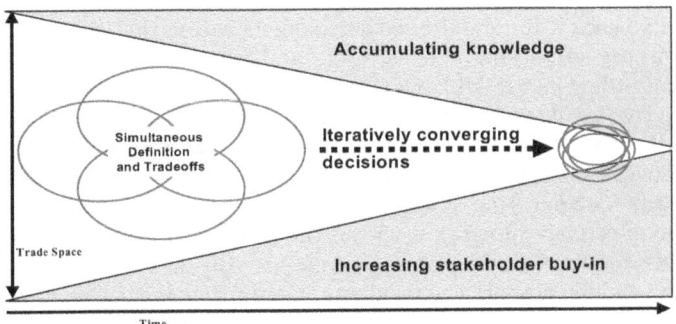

Fig. 2. The ITSEP Objectives

2.3   Accumulating Knowledge

Concurrent to the diminishing of the trade space, knowledge is iteratively growing about the Solution. This knowledge includes an increasingly detailed understanding of the following:

 - capabilities and limitations of COTS products
 - implications of the products on the requirements for the Solution and the end-user business processes as well as the planning necessary to implement any needed changes
 - architectural alternatives and integration mechanisms that bind the products together
 - cost, schedule and risk associated with implementing and fielding the Solution.

Keeping knowledge current about the marketplace is particularly important. This allows the organization to track trends that may affect the Solution over time and keep the need for stability in development and operations in balance with the volatility of the marketplace. In some cases, market events may invalidate earlier decisions (e.g., support for a product is dropped, a new product is introduced, or a feature is added to the product). While there is no easy resolution for such disruptions, early warning of impending changes will allow decisions to be made in a deliberate and careful way.

2.4   Increasing Stakeholder Buy-in

At the same time, the stakeholders must increase their buy-in and commitment to the evolving definition of the Solution. Creating an environment that includes the stakeholders directly affected by the change (or empowered representatives) allows ITSEP to quickly resolve discovered mismatches between the available COTS products, the desired end-user business processes, and the stated stakeholder's needs while simultaneously demonstrating that the Solution can be built within cost and schedule constraints and with acceptable risk. With increased understanding of available COTS products, end-user needs mature and change. The active involvement of end users is essential to ITSEP because the day-to-day activities that identify, evaluate, and select COTS products will shape the end-user business processes and define the functionality that will be delivered. At the same time, engineering stakeholders ensure that the COTS products considered can be effectively integrated within the broader organization's existing systems to meet required performance parameters. Business analysts must ensure that viable vendors support the products. Vendor involvement can provide enhanced visibility into the products' capabilities and potential insight for the vendors into the organization's needs.

3   ITSEP Framework

ITSEP uses a risk-based spiral development process to keep the requirements and architecture fluid as the four spheres of influence are considered and adjusted to optimize the use of available products. Each iteration, or spiral, is planned to mitigate specific risks in the project while addressing the most critical functions first. Iterations systematically reduce the trade space, grow the knowledge of the Solution, and increase stakeholder buy-in. Each iteration produces an executable representation of the Solution that exhibits the common understanding of the Solution that has been achieved to that point through negotiation between stakeholders and addresses the major risks in implementing the Solution.

Each ITSEP iteration, as shown in Fig. 3, begins with detailed planning for the iteration and ends with assessing whether or not the objectives in that plan were met. Iteration planning uses the current understanding of risk to establish goals and objectives, and defines the specific tasks as well as the cost, schedule, and resources specific to the iteration. Executable representation(s) are assembled in every iteration to demonstrate the adequacy of the Solution to meet the iteration objectives.

Unique to the development of COTS-intensive solutions are a number of inherently chaotic activities. These are the activities that continuously *gather* information from each of the four spheres and *refine* that information through analysis of the newly gathered information in the context of the evolving definition of the solution. As analysis proceeds, the need for more information and conflicts among the four spheres (mismatches) are identified. Mismatches are resolved through negotiation among the affected stakeholders to meet the iteration objectives. It may take many cycles of gathering and refining information within an iteration to produce a harmonized set of information that meets the iteration objectives in preparation for assembling the executable representation. While these activities are the same for every iteration, the focus, depth, and breadth are adjusted to meet the iteration objectives.

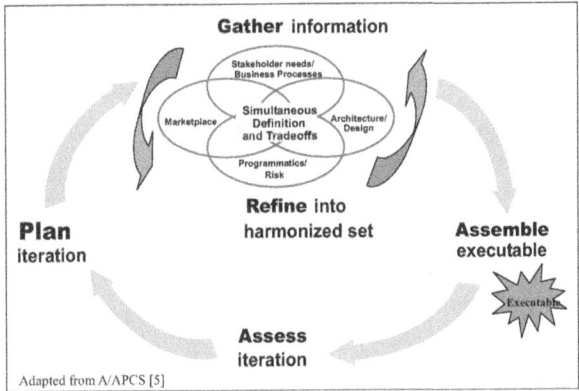

Fig. 3. An ITSEP Iteration

ITSEP iterations are managed, as shown in Fig. 4, by the RUP phases (inception, elaboration, construction, and transition) and anchor points (Lifecycle Objectives, Lifecycle Architecture, and Initial Operational Capability). Each phase consists of multiple ITSEP iterations. Iterations in each phase build on and strengthen stakeholder understanding of the available products and each product's impact on requirements and end-user business processes, architecture and design, and the cost, schedule, and risk of implementing this increment of the project.

Each phase has explicit objectives, activities, artifacts and phase exit criteria and ends with an anchor point that provides an opportunity to review progress, ensure continued stakeholder commitment to the evolving Solution, and to decide to proceed, change project direction, or terminate the increment.

The four phases are repeated for each project increment. Thus across the life of a project, many Solutions are created and retired in response to new technology, new products, and new operational needs; often with multiple increments being developed in parallel (although with varying timelines).

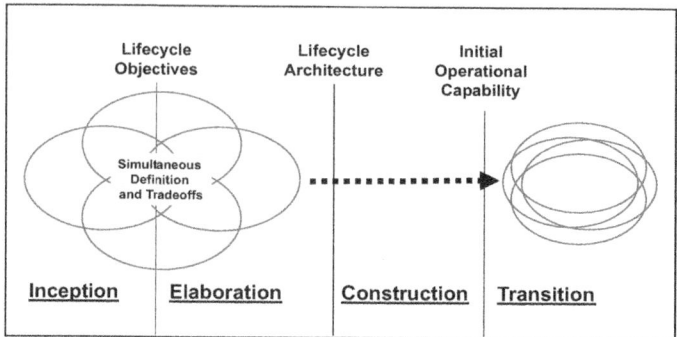

Fig. 4. ITSEP Phases

4   Using ITSEP

To meet the demands of COTS-intensive Solutions, ITSEP refines the RUP phases and anchor points:

- Requirements must stay fluid until the COTS product implications are under-stood – often until well within the Elaboration Phase.
- The analysis and design activities must start sooner – typically in parallel with the requirements activities.
- The project management activities include the management of vendor relationships.
- The business modeling is mandatory rather than optional.
- Activities are added to monitor the marketplace and evaluate candidate COTS products.
- Business, contracting, and organizational change activities are integrated throughout.
- An experimental facility is essential across all RUP phases.

The paragraphs below highlight the major ITSEP activities in each phase.

4.1   Inception Phase

The Inception Phase establishes a common understanding among stakeholders of the objectives for this increment of the project, consistent with the project's longer-term objectives. This common understanding, or scope, defines what the Solution for this increment will do and why. It provides a basis for planning the technical content of each of the following phases and for estimating the cost and time to develop the Solution.

The focus of the Inception Phase is on gathering information from the disparate stakeholders. This information includes

- A high-level understanding of the end-user needs, expectations, and constraints to be represented in stakeholder needs and end-user business processes. As Solutions are defined, stakeholder requests are challenged to ensure that each need and the implication of not meeting that need are fully understood.
- A market survey to understand the makeup, motivations, and products available in the relevant market segment(s). As COTS products are identified, the vendors of those products are examined for long-term viability and limited experiments of the products are conducted to evaluate its suitability.
- The constraints imposed by available technology and products as well as applicable standards, external interfaces, and any existing systems with which the Solution must interact.
- The cost and schedule targets for the increment, available acquisition vehicles for needed products and services, impediments to end-user business process change, and project risk.

The gathered information is refined through analysis and negotiation with appropriate stakeholders to form one or more feasible, albeit high-level, candidate Solutions. A candidate Solution is feasible if it describes a useful capability based on available products that can be integrated into the broader organization's architecture, in a reasonable period of time, at affordable cost, and for acceptable risk. As Solutions are defined, stakeholder requests are challenged to ensure that each need and the implication of not meeting that need are fully understood. The candidate Solutions are summarized in an initial business case and identification of the Solutions recommended for detailed examination in the Elaboration Phase is made. Executable representations demonstrate the feasibility of the candidate Solutions to meet the critical use cases (the primary scenarios of operation).

The Inception Phase ends with the Life Cycle Objectives (LCO) anchor point. This anchor point reviews the phase exit criteria, determines that the phase objectives have been met, validates stakeholder concurrence on the scope of this increment, and seeks approval to examine the most viable candidate solutions in greater depth.

4.2 Elaboration Phase

LCO marks a change in intensity. The basic activities for the Elaboration Phase are the same as those in the Inception Phase, but the level of detail is deeper and the level of resource commitment is significantly higher. The Elaboration Phase achieves sufficient stability of the requirements, end-user business process, and architecture; selects and acquires products; and mitigates risks such that a single Solution is identified with acceptable cost and schedule. The focus of the Elaboration Phase is on in-depth hands-on experiments with the candidate Solutions by engineers and end users. These experiments are conducted in a experimentation facility that represents, as closely as practical, the operational environment. As mismatches between what each candidate Solution delivers and the stakeholder needs are identified, they are analyzed to determine the extent and implications of the mismatch. Negotiations and tradeoffs among the four spheres of influence involving relevant stakeholders are conducted. Where possible, end-user business processes are modified and requirements negotiated to allow greater use and leverage of available products.

When the candidate Solutions are sufficiently understood, one Solution is selected that will become the basis for the Construction Phase. The selected Solution is further amplified, using the experimentation facility, until it is shown that the selected Solution has achieved sufficient stability in requirements and architecture as demonstrated in an executable representation.

The Elaboration Phase ends with the Life Cycle Architecture (LCA) anchor point when all stakeholders agree that the Solution provides sufficient operational value to stakeholders and can be assembled by the engineers for acceptable cost, schedule, and risk. At this point, all products have been selected and procured, any integration mechanisms to incorporate the COTS products and any other components are validated, and the cost and schedule for completion of the increment have been predicted within an acceptable range. All significant risks are eliminated or acceptable risk mitigation plans are in place.

4.3   Construction Phase

The focus of the Construction Phase is on preparation of a production quality release of the selected Solution approved at the LCA anchor point that is suitable for fielding. Any custom components needed are developed. Production rigor is applied to tailoring[2] products, integration code or data (including wrappers, glue, data sets, etc.) needed to incorporate products and custom components, and system testing. Additionally, the Construction Phase includes preparation of necessary support materials, including installation instructions, version descriptions, user and operator manuals, and other user and installation site support capabilities.

The Construction Phase continues the preparation of the business environment of the target organizations to facilitate the initial fielding of the Solution. This includes development of required policies and procedures, restructuring of the organization as necessary, implementation of the end-user business process changes for the initial rollout groups, and the establishment of incentives, user groups, and other mechanisms to encourage adoption of the Solution.

While every effort was made during the Elaboration Phase to stabilize the Solution and to address risks, inevitably some unanticipated changes may occur in requirements, products, and the architecture and design during the Construction Phase. In particular, because of the volatile nature of the commercial marketplace, new versions of the selected products will require detailed investigation as vendors add, change or remove functionality. Continuous monitoring of the marketplace and evaluation of new and changed COTS products is required to anticipate changes and determine an appropriate product upgrade approach.

---

[2] *Tailored* means non-source code adjustment necessary to integrate the COTS products into an operational system (e.g., scripts).

The Construction Phase ends with the Initial Operational Capability (IOC) anchor point. The IOC anchor point allows stakeholders to verify that a production quality release of the Solution is ready for fielding to at least a subset of the operational users as an initial fielding or beta test.

4.4 Transition Phase

The Transition Phase is focused on moving the Solution to a broader set of the user community. This requires that the users attain proficiency in the Solution and the end-user business processes that the Solution supports, are motivated to use the Solution, and are self-supporting in their use of the Solution.

The Transition Phase begins with an initial fielding, or beta test of the Solution developed in the Construction Phase. Following a decision to make the Solution release generally available, the Solution will be fielded across the user base. As required, bugs are fixed, features are adjusted, and missing elements are added to the fielded Solution in maintenance releases. Continued monitoring of the marketplace and other sources and is required to anticipate changes. Maintaining a experimentation facility for product evaluation to assess their potential impact is essential. Product obsolescence and Solution stability must be carefully balanced.

The Transition Phase encompasses continued support for the Solution. The Transition Phase ends when the Solution is retired and replaced by a new increment. The activities of this phase are required for support of the Solution even if support is provided by an organization different from the organization responsible for its implementation. In this case, it is incumbent on the implementation organization to transfer the knowledge that has been gained in the previous phases and iterations to the support organization.

5 Summary

ITSEP is more than a way to select a specific product; rather, it provides a way to develop, field, and support a coherent Solution composed of one or more products, any required custom code, and implementation of any changes required to end-user processes. ITSEP is designed to help organizations realize the promise of COTS while avoiding the pitfalls experienced by programs to date.

ITSEP has been documented [10] to provide detailed instruction in its use. Detailed goals, objectives, exit criteria, activities, and artifacts are provided for each phase and guidelines and artifact details are provided for activities that are unique to ITSEP. The basic concepts and structure of ITSEP have been tried out with several small projects. ITSEP is currently being used to support implementation of a large-scale reengineering project within the United States Department of Defense [11]. The process is ready for use with support of the process designers.

References

1. United States Air Force Science Advisory Board (AFSAB) report on Ensuring Successful Implementation Of Commercial Items In Air Force Systems. SAB-TR-99-03, (2000).
2. Brownsword, L., Oberndorf, P., Sledge, C.: COTS-Based Systems for Program Managers. (tutorial) Software Engineering Institute, Carnegie Mellon University, Pittsburgh, PA, USA, (1999).
3. Office of the Secretary of Defense: Commercial Item Acquisition - Considerations and Lessons Learned. USA Office of the Secretary of Defense Acquisition Deskbook, Discretionary Document.
   http://web1.deskbook.osd.mil/htmlfiles/DBY_dod.asp (2000).
4. Oberndorf, T., Brownsword, L., Sledge, C.: An Activity Framework for COTS-Based Systems. CMU/SEI-2000-TR-010. Carnegie Mellon University, Pittsburgh, PA, USA, (2000).
5. Carney, D., Oberndorf, P., Place, P., Brownsword, L., Albert, C.: Acquisition/Assembly Process for COTS-Based Systems (A/APCS). (briefing) Software Engineering Institute, Carnegie Mellon University, Pittsburgh, PA, USA, (2000.)
6. Oberndorf, P., Dean, J., Morris, E., Comella-Dorda, S.: COTS Product Evaluation (tutorial). Software Engineering Institute, Carnegie Mellon University, Pittsburgh, PA, USA and National Research Council Canada, (2001).
7. Kruchten, P.: The Rational Unified Process: An Introduction-Second Edition. Addison Wesley Longman. Inc (2000).
8. The Rational Unified Process, product version 2001.03.00. Rational Software Corporation (2001).
9. Boehm, B.: A Spiral Model of Software Development and Enhancement. IEEE Computer, May. (1998) 61-72.
10. Albert, C., Brownsword, L.: Information Technology Solutions Evolution Process (ITSEP): Tailoring the Rational Unified Process for Commercial-Off-the-Shelf (COTS) Products, CMU/SEI-2001-TR-011. Software Engineering Institute, Carnegie Mellon University, Pittsburgh, PA, USA, (2001).
11. Smith, J., Hybertson, D.: Implementing Large-Scale COTS Reengineering within the United States Department of Defense. ICCBSS Proceedings, Springer-Verlag, Berlin Heidelberg New York, (2001).

Lessons Learned Integrating COTS into Systems

Thomas G. Baker

The Boeing Company
P. O. Box 3707 MS 6M-HR
Seattle WA 98124-2207
tom.baker@boeing.com

Abstract. This paper presents lessons learned by the author over fifteen years of experience integrating COTS software into systems at The Boeing Company. One key lesson has been to distinguish development vs. customization vs. integration vs. configuration and understanding the corresponding impacts on tools, architectures, and even methodologies. Methodology impacts can destroy a project if they aren't recognized and mitigated in a timely manner. The paper walks through four COTS projects, discussing the challenges of each and how they were overcome. The COTS integration project involving a workflow engine provides an extreme example of methodology impact.

1   Introduction

Development of software systems is changing. Commercial Off The Shelf, or COTS, software is becoming an increasing part of our new systems. There is a wealth of experience, which has led to well-understood methodologies for developing software built upon a "standard" infrastructure. The infrastructure used to be an operating system and compiler, but that has evolved to now include middleware, widgets, object libraries, etc. Still, the end user's unique requirements, the business logic, has mainly resided in custom developed code. Our well-understood methodologies have adapted pretty well to this evolution. However, where the business logic resides in COTS software, where COTS software is the star of the show instead of the supporting cast, our methodologies and practices don't work nearly so well. We must add the following four aspects of COTS Management to our list of critical success factors.

The first aspect of COTS Management is "Selection Issues". These issues are generally well understood; they are similar to buying anything from a vendor. They include architecture, functionality, compatibility, platform, cost, etc. What is not so well understood is that the other aspects of COTS Management must also be part of the selection process. There is one additional selection issue that is frequently ignored – the ongoing cost in terms of user productivity by being forced to utilize the COTS supported business process. The usual focus is the cost of development and deployment. One last point here – talking to other customers who have used the same products/features that you intend to use is a big help in separating marketing from reality.

J. Dean and A. Gravel (Eds.): ICCBSS 2002, LNCS 2255, pp. 21–30, 2002.
© Springer-Verlag Berlin Heidelberg 2002

The second aspect of COTS Management is "Incorporation Issues". One of the major decisions to be made in designing a system utilizing COTS software is the level of coupling between the COTS software and the rest of the system. For this paper, I will use four levels:

- Configuration – "stand-alone" usage, add macros, templates, etc.
- Integration – glue together with other software, minimal internal changes
- Customization – modest enhancements of COTS software using vendor supported methods
- Development – significant enhancements or use of non-supported methods.

In general, a lower level of coupling is better – it's cheaper, less risky, and more flexible for future changes. It's also important to realize that different parts of the system may have different levels of coupling.

Another big consideration is the software engineering methodology to be used. Depending upon the level of coupling, methodology impacts can destroy a project if they aren't recognized and mitigated in a timely manner. In addition, implementation of a COTS software package may require tools, techniques, and expertise that may not be readily available.

The third aspect of COTS Management is "COTS Product Direction". This aspect deals with how the COTS software will evolve over time and how well that evolution will fit with your project's evolving needs. This aspect has varying degrees of importance for different projects. The factor that most people consider is what features the COTS software is likely to have in the future. Another often-ignored factor is architecture, both current and it's future direction. Topics such as compatibility, scalability, performance, and platform evolution are all part of architecture considerations. The vendor's track record, their plans and press releases, plus their vision of their future can all assist in this evaluation.

The fourth aspect of COTS management is "Vendor Relationships". The type of relationship required is very project dependent. For "configuration" projects, being a nameless consumer may suffice. In other situations, you need to be a VIP customer. For larger projects, especially those involving "development", a win/win partnership may be ideal. The vendor, of course, must be willing to engage in the type of relationship required by your project. Another factor in vendor relationships is their support to end-users and their support to developers for fixing bugs, both out-of-the-box bugs and customization bugs. Stability of the COTS vendor's company is often considered; stability of the COTS software price is also important and often neglected. Talking with other customers and attending user conferences are great ways to understand the type of relationship to expect with the vendor.

Now let's walk through four projects at The Boeing Company where COTS software was the centerpiece of the delivered system. We'll look at the role of COTS in each project, the challenges of each project, how they were overcome, and the insights gained into COTS Management.

2   Software Integrated Environment (SwIE)

The first project is the Software Integrated Environment, or SwIE. The project had a dozen developers. I became the project lead just prior to the System Requirements Review. Several COTS software engineering tools from several vendors were used. There was a bit of software development for the integrating software. Most of the coupling was at the integration level, with a lot of configuration work done on the resulting system. DoD-STD-2167, a software development methodology for mission critical systems, was used.

In the mid-eighties, producing embedded or mission critical software for government use meant that, in addition to architecting, designing, coding and testing, there was the additional task of documenting the software according to DoD-STD-2167. A study at the time by Barry Boehm indicated that slightly over half of the effort on a 2167 project was spent on the documentation portion of the job. Software engineering tools were beginning to be available, but each tackled only one aspect of the job and there was no communication between them. SwIE was to change that.

SwIE had two main purposes. The first was to reduce the cost of software development. It would do this by eliminating the need to manually enter the same information into multiple tools. This also meant that information entered into a design tool would not need to be manually re-entered into a document. Documents would be produced that were compliant to multiple, changing standards. DoD-STD-2167 was the initial target. The second main purpose was to "show the way" to tool vendors while serving Boeing's needs until they caught up.

SwIE was implemented as an integrating framework. Tools could be added, deleted, or upgraded as appropriate. Candidate tools had to: 1) be a good tool for the software engineers to use, 2) have some way to extract data from the tool, and 3) be capable of being driven by batch jobs for data extraction and insertion. Projects using SwIE were able to choose the combination of tools and standards that best fit their needs. Most of the tools were COTS tools but a couple of them were Boeing built. None of them were built with SwIE in mind. The primary store for data remained within the COTS tool where the data was originally entered. Custom software extracted data from one COTS tool for insertion into another. Let's take a look at how that was done.

The SwIE extraction software had a defined set of functions that it needed to perform against a COTS tool in order to perform the extraction. Some functions were navigational, e.g. move to the parent, locate the next child. Some functions extracted a particular type of information, e.g. a diagram, a requirement, or a note. The SwIE extraction software utilized a tool interface to support these functions. There was a custom-built tool interface for each COTS tool that had data to be extracted.

A language was developed to control the extraction software. It contained simple variables plus basic control structures such as branching and looping. It also could invoke the tool interface functions. Lastly, the language supported writing output to specified files. This could be "canned" text or information

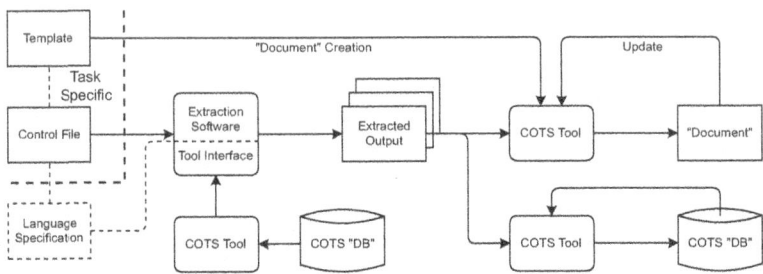

Fig. 1. SwIE Data Migration

extracted from the COTS tool. The files produced contained not only data to be inserted into the receiving COTS tool, but also the commands necessary to control the insertion.

Lastly, a control file, written in the extraction language, was written for each extraction task required. If the task required creation of a "document", a template would also be created. Alternate standards required a different set of templates and control files. However, there was a great deal of reuse among the control files.

SwIE achieved both of its purposes. Its use provided significant reductions in cost and flow time. For a while, it provided a significant competitive edge to Boeing Aerospace. It was in use for ten years, far beyond its expected life. Perhaps it was leading from too far in front. SwIE proved to be very adaptable over time. It supported five different documentation standards over its life span and a very wide variety of COTS tools.

The normal problem of "being at the mercy of the COTS vendor" was minimized because of the adaptability inherent within SwIE. The vendor of our first analysis tool dropped support for it shortly after our first release. This didn't hurt too badly because we had already integrated an alternate. As far as SwIE was concerned, the only difference was the Tool Interface. That was fairly easy because the new vendor had an extraction tool kit that they had used for testing. No other changes were required.

One thing we did differently that really paid off was how we treated the COTS vendors. The worst thing is not for your vendor to be unresponsive to your needs. The worst thing is for them to be so responsive that they go out of business! For many companies, doing business with Boeing can be like a deer doing business with a tour bus at night. They become fixated on Boeing's needs and forget about their marketplace. We worked very hard with our vendors on this point. We insisted that they not do anything to meet our needs that would not be part of their standard product offering. It also had to offer value to other customers for them to do so. In one case, we needed a change that met these "requirements", but the vendor could not justify making the change. We arranged to pay for the change to be made in return for additional product licenses.

3 Software Reuse Library (ReLib)

The second project took place in the early nineties. The Software Reuse Library, or ReLib, is a library for reusable software components. The project averaged seven developers. I joined the project shortly after it started and became the System Architect. ReLib started out at the configuration level of coupling but progressed to the development level. We used a methodology called P+ from DMR. It is similar to standard software development methodologies but with finer grained deliverables and data focused design techniques. ReLib provided storage, search, and retrieval capabilities. It also provided supplemental services, such as tracking component usage to permit users to be notified of upgrades. Initially, ReLib was implemented using software in the public domain. COTS Product Direction and Vendor Relationships did not exist. Support was minimal.

The system had a VT100 style user interface. Even at that time, such an interface was ancient and we immediately got complaints. So, the first upgrade was to replace the interface used by the end users of the library. We chose to implement the new user interface using the Web. Mosaic had recently been released and it appeared to be a good fit for our needs. We knew that distributing custom client software to our large user community would be more headaches that we desired. People liked the new interface and usage grew.

Our next challenge was the platform. The public domain software was written in Ada and required an IBM/AIX platform. That platform was non-standard in our part of the company so we borrowed one for a while. We acquired a standard (for us) HP platform and an Ada compiler to run on it. All we were planning to do was recompile the software. Well, we learned what the rest of the Ada community already knew – library incompatibilities are the scourge of Ada. We also discovered that, as far as we could find, nobody had ever run Ada on an HP before, much less this particular compiler and library! We had accidentally wandered into no man's land. We got it to work only because one person was absolutely determined not to let any software get the best of him.

Over time, additional capabilities were added. Users could browse various classification schemes to locate components of interest. Metrics were collected and made accessible to anyone. However, integrity of the library database remained a continuing problem. Finally, the database was reengineered and all related software, including the component installation software, was replaced. The Ada code was gone forever, as were the database integrity problems. The only trace of the original COTS package is the format used to submit a component to the library.

In many ways, this COTS experience was similar to maintaining any undocumented legacy system for which the previous software folks are no longer around. However, because it was officially a COTS project, we did not recognize this fact until we were well underway. There is one profound COTS lesson though: NEVER buy software before talking to people who have actually used it, even something as mundane as a "standard" compiler. Remember that marketing vs. reality point?

4   Electrical Change Tracking System (ECTS2)

The third project took place in the latter part of the Nineties. The project staffing varied between two and ten developers. I began the project as System Architect. The Electrical Change Tracking System (ECTS2) was to assist engineers and others in implementing changes in electrical/electronics systems on Boeing commercial airplanes. It was intended to be mainly a configuration project with pieces of customization. It turned out that there was a lot of configuration, customization, and development. There were four vendors involved. Surprisingly, there was very little integration work. COTS Product Direction and Vendor Relationships became significant hurdles.

The initial concept for ECTS2 was to build an Oracle Forms application to enable managers to see status of the work. However, such "status" systems are notorious for their poor accuracy and the overworked engineers were less than enthusiastic (tongue planted firmly in cheek) about entering status into yet another system instead of actually doing the work that they were being held accountable to get done. Further consultation with management and other users of the system gave rise to a better concept – a workflow management system that would help people get their work done while automatically collecting status and metrics for management. There would be a thousand users initially, but if things went well, it might be deployed to even more users. The user base had an extremely wide variety of platforms at their desks. I even found actual 3270 and ADM3 terminals! The only conceivable user interface solution seemed to be the Web.

At that time, no workflow vendors had a Web user interface. But we found one solid, extensible product for which a third party had written a Web interface. They also had written other software packages that extended the capabilities of the workflow vendor's product, task automation for example. The final system had eight COTS packages from four vendors as shown here:

Table 1. ECTS2 Components and their integration

Component	Supplied By	Level of Coupling / Type of Work
Web Server	COTS #1	Integration / Configuration
Database	COTS #2	Integration / COTS #3 = Configuration, populated tables; Boeing work = extended schemas, populated tables
Workflow Engine	COTS #3	Integration / Configuration
Process Definition	COTS #3	Integration / Loaded process definitions
Process Management	COTS #4	Integration / Used as is
Task Automation Capability	COTS #4	Integration / Small enhancement made by vendor for our use
Automated Task	COTS #4 + Boeing	Configuration / COTS #4 = added parameters Development / Boeing = built new agents
Web Interface	COTS #4 + Boeing	Configuration / COTS #4 = built web templates Customization / Boeing = wrote validation code, extended some OO methods, added a lot of custom capability, such as tabular data

Surprisingly, there were no significant interoperability problems (for us). The vendors recognized their "pecking order"; each adjusted their software as required to work properly with the snafus released by those "higher up". When we extended functionality in ways that were directly supported by the vendors, we had very few problems. On one occasion, we made a change in the vendor's code. When the vendor completely rearchitected their system, we were forced to rearchitect our customization. Ouch – the perils of the development level of coupling with COTS products.

Mergers and acquisitions among vendors caused them to spend their resources adjusting their systems to comply with their new owner's way of doing business, at the expense of supporting customers. One vendor initially had a relatively straightforward architecture and ended up with an architecture incompatible with Boeing's direction – but it was integrated with their new parent company's software. Support varied widely, even within the same vendor. One vendor located in Australia provided near miraculous support. One vendor located literally "down the street" was often non-existent. One big problem was "licensing hell" – the cost of the workflow engine tripled every year! That really plays havoc with ROI calculations.

However, the biggest problem we faced on this project came from a completely unexpected source. It was our software engineering development methodology! All methodologies/techniques make assumptions about the problem that they are solving and the environment that they are working in. The more efficient it is, the more focussed it is, and the more assumptions there are. That's true of most things, not just software methodologies and techniques. The key is this: prior to making a decision, know what the assumptions are and make sure they are valid in your situation.

For example, embedded software is part of a larger system. That system levies specific functional and interface requirements on the embedded software. Those requirements are the focus of embedded software development methods. On the other hand, Information Systems (IS) software supports a business process. Ergo, the business process and the data that the business process manipulates is the focus of IS software development methods.

We were implementing business processes. So, typical IS software development methods should work. Right?

Wrong. We tried our standard IS methodology. It didn't work. We tried some earlier, simpler methodologies. They didn't work. We tried a variant of MIL-STD-498. That didn't work. We tried ISO/IEC 12207. That was better, but still not successful. What we finally figured out after many months of trial and error is that we had four projects, not one. We were initially implementing three business processes; each was a separate project. In addition, there was a workflow infrastructure project.

The three business process projects were each driven by a business process, just like an IS development project. But they weren't development projects! They were "merely" configuring the workflow infrastructure. All that needed to be done was: 1) define the business process and data, 2) load it into the workflow infrastructure, 3) add the user interface, 4) test it, and 5) deliver it. There really wasn't any software development in the traditional sense.

The workflow infrastructure project wasn't a normal IS software development project either. It had no business process associated with it. It wasn't even like an embedded software development project. It didn't have any real requirements. There were some general requirements, but the COTS software satisfied these. Real software development requirements only became visible when a business process project couldn't be implemented because something was missing from the infrastructure. And even these requirements couldn't be called complete. Implementing exactly what a particular business process required would likely mean that a subsequent business process implementation would run into similar limitations. The trick was to take a particular business process requirement and generalize it to solve the class of problems, while making sure that the resulting solution was still one that mere mortals could utilize. We foresaw some of these requirements, but by no means all of them. As additional business processes were implemented, "missing pieces" became fewer.

5   Define and Control Airplane Configuration / Manufacturing Resource Management (DCAC/MRM)

Define and Control Airplane Configuration / Manufacturing Resource Management, or DCAC/MRM, is Boeing Commercial Airplanes' business process reengineering initiative.The new information system supporting the new business processes consists of several large pieces of COTS software, a lot of COTS infrastructure, plus a lot of custom built integration software and COTS customizations. Some parts are almost pure development. With the numerous vendors, managing COTS Product Direction and Vendor Relationships is a major undertaking. We've been working at it for over six years; peak employment was over 1000 people committed full time to the project. It currently manages most airplane parts. Early in 2002, it will start managing airplane configurations. While the project was begun during a weak market for airplanes, implementation is coinciding with near peak production. The challenge has been compared to putting a new set of wings on a 747 – while it is on a flight from New York to London.

In late 2000, I became chief System Architect for the Product Data Manager, or PDM. PDM is the central repository of part and airplane configuration data within the DCAC/MRM system. As such, it is at the heart of DCAC/MRM. While my experience has been from the PDM viewpoint, it is so wrapped up in the DCAC/MRM project that from a COTS perspective, one is merely a subset of the other.

The DCAC/MRM project is unique in many ways. Size is obviously one factor. Complexity, especially in terms of interrelationships with other processes and systems, is another. Because it was a business process reengineering project with an information systems component, solid detailed requirements were almost non-existent early on. Strangely enough, that didn't really matter. Boeing understood right away that "Vendor Relationships" were key to the success of the effort. COTS vendors had to be large, "rock-solid" companies. They had to have a proven product that could scale to this size task and be compatible with the standards we had chosen for integrating the COTS products. The product also had to be flexible and extensible. Lastly, Boeing demanded a commitment from each vendor to the success of DCAC/MRM. With these as "requirements", the list of possible COTS vendors for each component of the DCAC/MRM system was quite short. If we had generated some detailed functional requirements, it is quite possible that no COTS products would have qualified for any part of the system.

One of the policies adopted by the DCAC/MRM project early on has made a big difference. Having picked the COTS software, we would utilize the COTS capabilities wherever we could, even if that meant not doing things the way we might otherwise want to. Development of new capability within COTS software was a last resort. This meant that a lot of functional requirements that would normally be levied on an information system in support of a business process were negotiated to adapt to the capability within the COTS software.

Because of the joint Boeing/vendor commitment to the success of DCAC/ MRM, "Vendor Relationships" and "COTS Product Direction" issues are minimized. Since architecture and architecture direction issues were part of the selection criteria, specific functionality is the most significant remaining issue. Even this is minimized with the aforementioned policy. By the way, you really know a vendor is committed to your project when you walk into their office and see a big plaque honoring their strategic partners. On the plaque, there are HP, Oracle, and DCAC/MRM – there's no mention of Boeing.

Lack of a good COTS methodology has hurt this project. A lot of decisions were "What makes sense right now for this issue? OK, let's do it and move on". Analysis paralysis did not exist. The result was that a lot of information about the system existed only as tribal knowledge – and a lot of tribal members have moved on. We are now dealing with very long learning curves and scarcity of experts in many areas. There are reverse engineering tasks being done in key areas of the system. It has become a legacy system before it has been fully implemented. On the other hand, a management attitude of "Let's make sure we make the correct, optimal, long term decision" would probably mean nothing would ever have gotten done. Nobody could have foreseen how big, messy, and tough this project would turn out to be.

6   Conclusion

I'd like to summarize with a table of the highlights of COTS Management Aspects and the corresponding project experiences we've just been discussing.

Developing a system that utilizes COTS software at the centerpiece of the system has challenges over and above those that only use COTS software for infrastructure. Diligent attention to COTS Management can control these challenges. The key is adaptation. The methodologies, techniques, and support must be adapted to COTS usage. We must be vigilant in ferreting out work that

Table 2. Summary of COTS Management Aspect Experiences

COTS Management Aspect	SwIE	ReLib	ECTS2	DCAC
Selection Issues				
Architectural, functional, compatibility, cost, etc	+	-	+ +	+
User productivity cost	+ +	- -> +	?	? ?
Marketing vs. reality	+	- -	- -	-
Incorporation Issues				
Level of coupling	I + D	Co-> D	C0+Cu	Cu&D
Impact of (not) understanding level of coupling	+	-	- -	-
Impact of methodology vs. level of coupling	0	-	- -	- -
Availability of tools, techniques, expertise	-	- -	-	- -
Learning Curve	0	0	-	- -
COTS Product Direction				
Features	+ +	N/A	+	+
Architecture	N/A	N/A	- -	+
Vendor Relationships				
Level of involvement, support	+	N/A	+ / -	+
Vendor stability	+	N/A	-	-
Cost stability	+	N/A	- -	+ / -
Overall COTS Experience	+	-	- -	0

adds no value. A methodology that hasn't been properly adapted to COTS software and the project's level of coupling is an excellent place to start. Adapting project management brings additional benefits. Adapting the requirements and customers is harder but brings even bigger rewards.

Risk Reduction in COTS Software Selection with BASIS

Keith Ballurio, Betsy Scalzo, and Lou Rose

Software Productivity Consortium, Herndon, Virginia, U.S.A.
{ballurio, scalzo, rosel}@software.org

Abstract. Organizations are moving toward COTS-based software development with limited success. The quality of resulting systems is not measuring up to expectations. Transitioning to a new development paradigm requires many kinds of changes, but the most important concerns the development process. A well-defined approach tailored for COTS-integration is needed. The Base Application Software Integration System (BASIS) is an approach that improves the architecture of COTS-based systems by determining the best integration sequence for the chosen COTS products. The best sequence is determined by synthesizing objective product evaluations, emerging practices in integration technologies, and business priorities. By balancing practices, technologies, and priorities with BASIS techniques, organizations can manage integration risk and make the transition to COTS-based development more successful.

1   Introduction

The software industry today favors a COTS-based approach to software development, and many organizations are in the process of transitioning teams to the new development paradigm. In the adoption of any new technology, there is a risk of lower product quality, higher project costs, and extended development schedules. The Software Productivity Consortium currently sponsors several projects that focus on reducing risk in COTS-based software development. One project reduces the risk of selecting inappropriate COTS components by defining a method for evaluating software products, the Component Evaluation Process (CEP). Another project reduces the risk of downstream integration problems through early assessment of the compatibility between a chosen COTS product and an existing enterprise system. A third project, Phased Integration for COTS products (PIC), reduces risk throughout the development lifecycle by defining built-in checkpoints, incorporating best practices of industry leaders, and recommending proven measurement techniques. One part of PIC is a technique that includes support for sequencing the integration of COTS products. The technique comprises component evaluation, state of the art practices in integration technologies, and sound computational methods for identifying interface mismatches. This technique is the subject of this paper and is called the Base Application Software Integration System (BASIS).

J. Dean and A. Gravel (Eds.): ICCBSS 2002, LNCS 2255, pp. 31–43, 2002.
© Springer-Verlag Berlin Heidelberg 2002

The remainder of the paper is organized to provide an introduction to the main concepts of BASIS. In Sect. 2, background material is presented that gives a context for the rest of the discussion. Similar work is briefly outlined and compared with the BASIS approach. Section 3 will present the major parts of BASIS while explaining the contributions of each phase to the development lifecycle. Section 4 will emphasize the most important concepts that distinguish BASIS from other techniques.

2 Background

The dream of building software systems in minutes or hours with pluggable components has been around for many years. In the 1980's, Brad Cox coined the term "software ic" in the attempt to make an analogy between hardware components and software objects [2]. When object technology did not produce the expected results by the mid 1990's, organizations looked toward components, as defined in OLE and COM by Microsoft Corporation and in Java with Java Beans by Sun Software. The new vision of software development foresaw an approach where developers would search for online resources, visually drag components from a repository into a development tool, and then plug the components together for the new or modified application.

While some claim to have realized this dream, most organizations are grappling with many issues surrounding the new paradigm. Brereton and Budgen defined a framework for classifying the issues into categories of product, process, business, or people skills as viewed from the perspectives of component providers, component integrators, and software customers [1]. They found that the primary issues for component integrators include:

- Component selection
- Vendor selection
- Component interoperability
- Mixing quality attributes
- Maintaining quality over time
- Making tradeoffs between requirements and component capabilities
- Finding good tool support
- Implementing requests for change
- Project management

Although the Consortium is working to solve most of these problems, this paper will address only the first three issues, excluding the early market survey.

Other efforts addressing some of the same issues as BASIS include work by Yacov Haimes and Wilfred Hansen. Haimes developed a risk identification framework for large-scale and complex systems. The hierarchical holographic modeling (HHM) framework provides a tool that supports any risk identification process. He has used this framework for modeling risk identification in systems integration. The framework includes seven categories for sources of risk: software development, temporal, leadership, environment, acquisition, quality, and technology. After risks are identified from all perspectives, they are ranked with the risk filtering and ranking method (RFRM) that defines a process for filtering, prioritizing, and managing risk scenarios from multiple overlapping perspectives of a large-scale system [3].

Hansen developed a generic process for evaluating COTS software at the Software Engineering Institute called QESTA, from quantification, examination, specification, transformation, and aggregation. In this 5-step process, the stakeholders' goals, priorities, and environmental context are used to produce evaluation metrics that contribute to a final decision value when applied to a group of candidate COTS products. The method obeys standard measurement principles and provides a continuous thread of work that can be used to trace end results back to the stakeholders' specifications [7].

While this work has much overlap with BASIS, there are several features in BASIS that provide added value. With BASIS, organizations will be able to:

- Understand the impact of a COTS supplier on system stability
- Exploit the power of the latest research in architecture mismatch and resolution
- Determine the best sequence of integration for the products that survive evaluation
- Enhance the corporate software development process with repeatable procedures specific to COTS software

With this understanding of the unique benefits of the BASIS approach, the next section discusses the approach in greater detail, showing how each part fits within the context of an existing defined software development process.

3 BASIS

The greatest benefits of BASIS include product selection and integration sequencing, requiring several activities to be performed before using the BASIS technique. In fact, BASIS uses the products of several lifecycle activities, such as requirements analysis, ongoing market surveys, logical design, and enterprise architecture specification. In order to support the objectives of the project, BASIS needs to use the negotiated objectives and requirements from early systems analysis. Ongoing market surveys identify COTS components that are potentially suitable for use within a particular product domain, so this group of products and vendors becomes the initial product domain to which BASIS is applied. Logical designs produce the early architecture descriptions that enable product down selection based on determined interface requirements. The enterprise technical architecture provides the standards that are the foundation of all products of the enterprise and therefore help to eliminate COTS components that do not comply. In this context, the BASIS approach can be started whenever most project requirements are defined and an initial COTS product domain is available.

In a nutshell, the BASIS approach includes three steps. First, the Component Evaluation Process evaluates candidate components against customer requirements to determine how well the components' capabilities support project requirements. Unsuitable products are eliminated from the process while the others stay for further evaluation. The remaining component vendors are subjected to the Vendor Viability Process and are evaluated against criteria such as maturity, customer service, and cost/benefit ratio. Again the field is reduced if some vendors do not meet rating thresholds. Finally, the amount of effort required to integrate each of the products into the existing or developing system is estimated by calculating the Difficulty of Integration index. The survivors of this filter are prepared for final selection by computing a number that merges all of the factors together into a single, prioritized index of suitability. This index, called the BASIS indicator, is not an absolute measure of value, but it does provide a way to compare COTS products against each other so that an objective decision can be made.

3.1   Component Evaluation Process

The Component Evaluation Process [8] is comprised of five top high-level activities:

- *Scope Evaluation Efforts*. This activity sets the expectations for the level of effort required to complete the remaining activities in the evaluation process and provides an estimate for the number of packages that will undergo the search, screen, and evaluate cycle.
- *Search and Screen Candidates*. Searching for candidate packages requires an initial *"must have"* criteria be defined. This is typically based on the project's required functionality, conditions, and definition of concerns. It is kept as broad as possible so to not restrict initial search conditions. Upon locating the candidate packages, initial screening of these candidates is performed by setting minimum thresholds for the search criteria that each candidate package must meet. This screening filters out the high risk packages, leaving the best products for later evaluation.
- *Define Evaluation Criteria*. This activity produces the detailed criteria necessary to support a repeatable and systematic evaluation. Definition of criteria is used to refine, formalize, and expand initial search criteria in order to ensure the functional, architectural, performance, and financial characteristics of the candidate packages. Weighting is established for all evaluation criteria with respect to the level of importance for the development project.
- *Evaluate Component Alternatives*. This activity conducts a detailed evaluation of the alternative products to assess how well the packages meet defined criteria. Evaluation scenarios are developed to evaluate the packages within the project's context. To ensure consistent comparison, the same scenarios are executed on all packages. The evaluation of packages is performed

based on available data from multiple sources, such as hands-on experience, third party literature, or vendor demonstrations. The *credibility* is measured by how well the package is understood. Essentially, it qualifies the source of the information.

- **Analyze Evaluation Results**. The evaluation process produces data on how well each alternative product meets defined criteria. The analysis may consist of activities to compare and contrast rankings of alternatives based on project priorities. Sensitivity Analysis is used to help evaluators understand the impact of certain criteria, or groupings of criteria, on the ranking of alternatives and may be iterative.

In summary, the Consortium's Component Evaluation Process was developed to help avoid common pitfalls associated with evaluation and trade studies while assisting evaluators with package (component) selection. It is generally applicable to all types of components and adapts methods to assist with decision support. The process stresses the creation and maintenance of a repository for capturing evaluation data and lessons learned for future use.

3.2 Vendor Viability

Successful products within any market space must meet several conditions in order to maintain success. They must exhibit good technology, good marketing, good organization, and adequate capitalization. The single most dominant element driving the COTS market today is the financial bottom line. Vendors must demonstrate product superiority, differentiation through product updates, and acceptable performance within in the market space so as to establish a profit margin. The relationship a COTS vendor has to a market space is based on the size of the market divided by the number of vendors with products being marketed in the space. Many other factors must be analyzed to better describe vendor viability, such as:

- What development strategies has the vendor chosen?
- Do they develop for client system, server-system, Microsoft system, Sun ....?
- How complete is the product with respect to the domain and to competition?

Understanding these issues for every COTS vendor provides insight into the potential life cycle of the product. In addition, other factors such as:

- Does the vendor demonstrate sufficient product superiority?
- How responsive has the vendor been to product updates?
- How has the product been supported in the past?
- What are the plans for the product in the future?
- What is the current development strategy?

Vendor Viability, a critical and often overlooked aspect, should examine both the management and financial strength of a vendor. If a vendor is supplying a strategically important system upon which a large sum of development dollars is going to be spent, then it must be assumed that the importance of the vendor responsible for the product is of strategic importance. Minimally, a vendor's viability criteria should evaluate the overall financial viability of the product vendor from both the macro and micro market level.

3.2.1   Vendor Viability Value. The process to establish a Vendor's Viability value (VV) uses a value table to provide a rating for each of five important factors. As research on each vendor proceeds, material is collected on each of the factors listed. When all the evidence is weighed against professional experience and project requirements, then the most likely rating for each factor can be obtained from the Vendor Viability Table and the accompanying definitions. The critical factors are:

- *Financial Viability*: Overall financial health, including such factors as sales revenue, variable cost, fixed cost, and assets and liabilities. The value ratio is based on the combination of these factors using standards practices of financial health.
- *Market Stability*: Overall status in product domain, including marketing position and product position in the market related to overall market potential. Typically this value is based on the number of customers to the number of potential customers available, total product revenue in market space, installed base, and years in market.
- *Management Viability*: Status and capabilities of management team, including company directors, marketing managers, product managers, development managers, general managers and consultants, where applicable. Value ratio based on management total years of experience, achievements, and time in position(s).
- *R&D Viability*: Research and Development, what ratio of dollars spent are placed back into company to expand on current system.
- *Product Support*: Status and capabilities of product support.

Property value definitions:

- *poor*: Not achieving an adequate standard, substandard value in market, not profitable or non existent. Overall improvement for current standing in market domain not witnessed for an extended period of time. Value ratio is between 0% and 9%.
- *low*: Achievements extremely low, value in market space low and profitability marginal or stationary. Overall standings in market domain speculative, improvement potential speculative. Value ratio is between 10% and 39%.

- **medium**: Achievement average, value in market space low to medium and profitability marginal or growing. Overall standings in market domain improving, improvement potential medium however positive. Value ratio is between 40% and 59%.
- **good**: Achievement average to good, value in market space medium to good and profitability growing. Overall standings in market domain good and growing, improvement potential good. Value ratio is between 60% and 79%.
- **very good**: Achievement very good, value in market space very high and profitability very good. Overall standings in market domain in top percentile and growing, potential good very good establish best in bread products and financially sound. Value ratio is between 80% and 100%.

3.3   Difficulty of Integration

The last filter of BASIS determines an estimate for the effort required to integrate each potential component into the existing system architecture. The estimate of integration complexity considers several factors. The connection of two software components may or may not result in an architectural mismatch. The complexity of any identified mismatch may be very small, requiring little effort to resolve, or the mismatch might be severe and require a substantial amount of analysis in order to design a maintainable resolution. Similarly, mismatch resolutions vary considerably in approach and in difficulty of implementation. The final estimate, which combines all these factors, describes the complexity of integrating a COTS component into the current system and is called the difficulty of integration factor (DOI). An important tool that helps determine this factor is called the Interface Point table.

3.3.1   Interface Point Table. The Interface Point Table (IPT) collects and organizes properties that describe the major interface points of a particular COTS product. The information compiled by the IPT is required to compute the Difficulty of Integration factor (DOI) for a COTS product. Figure 1 illustrates a number of important terms and shows how they will be used in this paper. The figure shows a software component that is composed of three additional components that communicate through individual connections. These terms are defined for this discussion as:

- A *component's interface* is defined as the set of interfaces published by the component that specify all possible roles that the component can assume.
- A *role* describes the behavior of a component within a specific context. Each role will have a set of action interfaces, one of which is shown in the figure within the dotted rectangle.
- Each action interface within a role is an *interface* point and is associated with a single entry or exit point, sometimes called a requirement or a service. The interface point defines the type of connection, or interaction protocol, that is needed to support interaction with another component. The interface point also specifies the type of data received and reported.

- Components communicate through a *connection* which is like an information conduit, spontaneously created at runtime to contain and direct the information flow that defines the interaction. The type of connection depends on the system architecture, and examples include a function call, a spawn, shared data, or a data trigger.

Using this terminology, a component has a collection of role interfaces, each of which describe behavior using multiple interface points. Figure 1 shows only one possible role interface. Each interface point includes a number of input and output parameters that must be satisfied to establish a successful connection with the component.

An architectural mismatch occurs, meaning a connection cannot be established, when the type of an interface point, or any of the associated parameters, do not agree with those of the component attempting the connection.

The DOI estimates the complexity of integrating a component into a system architecture that may have multiple architectural mismatches. This means that the interface point for each possible connection to that component must be examined for architectural mismatch. The DOI aggregates all the connection complexities into a single index for the component. The complexity of any interface point comprises three separate factors: the inherent complexity of the interface point (IPC), an associated potential architectural mismatch for connecting to the interface point, and the difficulty of the mismatch resolution (MRD). The Interface Point Table, shown in Table 1, collects the information for all the interface points in a component along with the associated complexities needed by the DOI formula.

Table 1. Interface Point Table

COTS Product Name		Mismatch Identification & Resolution			Connection Indices
Interface Point Name	Interface Point Complexity, (IPC)	Mismatch IDNumber	Resolution Name	Mismatch Resolution Difficulty, (MRD)	Connection Complexity Index, (CCI)

The process of computing the DOI is not difficult. Understanding the complexity of any component interface is the first step toward understanding the effort of integrating the component with other software. The complexity of using any COTS product in a given system architecture, the DOI, can be estimated as the average of the connection complexities of all interface points within all component interfaces. Consider the following steps:

1. Select a component from the group of potentials, and identify the specific role interfaces that will be needed for the current project, as well as possible extensions in future work.

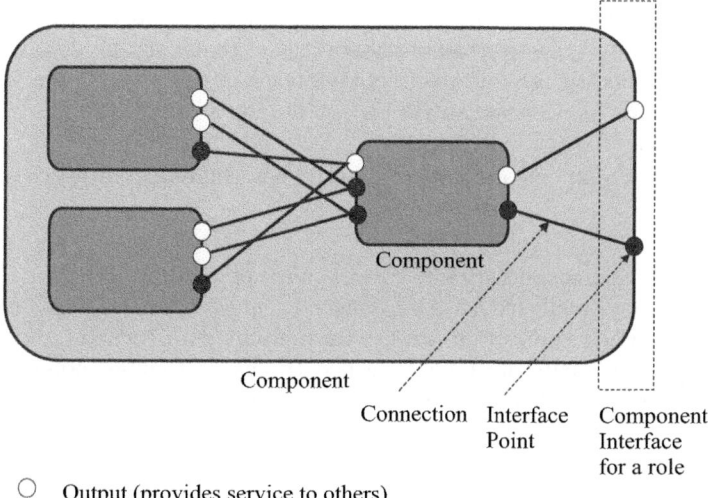

Output (provides service to others)

Input (requires service from others)

Fig. 1. BASIS Terminology

2. Each required role interface identifies a set of interface points for mismatch consideration. Each interface point could generate several potential mismatches.
3. The difficulty of integration will vary with context, so connections between the component and all parts of a given system must be identified for mismatch consideration.
4. Each role interface can support multiple connections, but the designation of roles is not central to the task of computing the integration complexity. This means that roles do not play a central part in determining integration complexity once the unique action interfaces are identified.
5. Each interface point is unique, so each is given a textual mnemonic which is entered into the first column of the IPT.

An interface point signifies a potential connection with a target component, so the inherent complexity of an interface point (IPC) is related to the coupling complexity incurred by that connection. Coupling with another component can be measured in terms of data types or methods. Using the Chidamber and Kemerer metrics suite as a foundation, Wei Li defined metrics for both types of complexities, Coupling Through Abstract Data Type (CTA) and Coupling Through Message Passing (CTM) [6]. Since an interface point is often just one service call, the inherent measure of complexity focuses on the data types required to effect the call.

Coupling Through Abstract Data Type (CTA) counts the number of classes that are used as abstract data types in the data-attribute declaration of a class.

For an interface point, the corresponding coupling measure will be the number of abstract data types (or complex data types) that must be declared in the data-attribute declaration of a source component in order to connect with a target component. As a result, an IPC is computed as:

IPC = the number of complex data types declared in order to connect with a target

After this rough estimate of inherent complexity is determined, the interface point is analyzed to determine how many and which connections it will support. Each connection implies interaction with a target component, so all target components must be identified to ensure that all potential mismatches will be revealed. For instance, two components may assume different underlying platforms so that one of them would need to change to accommodate the other's expectations. Another example would be when a source component tried to access data which was considered private by the target component.

Mismatch identification is performed using the procedure defined by Gacek [4]. Each interface of the required component will suggest one or more types of connection that can be used to pinpoint specific mismatches. Once the connection type is known, such as call, spawn, or trigger, then all of the mismatches associated with that connection type are potential mismatches for the connection. When the mismatches are examined and irrelevant ones are filtered out, then the identification codes of the potential mismatches are entered on successive rows of the IPT table in column labeled 'Mismatch ID Number'. If there are several potential mismatches, then the same interface point will have multiple entries.

For each mismatch, the potential resolution techniques must be considered against project constraints so that an appropriate choice can be made. The possible resolutions derived from Deline are shown in Table 2 [5]. Each mismatch resolution technique has a weighting factor that describes the difficulty with which that solution can be implemented. When the simplest resolution appropriate for a given mismatch has been selected, then enter the name on the same row under the column labeled 'Resolution Name' and place the associated weight from Table 2 in the column 'Mismatch Resolution Difficulty'.

Table 2. COTS Resolution Complexity Factors

Type of Resolution Technique	Relative Complexity
Bridge - Online	5
Bridge - Offline	4
Wrapper	6
Mediator	8
Negotiation - Unilateral	6
Negoatiation - Bilateral	8

The complexity index for each connection and architectural mismatch combination listed in the IPT (each row) is estimated with (1). The formula scales the interface complexity to the range of the remaining factors. The same procedure for calculating CCI is followed for each connection required to integrate with the COTS product, and the complexity indices are added to subsequent rows of the IPT.

$$CCI = truncate\,(10 * (IPC/ub) + .9) + MRD. \tag{1}$$

where:

IPC is the inherent Interface Point Complexity
MRD is the Mismatch Resolution Difficulty, a value between 1 and 10
ub is the upper bound of IPC, not less than 10
CCI is the Connection Complexity Index for one interface point

After all potential connections to a particular target COTS product have been examined and results documented in the IPT, then the Difficulty of Integration (DOI) for that COTS product can be determined.

3.3.2 Difficulty of Integration. The Difficulty of Integration indicator for a particular COTS product is a relative indicator of the product's integration complexity. A separate DOI is computed for each COTS product that is part of the decision process. The DOI formula is simply the average of all Connection Complexity Indices, as shown here:

$$DOI = \frac{\sum_{i=1}^{nrows} CCI\,(i)}{2 * nrows}. \tag{2}$$

where:

i is a particular row in the IPT
$nrows$ is the total number of rows in the IPT

Once the difficulty of integration has been estimated for each COTS product, then the values for CEP, VV, and DOI are inserted into the BASIS table to determine a *relative* recommendation index for each product based on all factors. Using the BASIS indices to make an informed decision on which products to include in the foundation can greatly reduce the uncertainty and subjective bias that is sometimes involved.

3.3.3 BASIS Table. After all potential COTS products have values for EV, VV, and DOI, then the BASIS table can be filled in. Using this table, a final computation can produce relative indicators for which products should be chosen for the foundation architecture of the integrated system. This indicator is named the BASIS Factor (BF).

42   K. Ballurio, B. Scalzo, and L. Rose

Table 3. The BASIS Table

Product Name	CEP Value (EV)	Vendor Viability (VV)	Difficulty of Integration (DOI)	BASIS Factor (BF)

Once the BASIS Table is complete then the deciding factors can be computed for each product with the following formula:

$$BF = truncate\left(\left(Pr_1 * EV/10 + Pr_2 * VV + Pr_3 * DOI\right)/3\right) + .9). \qquad (3)$$

where:

Pr1, Pr2, Pr3 are Business Priorities assigned as parameter weights
BF is a number scaled between 1 and 10 inclusive

Product comparisons are made using the relative BASIS factors at the end of each row. Choose the products with the lower values, but integrate the components from most to least complex so that risk items are revealed and mitigated sooner rather than later.

4 Summary

With COTS-based software development gaining in popularity across the industry, organizations are looking for techniques to support their transition. Standard development processes do not cover the special needs of COTS products and do not take a preventative approach to problem and risk avoidance. BASIS is an approach that is focused on the issues surrounding COTS software and can provide some of the missing pieces to a defined software development process.

One of the first challenges of COTS development is deciding which components are most suitable for a given project. The Component Evaluation Process, a sub-process within BASIS, supports developers by setting boundaries for a product search, defining evaluation criteria that cover factors such as functionality, architecture, performance, and financial value. Using this defined repeatable technique will help organizations choose the best products for their particular integration effort.

Once a field of best of breed components has been created, then the vendor relationship needs to be evaluated. The Vendor Viability technique within BASIS helps organizations filter the set of products by examining important factors that characterize the product supplier. These factors include financial viability, market stability, management viability, research and development viability, and extent of product support or maintenance contracts. Researching and examining these factors for each vendor will eliminate those who are not using advisable business and marketing practices that will ensure a long product life.

Understanding architectural mismatch is critical to the success of COTS software development. In spite of the marketing hype, not many components are of the plug-and-play variety. One of the most important aspects of BASIS helps to identify potential mismatches between component interfaces and suggests several possible techniques for avoiding or correcting the problem. Based on the latest research by Gacek and Deline, BASIS defines repeatable procedures that walk team members through these critical decisions.

Combining the results of the component evaluation process, the vendor viability process, and the mismatch identification process provides a final risk indicator that serves to order the integration sequence of the chosen components. By integrating the software that has the highest amount of risk in the beginning of the project, the team can identify and eliminate many problem issues before too much time is lost.

The integration of these techniques in BASIS provides value that cannot be found in existing software development processes. Many publications point to examples of isolated techniques, but none have integrated all aspects into a package that can be used by any organization with a defined process in place. Organizations that adopt BASIS will enhance the probability of success in their COTS-based software development projects.

References

1. Brereton, Pearl, Budgen, David: Component-Based Systems: A Classification of Issues. IEEE Computer 33, (2000), 54-62.
2. Cox, Brad: Object-Oriented Programming. Addison-Wesley, Reading (1986).
3. Longstaff, Thomas A., Chittister, Clyde, Pethia, Rich, Haimes, Yacov Y.: Are We Forgetting the Risks of Information Technology?. IEEE Computer 33, (2000), 43-51.
4. Gacek, Cristina: Detecting Architectural Mismatches During Systems Composition. Doctoral Thesis, University of Southern California, (1998).
5. Deline, Robert: Resolving Packaging Mismatch. Doctoral Thesis, Carnegie Mellon University, (1999).
6. Li, Wei: Another metric suite for object-oriented programming. The Journal of Systems and Software 44, (1998), 155-16.
7. Hansen, Wildred J.: A Generic Process and Terminology for Evaluating COTS Software. Proceedings of TOOLS 30, Technology of Object-Oriented Languages and Systems, Santa Barbara, California, IEEE Computer Society, Los Alamitos, (1999), pp. 547-551.
8. Polen, Susan M., Louis C. Rose, Barbara C. Phillips: Component Evaluation Process. Software Productivity Consortium, SPC-98091-CMC, Herndon, (1999).

European COTS User Working Group: Analysis of the Common Problems and Current Practices of the European COTS Users

Gorka Benguria, Ana Belén García, David Sellier, and Sandy Tay*

European Software Institute (ESI)
Parque Tecnológico, Edificio 204
E-48170 Zamudio (Bizkaia), Spain
{Gorka.Benguria, Anabelen.Garcia, David.Sellier, Sandy.Tay}@esi.es

Abstract. The use of commercial off-the-shelf (COTS) software is increasingly becoming a necessity for many European organisations. But this necessity introduces new problems and changes for all levels of the organisations both from the business point of view and the technical point of view. Funded by the Information Society Technologies Programme of the European Commission, the European COTS User Working Group (ECUA) was born to address common problems faced by European COTS users, achieve consensus on their solutions and produce a favourable impact in the overall COTS market. This paper is written based on the discussions of the Special Interest Group Sessions on the COTS Issues From the Business and the Information Technology (IT) Perspectives at the First ECUA Workshop, held at the European Software Institute, Zamudio, Spain on 31 May - 1 June 2001 in which over forty participants from all over Europe (and one from Canada) participated.

1 Introduction

The use of commercial off-the-shelf (COTS) software components is becoming an economic and strategic necessity for many European organisations in a wide variety of application areas including finance, defence, medicine, logistics, administration, manufacturing, and commerce. However, employing COTS components in building applications is not a painless business. As the COTS software market develops, COTS users must face new challenges to successfully and effectively integrate commercial software components in applications and systems.

The Information Society Technologies (IST) Programme of the European Commission (EC) funds the creation of the first vendor independent organisation of its kind in Europe, arguably in the world, the European COTS User Working

---

* We wish to thank all the participants of the first European COTS User Working Group Workshop who shared their actual CBS development experiences with us during the discussions. This document could not be have been written without their contribution.

J. Dean and A. Gravel (Eds.): ICCBSS 2002, LNCS 2255, pp. 44–53, 2002.

Group (ECUA), coordinated by the European Software Institute (ESI). The objective of ECUA is to group, study and analyse the common problems and current practices of the European companies using COTS products in order to find shared solutions and to achieve consensus in an attempt to produce a favourable impact on the overall COTS market. The members of ECUA are mainly based in Europe but membership is open to organisations with an interest in COTS all over the world.

Three ECUA workshops are planned from January 2001 till June 2002. This paper is written based on the discussions of the Special Interest Group (SIG) sessions from the 1st ECUA Workshop held on 31 May - 1 June 2001 in the European Software Institute, Zamudio, Spain. Over 40 participants from all over Europe (and one from Canada) participated in the 1st ECUA workshop.

Two parallel SIG sessions were held – COTS Issues from the Business Perspective (Business SIG), and COTS Issues from the Information Technology Perspective (IT SIG). The format of the SIG sessions was based on open discussions moderated by SIG Chair and Vice Chair elected from the ECUA Members where participants shared their actual experiences in COTS-based development.

2   Business Perspective

The Business SIG participants agreed that CBS development involves, in addition to a technical change, a transformation at a business level. The COTS paradigm brings in new activities and relationships that need to be performed in an effective and efficient way to fully benefit from using COTS.

The domain of non-technical activities related to CBS development covers activities such as finding appropriate COTS, evaluating them, managing relationships and agreements with vendors, establishing new business strategies, etc. Companies need to implement processes, techniques, mechanisms and tools that allow them to make the right business decisions. The Business SIG participants raised many questions about selection criteria, contract/licence management, vendor relationships, organisational roles and skills, and the impact of COTS on the business strategies.

By the end of the Business SIG session, the participants agreed that using COTS poses the following seven groups of business related problems: glossary or common vocabulary, COTS identification, process and methods, change management, contracts and legal issues, cost analysis, and the certification or guarantee from COTS providers.

2.1   Glossary

There is not a common understanding of COTS related terms. So identification and elaboration of a common COTS vocabulary to facilitate communication within the COTS users community is necessary. It was, however, agreed that there are already glossaries defining COTS related terms. One of the tasks of the working group will be to gather these terms so that the future discussions will be based on terminologies of common understanding.

2.2   Identification

The difficulty to find suitable COTS in the marketplace and to characterise COTS is one of the major problems during the COTS acquisition phase. COTS product descriptions from the vendors are mostly insufficient; thus finding out the features and evaluating if the COTS product fits the system requirements is made difficult for the COTS users. Moreover, the COTS variety and the lack of classification (to characterise them) make the COTS research very difficult. The lack of appropriate methods to evaluate COTS products has an effect on the whole system life cycle.

Experiences show that COTS identification is more mature in big companies where some kind of process is more likely to exist for COTS selection. In the military field there are also mature processes but they are not usually accessible by the general public. On the contrary, in most civil projects and small- and medium-sized enterprises (SMEs), the identification, characterization and evaluation processes are performed in an ad-hoc fashion and the technical people usually make decisions, based mainly on their technical knowledge.

2.3   Process and Methods

Incorporation of new COTS products into projects implies that the project manager now has to improvise many activities because defined processes and methods to introduce COTS products into the project usually do not exist. Sometimes people are reluctant to use COTS because it implies a loss of control on what the system does. This is related to the cultural change necessary to change the development paradigm. This change can be facilitated with well-defined processes and methods.

2.4   Change Management

Management and control of the COTS-based development projects is associated with the following difficulties: maintain the system updated with the last COTS version (difficult to plan in advance the system upgrading), incompatibility between different versions (change of features, impact of the new version on the system), disappearance of the COTS product from the market, adaptation (learning) of the employees. Changes on the system requirements can obsolete some COTS products. Furthermore, the lack of standards has an impact in the replacement effort, the need of training, the dependence on the vendor, and the level of competitiveness.

There are reference process models such as SW-CMM, and the newer CMM-I, which establish best practices for change management. These best practices could be integrated into the company methodology and processes for CBSs development, providing a mechanism to seamlessly manage and control change.

2.5   Legal Issues

The contractual aspect of COTS is also a key issue for COTS acquisition. The COTS contract establishes conditions to use the COTS, even states conditions that spell out how resellers or integrators on how the final COTS-based product can be used or sold. Therefore, contract conditions such as licenses, distribution authorisation, duties and rights of both parties should be carefully analysed. They are not always negotiable, placing COTS users in an uncomfortable situation.

Using COTS products influence also the way managers work because they have to deal with as many contracts as COTS products they use. Project managers typically have not the knowledge to evaluate a COTS contract that may require the knowledge of a lawyer resulting in misunderstandings and unawareness of ultimate consequences of contract conditions. Another relevant point is the lack of protection for COTS users because usually COTS providers do not assume any responsibility for damages caused by a fault in their COTS products.

2.6   Cost Analysis

The evaluation of the economic feasibility and convenience of using a certain COTS against other options such as subcontracting, or developing in-house can be a challenge for the business units. These aspects include how to estimate the cost of the system to be developed taking into account: COTS price, evaluation effort, training, adaptation and integration effort, upgrades and maintenance effort, and estimation of the cost of the changes once the system is running. Mostly, companies have not the appropriate cost model to perform an efficient evaluation of the COTS cost.

The cost benefit analysis for a COTS acquisition should take into account parameters and issues related to the whole COTS life cycle, including training, evaluation, adaptation, integration, maintenance, etc. Therefore COTS economic feasibility should be assessed using specifically customised cost models. Moreover the cost of developing the COTS integration platform is usually not taken into account in the estimation of the cost of the overall system.

2.7   High Integrity

Today perceived COTS quality is directly linked to the confidence that the acquiring company has in the COTS vendor. This may be enough for some applications, but there are other application domains like military, nuclear, medical, aeronautical, etc. where a failure in a COTS influences the safety of human lives. These companies need a complete certification and some guarantees from COTS vendors that the COTS product fulfils the safety requirements. But a company usually acquires a COTS product based on the features that the COTS vendor assures that the COTS product complies with, but the company doesn't have any guarantee that this is true apart from what the vendor says. The COTS user is also ignorant of the development process that the COTS editor follows.

3   IT Perspective

The IT SIG participants decided to focus on the influence that COTS products have on the software development processes. The requirements, design, implementation, testing, and maintenance undergo changes with the integration of COTS products. It is clear that these changes influence at the same time the mechanisms, techniques, practices and tools of the software process.

The traditional waterfall software development process does not work well for a CBS. Using COTS products introduces some new phases (COTS acquisition for example) or extends current phases (COTS testing or COTS integration) of the software development life cycle.

The issues identified by the IT SIG participants as essential for further analysis are: COTS acquisition including evaluation and qualification, COTS comparison risks, COTS acceptance, integrator role, requirement role (legacy integration).

3.1   COTS Acquisition – Evaluation and Qualification

COTS acquisition refers to the difficulty to find the high quality product that is the right fit for the CBS to be developed. From a user point of view COTS acquisition means that the COTS product has to meet requirements for: COTS functionalities, COTS support from the vendor, and COTS quality.

The COTS acquisition phase deals with a set of problems as lack of COTS visibility (black box), lack of COTS processes visibility (quality of the software vendor's development process), less than adequate documentation, vendor's reluctance to certify COTS, quality of the COTS, lack of product availability, lack of useful and relevant information on vendors' web sites. COTS performance testing can be deceiving when running on a large scale. Integrating different COTS products may bring interoperability problems.

A large part of the evaluation is made from the COTS provider documentation but usually the COTS documentation is insufficient to provide the COTS users the certification required to show that the COTS product is suitable for the system. Insufficient documentation is always a cause of extra evaluation effort for COTS users.

3.2   COTS Comparison Risk

Evaluation of COTS products often must contend with comparing products that are not entirely comparable. Furthermore, some COTS products may themselves impose additional requirements on the systems. The evaluation and comparison criteria should therefore be rooted in the characteristics and needs of the system that will use the product, but what about the derived requirements that would be imposed by COTS and that are usually unforeseen?

Experiences show also that COTS-comparison requires a lot of time and work because it implicates extra work in the testing phase such as functionality tests or/and integration test.

3.3 COTS Acceptance

It is always very difficult to determine the absolute quality and appropriateness of a COTS product. It is clear that the value of a COTS product and its fitness for use is entirely wedded to the system context in which it will be used. So, when should the COTS product be contractually accepted?

Sometimes a user has contractually accepted the product before the final system has been built. As a protection for the users, perhaps, the COTS product should only be accepted contractually when user acceptance test has been performed.

3.4 Requirements Role-Legacy Integration

Frequently switching to CBSs introduces problems associated with how to integrate a new COTS product or a new CBS into an existing infrastructure or system environment with legacy systems.

There is a widespread agreement on the importance of requirements specification. When specifying the requirements of the system, some awareness of the available COTS products, their functionality, constraints, and design assumptions should be available to the authors of the requirements documents.

But what about system requirements imposed by the required integration with the legacy systems, the current software architecture, and the current hardware infrastructure? Can they be relaxed? Should requirements be balanced between the systems requirements on one hand and the intention to use COTS on the other?

3.5 Integrator-Expectation versus Reality

A COTS product will almost never fit perfectly in a complex system, in the sense that it usually cannot easily plug-and-play. Some degree of misfit is inevitable. The interactions between multiple COTS products integrated into a final system also play an important role in the CBS development.

But is this fact currently assumed? Could the users evaluate in advance the misfit, analyse the impact and see whether it can be accommodated? The extensive use of COTS implies a shift in the domain of the expertise required, especially for integration experts.

4 Summary of Working Group Discussions of the European COTS Problems and Current Practices

The SIG participants came from many different business sectors including banking, hospital, telecommunication, and aerospace industries. There was a good representation from various research centres and universities. The countries represented were Austria, Belgium, Canada, Denmark, France, Hungary, Ireland, the Netherlands, Spain, and Sweden and the United Kingdom.

Participants who attended the workshop had different problems, needs and expectations. The COTS practitioners must face a whole new set of problems in all phases of the software development life cycle ranging from the acquisition and selection of the COTS products to its integration and maintenance in the system. Thus they concentrated on finding solutions to their problems, making contacts with other COTS users and sharing their actual experiences. The researchers, on the other hand, were more oriented to sharing their knowledge and learning current practices and skills to manage COTS based system.

In the following sections, the practical experiences of the workshop participants are documented. After each section, the comments from fellow participants are summarised.

4.1   Cost Evaluation for High Integrity Technology Application

This company has a high level of requirements for the quality of the COTS product. The evaluation of COTS in this company generally follows these three steps defined: functionalities evaluation, COTS provider support evaluation and COTS quality evaluation.

The COTS functionality evaluation generally corresponds to an analysis of the documentation provided with the COTS product. The COTS provider has to assure that the COTS user(s) will have full support during the whole life cycle of the system and the product has been in the market long enough. Furthermore, the vendor company must have a reasonable history in existence so the possibility of it going out of business is reduced and upgrades to the product in the future will be possible.

If the vendor does not certify the COTS product, the COTS qualification can be based on the analysis of the documentation supplied by the COTS provider such as quality assurance documentation, design documentation, testing coverage measurements, etc. Unfortunately, this kind of documents is not always distributed.

Sometimes, due to the lack of certification, test plan and black box testing can be used to replace certification but this situation does not happen very often. The utilisation of the same COTS product in a similar application in some other companies or in a different application but in a similar company can be a proof as well. Generally, the COTS users of the company do not retest the COTS product itself if it is certified but a high level of testing after integration is performed.

If the COTS product is appropriate for a particular application but not certified to be integrated in the system, this company may participate in a certification process together with the COTS provider. This participation can be either a financial or a technical participation, or both. The financial participation in the certification process is effective only if the cost of the COTS plus certification process is still cheaper.

Group comments: the SIG participants agreed that if the vendor company is compliant with CMM, ISO 9000, or SPICE, it is considered having demonstrated the quality of the software development process. The SIG participants also noted that the prospective COTS buyer paying for certification is not commonly heard of or done in their companies.

4.2   CORBA COTS Acquisition

The situation of the company was it needed COTS that could run on many different operating systems (CORBA). This one was the first elimination criteria. The searching has been made on the Internet by looking at the description on the company web pages and eliminating candidates if the web pages do not reflect that their product runs on a particular platform. Finally, the company chose a product that was shipped with the source code to have the possibilities to recompile on different operating systems required.

Group comments: a discriminator was found in the evaluation process that is the key of this case.

4.3   Beta-Testers Network to Evaluate a Product

One of the participants reported an experience of being a Beta customer as a way to get familiar with the functionalities that a product has and how to solve the problem found during the beta-testing phase. The participant felt that being a Beta customer allowed them to have more influence and better support at that stage. The product was used on several projects in house forming a network of beta testers. A mailing list of these beta-testers was established. If a problem was detected (documentation, testing...), the description of this problem was sent to the other users of the product. The problems were logged on a place accessible by everyone on the mailing list.

It was very useful because the users did not have to waste time to find out if the problem is a bug or a missing feature. An evaluation was done several ways. It was not as important to have all the features but all the existing requirements must be met. This system was also a good help for vendors because they can base the future functional requirements from the information provided by the beta-testers.

4.4   Voice Recognition System COTS

The evaluation of the voice system is first based on the technical documentation. If the COTS documentation is not good enough, some black box tests are performed to evaluate the performance of the COTS products. The result of the black box tests can be compared to other results provided by other COTS providers (or other black box tests). Some other tests can be performed, according to the result of the black box tests, after the integration of the COTS in the system.

It is both effort and time consuming to determine if a COTS product is suitable for your system. The black box tests show that requirements are fulfilled but do not prove that the component is compatible with the system or the other COTS components. Moreover, testing the new COTS product within the system can sometimes imply the entire integration of the COTS product into the application in context.

Group comments: Developing when the users are evaluating implies that the evaluation is not finished until the system is built. But also the system is not finished until the evaluation is finished. This is a circular relationship. It can be a problem if the users have very specific requirements. At a certain moment the decision to quit the evaluation phase has to be made.

Sometimes the COTS users have to take a risk. The risk can be reduced but it has to be taken. The COTS users have to make a decision that enough evaluation has been done and they have to live with the COTS product that they have chosen. There are always risks in evaluations. COTS users cannot spend the whole project on evaluations. Proceed with a product based on the information that the user has. Normally, the COTS supplier and integrator have the responsibility of assuring the COTS will be working.

4.5   COTS for Hospital IT

The participant highlights how sometimes localised vision may cause incompatibility between different COTS components that need to be integrated together. In some hospital each department has certain autonomy to choose the appropriate COTS components. The result of this policy is that the choice of one department influences the choice of the other departments for some components are not compatible with the COTS desired by another department (may not be the most reliable).

As an attempt to improve the first policy, a two-level method was proposed: corporative level and department level. Instead of allowing a department to choose its COTS products then proceed to the next department, the selection process will run in parallel. The process consists of several phases: each department selects a COTS product that matches the minimum requirements and submits the request to the corporate. Then the corporate will propose different combinations and send the proposal back to the department for evaluation. Since this is still an ongoing process, one cannot tell if it will be successful.

Group comments: It is important to test if the COTS products required by different departments are really compatible with each other. It is wise to choose a COTS product based on a global view or a corporate view instead of a local or departmental view especially if the COTS is to be integrated with other applications in the company. The SIG participants feel that the second approach is definitely better than the first one.

5   Conclusion

The number of European companies using COTS is growing very rapidly. An increasing number of systems include components acquired in the component market. Small and medium-sized organisations are more dependent on COTS components.

Using COTS products implies important changes for an organisation that affect all levels of the organisation (business units and software development) and introduces problems and changes that can have an important influence on the benefits of using COTS.

The major problems faced by the business units are the difficulty to identify the suitable COTS on the market, a lack of knowledge to evaluate the cost of using COTS in their CBS, the contractual problems with the COTS providers and the problems linked with CBS project management.

For the technical departments, all phases of the life cycle are affected with the introduction of COTS product in the system. The most affected phases by using COTS products are: acquisition, evaluation and qualification of COTS products, integration of the COTS in their product and the testing phase (black box).

Because of country, language, and cultural barriers, the European companies may have a unique set of problems compared with their North American counterparts. The final results of the working group will only be available after the last of the series of workshops that is held in May 2002. The Working Group welcomes new members from the international community. If you are interested in becoming a member of ECUA, please email ecua@esi.es or visit its homepage on http://www.esi.es/ecua to download the Member Application Form.

Combined Selection of COTS Components

X. Burgués, C. Estay, X. Franch, J.A. Pastor, and C. Quer

Universitat Politècnica de Catalunya (UPC)
c/ Jordi Girona 1-3 (Campus Nord, C6) E-08034 Barcelona, Spain
{diafebus, el_estay, franch, pastor, cquer.0}@lsi.upc.es

Abstract. In this paper the problem of the combined selection of COTS components is analyzed in organizations of a specialized nature. This is currently a process of great interest: once many organizations have implemented recently ERP systems for supporting their central management areas, they need to select specialized components for other more particular business areas. We propose a model of combined selection of components based on the distinction of two levels. At the global level the combined selection process takes place, and it includes the initial planning, the enactment of the individual selection processes, the proposal of scenarios to evaluate and the final selection of COTS components. At the local level we locate all the individual selection processes of the different particular business areas, under the supervision of the process at the global level. The model presented here arises from the observation of an ongoing real case.

1 Introduction

Software development based on COTS (Commercial Off-The-Shelf) components [1,2] has acquired in the last years a great and growing importance in software engineering. This kind of development presents some risks, being the incorrect selection of components one of them.

Several methodological proposals have been formulated to improve effectiveness of the individual selection of COTS components [3,4,5]. This modality of selection appears in a great number of situations where one product is required to cover a specific functionality, such as a mail service or a graphical library.

Nevertheless, there exist other COTS component selection contexts that present relevant aspects that are not dealt with by the above methodologies. One particular situation is the one of an organization composed by different areas in the process of renovating their information systems through the selection of adequate COTS components. In this case, the renovation should not be a simple juxtaposition of several individual selection processes, one for each organizational area. Since many interacting factors influence the overall selection, these factors should be considered from the beginning of the selection process, in order to avoid products selected for an area negatively interfering with other products previously selected for other areas, and to avoid undesirable restrictions for future selections.

J. Dean and A. Gravel (Eds.): ICCBSS 2002, LNCS 2255, pp. 54–64, 2002.

This paper proposes a process model for the *combined selection of COTS components* to be used in situations such as the above one. The adjective *combined* not only means "the selection of a set of COTS components", but also "the indivisible and concurrent selection of them". Two levels compose the model. A global level is responsible of negotiating the overall process of combined selection, by firing individual selection processes for each area, supervising their evolution, controlling the viability of their results, and finding the best combination in the resulting proposals. At the local level, the different individual processes take place, under the supervision of the process at the global level. One of the relevant effects of this approach is that the individual selection processes evaluate components according to their specific requirements without really selecting them, while the final decision is taken at the global level. Thus, we believe that a final decision can be made in a more integrative, collaborative and conciliatory way, while caring for global and local selection goals.

Our proposal arises from a real ongoing combined COTS selection case in a big hospital in the Barcelona area in which we are involved by means of a collaboration agreement.

2 A Context for the Combined Selection of COTS Components

The areas and processes found in any organization may be classified as:

– Generic, common to a great number of organizations (for example, purchase orders and after-sale service).
– Highly specific, oriented to satisfy the product or service particularities within their vertical industries and markets.

Our process is oriented to those organizations where the second kind of areas and processes prevails (see Fig. 1). We name them *organizations of a specialized character (OSC)*.

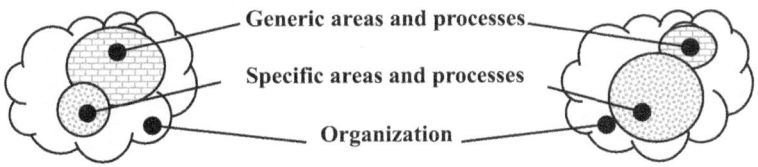

Fig. 1. Organization non-fully specialized (left) vs OSC (right)

There are different types of software that support the areas and processes of an OSC (see Fig. 2, left). Generic areas and processes are mainly supported by *basic management applications (BMA)*, such as ERP (Enterprise Resource Planning) systems [6]. Specific ones are covered by *vertical applications (VA)*, which are software products specialized for the specific areas and processes of the OSC; they play a prominent role in this kind of organizations. Two additional types of software products are *decisional applications (DA)*, such as data warehouses; and the *underlying technology (Tech)*, such as database management systems and middleware. Figure 2 (right) shows different ways for vertical applications to interoperate between them and with other types of software products.

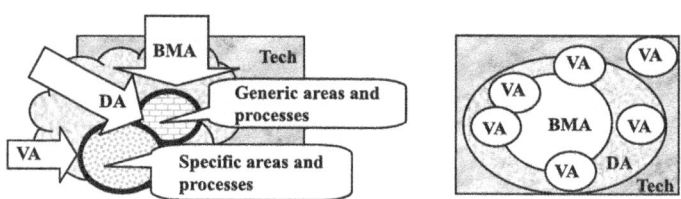

Fig. 2. Software types, areas and processes (left) and a possible underlying architecture (right)

The real experience we are involved in takes place in an OSC. This organization has as target the renovation of its information systems through the selection and implementation of COTS components, developing only the software needed to integrate them. This decision has been taken for reasons of cost and reliability. Software renovation started with the selection of an ERP system as the basic management application. Afterwards, an extensive set of vertical applications is currently being selected for each of the specific areas and processes of the OSC, each one with its own requirements. This is the phase of the OSC information system renovation that we address in this paper (see Fig. 3). In the selection process of these vertical applications some prior underlying technology requirements must be satisfied, while the same selection process could add some new technological requirements. In fact, the selection of both the middleware and the decisional applications were scheduled as the final selection processes, subordinated to the selection of the vertical applications.

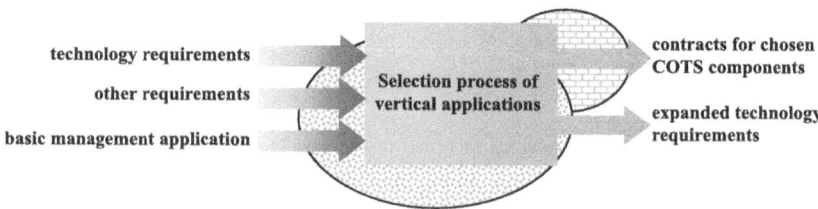

Fig. 3. The selection process of vertical application in the considered organization

3 The Selection of Vertical Applications as a Combined Selection

In our opinion, a key success factor for the selection process of vertical applications for OSCs consists in addressing the task as a combined selection of a set of components. This vision is justified by the fact that the set of the best individual products for the specific areas does not have to be the best global solution, as we argue below.

The selection of a vertical application starts with a set of requirements obtained from various information sources. Most of these requirements come from the particular area or process to be supported, but there are also requirements from a more general context. We may classify the requirements as:

- **External requirements**. They are external to the organization and usually imposed by technical or political institutions, standards, laws, etc. For instance, personal data protection laws.
- **Corporate requirements**. Arising from the very OSC under consideration. Usually, they will be established in the initial phases of a new information systems and technologies strategic plan, before the selection process of vertical applications starts. For example, the providers of the selected components may be required to have a permanent site in the same city as the OSC.
- **Interaction requirements**. They determine technological needs for the communication of the vertical applications among them and with other components.
- **Local requirements**. They are specific to each of the areas, processes or departments. They can be refinements or adaptations of non-local requirements, but mostly they will be new specialized requirements, which may be functional, technological, or strategic.

Out of the above requirements categories, just the last one is related to the specific local environment of a vertical application. A combined study of the rest of requirements (which we name *global requirements*) fits better to their nature, both from a conceptual point of view (global vision for global requirements) as from a practical one (the global requirements are analyzed only once and not repeatedly in each area). Moreover, there are global requirements that very rarely can be transformed into local requirements. Some examples follow:

- Rather than trying to divide *a priori* the foreseen global budget among the diverse areas, it is the combined cost that should be adjusted to the overall budget settled down. A combined supervision of the candidates managed by the different areas will favour the detection of any deviation in this aspect, and it will allow to adjust it as soon as possible during the selection process.
- COTS components usually need to be parameterized to the particular requirements of the buying organization. This is why we believe that not only their producers, but also the candidate implementers should be considered

in the evaluation and selection. In addition to the reliability of producers
and implementers, it will probably be interesting to minimize their number
for different reasons: technological (the interoperability should turn much
easier when it involves a smaller number of producers), managerial (the
setup and monitoring of the implementation process will obviously be easier) and negotiation-related (the dispersion of producers and implementers
could harm the overall negotiation of contracts when diminishing the business volume with each of them).

– A basic compatibility requirement should be established: interoperability
among components and with the underlying technology should be possible. For example, a combined selection including two products that require
different underlying database management systems will not generally be acceptable. In addition, the connection of the vertical applications with the
chosen basic management applications should be considered.

Another point supporting the existence of a global view of multiple selection
has to be with the relationships between the chosen products and the involved
areas. The result of the selection process will be a set of individual COTS components, where one or more components may cover more than just one specialized
area or process. This situation can happen given several circumstances; for example, when requirements of more than one area or process are satisfied by one
single product. Coordination of the individual selection processes carried out in
the involved areas would be helpful to detect and manage this situation.

It is important to point that our proposal practically forces to execute the
individual selection processes simultaneously or at least within a very short period of time (to avoid an unacceptable duration of the process). This could be
negatively considered because it prevents learning about the process and about
events not previously foreseen as the process goes on. However, this situation
is not specific of our approach: in general any combined selection process is
constrained by temporal limitations and by the availability of human resources,
which will also impose overlapping constraints among the individual selection
processes.

4   The Global Level of the Combined Selection Process

From the discussion above, we propose a combined selection process that takes
place at two different levels: the *local level*, corresponding to the OSC areas,
where the *individual selection processes* progress; and the *global level*, corresponding to the OSC as a whole, where a *global selection process* coordinates
the individual ones.

4.1   General Vision of the Global Level

The global level is responsible of selecting the set of vertical applications that
will cover the established high level needs. To carry out this mission, the global

selection process supervises the evolution, and synchronizes the results, of the different individual selection processes. The global level consists of four phases:

1. Initial planning of the combined selection process and enactment of the individual selection processes.
2. Configuration of the scenarios to be evaluated.
3. Evaluation of the scenarios.
4. Selection of the vertical applications.

Figure 4 shows the sequence among these phases as well as the interactions between the global and the local levels[1].

4.2   Initial Planning and Enactment of the Individual Selection Processes

In this phase the following activities are carried out:

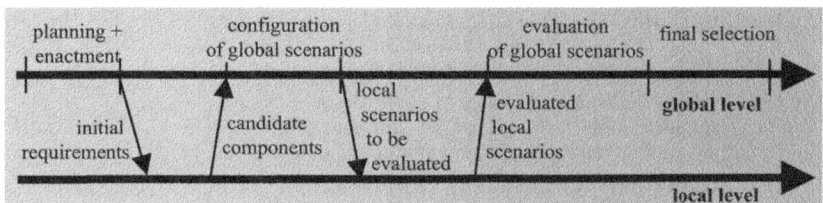

Fig. 4. The global level and its interactions with the local level

- Configuration of selection and evaluation teams. Our two-level approach leads to the establishment of at least one team dedicated to the global selection level (*selection team*) and one for each individual selection process (*evaluation teams*). Care should be taken with regard to the respective compositions of these teams. In particular, a good coordination between the selection and the evaluation teams should be guaranteed. A straightforward form of doing this consists in the integration of people from global and local levels (for example, including those people responsible for the evaluation teams in the selection team).
- Temporal planning of the milestones of each of the global level phases, taking into consideration the established timeframes within the information systems and technologies strategic plan.
- Temporal scheduling of the different individual selection processes. This is important if it is impossible to carry them out simultaneously or if there are areas particularly critical or complex.

---

[1] Inputs and outputs of this process are detailed in Fig. 3.

- Analysis, completion and prioritization of the initial global requirements already settled down in the information systems and technologies strategic plan. This point is especially important, since very restrictive requirements endanger the selection process [7].
- Selective transmission of these requirements to the individual selection processes that will take place in the areas and processes to be addressed.

4.3   Configuration of Global Scenarios

As a first partial result, the evaluation teams will propose to the selection team an initial set of candidates for their respective areas, once discarded the clearly unsatisfactory alternatives. An explanatory report should be included justifying each candidate suitability, based on the expected compliance with respect to the global and local requirements. Also, the report must include other relevant information useful for the global level: price, producer, platform, etc. From these partial results, the selection team is responsible of configuring several *possible scenarios*.

In general, we can speak of *global scenarios* formed by the combination *of local scenarios*. The local scenarios can be focussed from the point of view of the products and of the areas or processes considered:

- A scenario can consist of one single product or the combination of several ones.
- A scenario can be bounded to just one area or process, or it can affect several of them. In this second case, the evaluation teams of the involved areas or processes should obviously work together or coordinate their related areas or processes.

In Fig. 5, three different global scenarios are shown for the case of three areas. The first one presents the simplest situation (all the local scenarios consist of a single product specialized for a single area). The second and third are *inter-area scenarios* and this can suppose a management problem of the selection process. In the second one a product is evaluated more than once; so the same criteria may be evaluated in a different way in different scenarios without a convincing justification. Finally, in the third global scenario one of the local scenarios embraces two areas, avoiding partially the previous risk but requiring a strong coordination.

The determination of scenarios may involve interactions with producers and implementers, mainly in case of inter-area scenarios, to ensure the correct coordination of products from different producers and/or with different implementers if they are finally chosen.

4.4   Evaluation of Global Scenarios. Final Selection of Vertical Applications

Once the evaluation teams evaluate the local scenarios, they communicate to the selection team their results. Starting from here, the global scenarios are

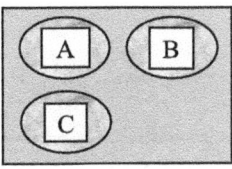 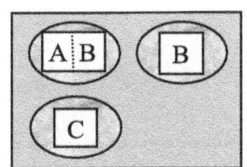 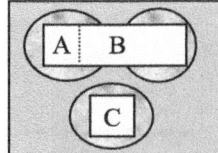

Fig. 5. Scenarios (circle: area/process; rectangle: scenario; A, B, C: components)

evaluated considering factors such as those enumerated in Sect. 3. The result of this evaluation determines the COTS components chosen. Afterwards, it will be appropriate to negotiate the full details of the contracts regarding acquisition, implementation, installation, and maintenance. The technological requirements generated by the selected components are also collected.

4.5 Cycles

The description that we have presented of the global level allows us to clearly establish the phases in this level, but it does not consider a usual feature of most software processes, including ours. Namely, the existence or possibility of *cycles* in various points of the process.

We identify two types of cycles: cycles between phases at the global level, and cycles between the global and the local levels. Among the reasons that generate cycles, we mention:

- The requirements can be refined when candidates are explored and also during the process of evaluation of the scenarios (see cycles **a** in Fig. 6). From some requirements, candidates are discarded; the candidates that remain are more thoroughly explored, so giving place to new requirements that draw needs and opportunities that had not been previously considered.
- The final selection may fail not due to process errors, but because of unsolvable problems appearing during contract negotiation. In this case, the last phase of the process should be recaptured with the next best-evaluated scenario (see cycles **b** in Fig. 6).
- The initial proposal of candidates can demand diverse interactions between both levels (see cycles **c** in Fig. 6), either because the global selection process requires more information about some of the proposed candidates, or because it considers that there are too many (or too few!) candidates.

Furthermore, the evaluation of scenarios can be addressed as an incremental and iterative process. Notice that a given scenario considered temporarily feasible could become inappropriate in later stages. For example, if the first scenario presented in Fig. 5 is evaluated positively, the other two could be discarded for being inter-area ones, in case that this kind of scenarios are to be avoided.

It is worth remarking that these cycles are difficult to avoid in any multiple selection process, regardless of being two-level or not. Also we would like to point

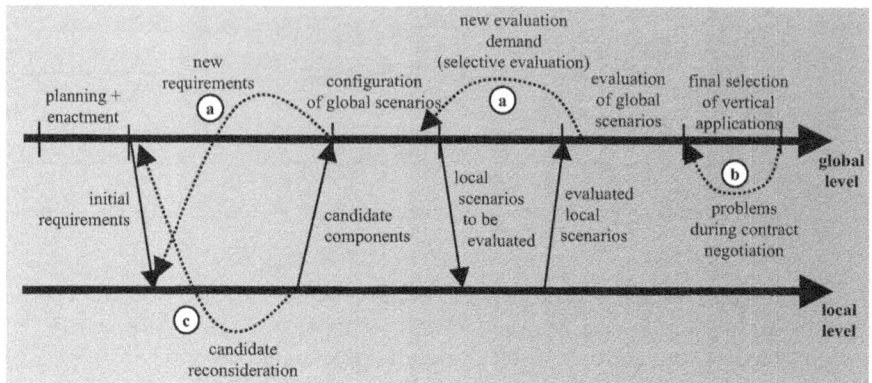

Fig. 6. The global level considering cycles (dashed lines)

out that most of them (with the notorious exception of contract negotiation) may be considered beneficial to obtain a greater knowledge of the domain and to better organize an control the evolution of the selection process.

5   The Local Level of the Combined Selection Process

For the elaboration of our proposal, aside of taking into account previous experiences of our team in the field of ERP systems selection [8,9], we have analyzed several methods that would be applicable at the local level of our approach. Two of the most widespread methodologies in this field are PORE [4,5] and OTSO [3].

The PORE methodology has reinforced our eminently iterative vision of the process: given a set of initial requirements, some candidates are discarded, while the candidates that remain are more thoroughly explored to discover new requirements, and beginning a new cycle. Thus, by enlarging our knowledge on the area and our requirements altogether, we may decrease at the same time the number of candidates until obtaining the most appropriate. OTSO does not incorporate any cycle at all in the model, but proposes a transfer of knowledge from an individual selection process to the next one. Nevertheless, we do not make this in our proposal because we consider that this knowledge transfer is interesting in the framework of the referenced method (*experience factory*), but not under the context explained in this paper: the overall renovation of information systems in a short period of time, which is a process with very low frequency in the context of any organization, especially OSCs.

6   Conclusions

In this paper, we address the problem of the combined selection of COTS components in organizations of a specialized character. We provide the main reasons for not managing this selection task as a simple juxtaposition of individual selection processes. Rather, we propose a process model for combined selection of components based on the distinction of two levels, a global one corresponding to the combined selection itself, and a local level where all the individual selection processes take place in specific areas, processes or departments.

We believe that the most relevant points in our proposal are the following:

- We have captured the need of coordinating diverse individual selections of COTS components when they converge in space and time within the same organization. Good coordination is a critical success factor for a combined selection process. Otherwise, the selection could not be good enough (not including fundamental global aspects or taking decisions too early) or the process could take more time than expected (reconsidering previously taken decisions when they become incompatible with components selected in other areas). Although some authors have already commented about the convenience of this type of model [10], we have not found yet any similar one in the literature. The distinction of two levels addresses this idea in a natural way, distributes the responsibilities appropriately and favours the coordination and the follow-up of the separate tasks.
- The generic characterization of the local level, without formulating any rigid internal organization, provides a flexible way to adapt our selection process model at this level to the specific characteristics of each area.
- The cyclic nature of the selection process is introduced in our proposal, which adapts to the realistic evolution of selection processes, and provides for their enrichment and improvement in an incremental way.
- The applied character of the proposal arises from the observation of, and participation in, several real experiences of comprehensive software selections for a varied set of organizations. More specifically, our mentioned participation in a real combined COTS component selection for a major hospital.

Our future work involves several related areas. For instance, we plan to extend our proposal by:

- integrating hierarchies in the model, both for the global level (intermediate units) and for the local levels (complex areas);
- analyzing matrix-like organizational structures which involve overlapping of areas;
- determining accurately the influence of the size of the components in the model, as well as of other relevant factors (temporal constrains, team composition, etc.);
- formalizing some parts of the process model, for example, by means of UML; and,
- studying with more detail the inter-area scenarios.

References

1. Software Engineering Institute, Carnegie Mellon University: Annotated Bibliography of COTS Software Evaluation. Available at
   `http://www.sei.cmu.edu/cbs/papers/eval_bib.html`, (1998-1999).
2. J. Dean, P. Oberndorf, M. Vigder (eds): Proceedings of the 2nd Workshop on COTS Software. Limerick (Ireland), June (2000).
3. J. Kontio: A case study in applying a systematic method for COTS selection. Proceedings 18th International, Conference on Software Engineering (ICSE), Berlin (Germany), March (1996).
4. N. Maiden, C. Ncube: Acquiring requirements for COTS selection. IEEE Software 15(2), (1998).
5. C. Ncube: A requirements engineering method for COTS-based systems development. PhD Thesis, City University, (1999).
6. J. Verville, A. Halingten: Acquiring Enterprise Software. Prentice Hall PTR - Enterprise Software Series 2000.
7. C. Ncube, N.A.M. Maiden: Procuring Software Systems: Current Problems and Solutions. Proceedings 3rd International, Workshop on Requirements Engineering (REFSQ), Barcelona (Spain), June (1997).
8. J.A.Pastor, X. Franch, F. Sistach: Methodological ERP Acquisition: the SHERPA Experience. 1st World Class IT Service Management Guide (2nd edition), tenHagenStam, (2001).
9. X. Burgués, X. Franch, J.A. Pastor: Formalising ERP Selection Criteria. Proceedings of 10th IEEE International, Workshop on Software Specification and Design (IWSSD), San Diego (California, USA), November (2000).
10. C. Ncube, N. Maiden: COTS Software Selection: the need to make tradeoffs between system requirements, architectures and COTS/Components. In [2].

Identifying Evolvability for Integration

L. Davis and Rose Gamble*

Software Engineering & Architecture Team
Department of Mathematical and Computer Sciences
University of Tulsa, 600 S. College Ave., Tulsa, OK 74104
{davisl,gamble}@utulsa.edu

Abstract. The seamless integration of commercial-off-the-shelf (COTS) components offers many benefits associated with reuse. Even with successful composite applications, unexpected interoperability conflicts can arise when COTS products are upgraded, new components are needed, and the application requirements change. Recent approaches to integration follow pattern-based design principles to construct integration *architecture* for the composite application. This integration architecture provides a design perspective for addressing the problematic interactions among components within the application environment. However, little attention has been paid to the evolvability of these architectures and their embedded functionality. In this paper, we discuss the need for design traceability based on the history of interoperability conflicts and resolution decisions that comprise the integration architecture. Additionally, we advocate that certain functional aspects of a pattern can be pinpointed to resolve a conflict. Combining these two aspects of integration architecture design, we illustrate that often evolution is possible with minimal changes to the integration solution.

1 Introduction

Integration of software components is a well-accepted approach to address the various issues associated with in-house development of complex systems. However, it is not always a simple process. Both industry and academia are developing techniques, methodologies, and products to alleviate the problems surrounding building composite applications. One central point to be considered is how the inclusion of COTS products impacts interoperability. There is no doubt that in most cases, COTS products offer well-tested, vendor-supported software that would be burdensome to build in-house. Though such in-house development is performed (often because a product won't integrate properly), it can significantly increase development cost, while at the same time decreasing reliability and support.

There are many reasons why integration is difficult. Most have to do with the behavioral expectations of the component and its application environment.

* Contact author. This research is sponsored in part by AFOSR (F49620-98-1-0217) and NSF (CCR-9988320).

J. Dean and A. Gravel (Eds.): ICCBSS 2002, LNCS 2255, pp. 65–75, 2002.

Other reasons include a shortage of tools to aid professionals in an integration effort. They must often rely on instinct instead of a principled approach to build composite applications. As in all software development, there may be disagreement as to what requirements, components, or middleware choices are malleable. Misjudgment of requirements can lead to unexpected behavior or the use of unacceptable products.

Middleware products are being heavily marketed as complete solutions to all integration needs. They can be a perfect fit, integrating components smoothly. In other cases, however, vendor consultants are needed to train, assist, and/or configure the solution. Overall, there is still a great deal of guesswork and complexity in implementing middleware as it is usually considered after a failed integration attempt. Basic principles of requirements engineering and software design must be diligently followed to achieve seamless integration.

In general, patterns provide an implementation approach to problems in the form of repeatable solutions. Architectural and design patterns have been defined that underlie middleware frameworks. Some issues need to be addressed within patterns to facilitate their use for general component integration. Many viable patterns are not identified as integration patterns. Those that are often do not detail the interoperability conflicts that they resolve. Patterns also do not naturally identify closed box functionality, like COTS products, present in the implementation. Thus, there is a lack of direction in pinpointing patterns that are descriptive enough to assist in the implementation of a composite application.

Given that integration goes smoothly, evolution can generate additional component integration issues, while, at the same time, making others obsolete. These problems are magnified when a COTS product is part of an integrated application. In fact, COTS products are especially susceptible to evolution, including radical changes, due to the need to attain and keep a broad customer base.

Integration solutions should be altered minimally for the continued reuse benefits. To do this, it is necessary to know how and why an existing integration solution is impacted by evolution in order to design it more robustly. This requires an understanding of why a pattern is use, how it can change and its effect on integration.

In this paper, we use the history of interoperability conflicts and resolution decisions that comprise the integration architecture as a basis for understanding the design. We advocate that certain aspects of a pattern can be pinpointed to resolve a conflict. Combining these two aspects of integration architecture design, we illustrate that often evolution is possible with minimal changes to the integration solution.

2   Background

Maintaining a high-level of abstraction at which to relate a system design remains the basis for describing an architecture for software. Through *software architecture* a system's computational elements, their interactions, and structural constraints can be expressed at a high, yet meaningful, level of abstraction

[1]. Conceptual system issues can then be explained, discussed and modeled without becoming entangled in implementation and deployment details. Characteristics defined with respect to architectural styles include those that describe the various types of components and connectors, data issues, control issues, and control/data interaction issues [2,3,4].

Connectors have become increasingly important in software architecture analysis, forming the basis for component connection [5,6,7,8]. Explicit descriptions of connectors are desirable as these can allow for design choices among and analysis of existing interaction schemes, along with the specification of new connectors. This effort can allow designers the flexibility to choose the correct interoperability schemes in an integrated application.

Architectures and patterns that form middleware frameworks provide guidance to "in-house" integration efforts. Common patterns considered as integration patterns are the Proxy [10] and Broker that afford clients and servers location transparency, plug and play mobility, and portability [10,11]. Recent integration patterns, including the Wrapper-Façade, Component Configurator, and the Interceptor, represent repeatable solutions to particular integration problems [12]. Enterprise Application Integration patterns, such as the Integration Mediator [13] focus on integrating enterprise application components. These patterns provide functionality such as interface unification/reusability, location transparency/negotiation, and decoupling.

The most salient point to be made concerning integration patterns is their lack of connection between the interoperability problems requiring the use of the pattern and the reason the pattern resolves those problems. As more patterns are defined and their complexity increases, at stake becomes the understandability of the integration pattern and the history of decisions for its use. In short, in their current state, patterns do not focus on issues of integration solution evolution.

The evolutionary properties of components can be captured using principles of software architecture. One goal is to find an architecture to which other architectures can transition easily [1]. Though architecture migration is a plausible solution, it is not always feasible for all systems, especially COTS products where many properties are hidden. In a similar vein, researchers examine constraints on reconfiguring architectures to assess their response to evolution [15]. This illustrates that certain properties of components and connectors lessen the impact of change [16]. Certain architecture description languages support architecture-based evolution through the changes in topology [16], optionality [17], and variability [18].

Analysis methods exist to assess the evolvability and reusability of a component architecture. One method employs a framework and a set of architectural views [19]. The architectural views include information gathered during various system lifecycles as well as stakeholder requirements. Our research relies on static property analysis methods to evaluate characteristics of the architecture in an effort to identify potential interoperability problems [20,21].

3 Fundamentals for Understanding Integration Solution Design

Collidescope is a prototype assessment tool to provide developers with a means for evaluating integration solution design decisions [22]. The ultimate goal is to provide the developer with a visible link between interoperability problems, their causes, and their solutions. Collidescope currently implements the foundational underpinnings needed to determine potential *problematic architecture interactions* (PAIs). PAIs are defined as interoperability conflicts that are predicted through the comparison of relevant architecture interaction characteristics and require intervention via external services for their resolution [22]. Utilizing broad, but descriptive, architectural characteristics of the component systems provides dual benefits. They aid discovery of PAIs and the assessment of inevitable future conflicts brought on by evolution [23]. In fact, Collidescope does not require all component characteristics to have values. It can work with only a partial set. This feature is very important because little information may be known about a COTS product, especially one with which a developer has had little experience. Of course, some potential PAIs may be missed.

Figure 1 depicts two linked components, Alpha and Beta, in a composite application. Control structure, the structure that governs the execution in the system, is identified for each of the components. Alpha has a concurrent control structure, while Beta's is single-threaded. The application has values for many of the same characteristics as the component with a different granularity. For instance, the control structure of the application governs how the *components* coordinate their execution. We will return to application characteristics in Sect. 4.

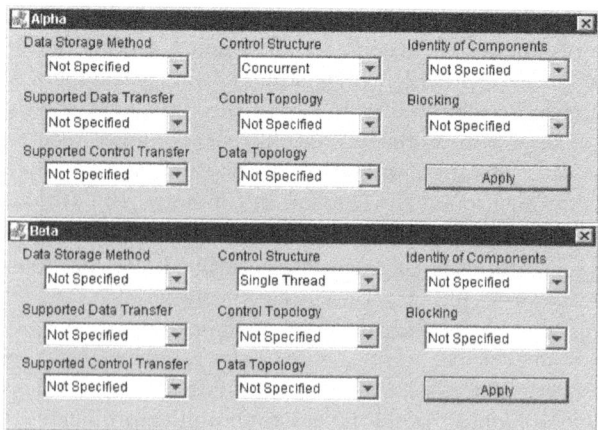

Fig. 1. Architecture Characteristics with Values for Control Structure

As a first pass analysis, Collidescope detects thirteen PAIs in one of three categories. These categories represent distinct issues that arise in component communication: expectations for data transfer, expectations for control transfer, and how interaction between components is initialized.

Two types of static analysis are performed [20]. The first is *component-component* analysis in which component characteristic values are compared. For *application-component* analysis, the application characteristics are compared with each component. Figure 2 displays the potential PAIs found by a component-component analysis using Alpha and Beta. In addition, we introduce an application, Omega, for application-component analysis. The name is in bold. The characteristic is in italics followed by a value. The number (1-13) is the conflict preceded by its category.

When comparing these characteristics it becomes apparent that communication between concurrent and single-threaded components will be difficult as single threaded components expect directed control transfer and block upon initiation. Concurrent components, on the other hand, run despite the execution state of other participating components.

Alpha		Beta	
Control Structure	Concurrent	Control Structure	Single Thread
4	Control Transfer	Sequencing multiple control transfers	
Omega		**Alpha**	
Control Structure	Single Thread	Control Structure	Concurrent
4	Control Transfer	Sequencing multiple control transfers	
Omega		**Alpha**	
Control Topology	Hierarchical	Control Structure	Concurrent
1	Control Transfer	Restricted points of control transfer	
Omega		**Alpha**	
Data Topology	Hierarchical	Control Structure	Concurrent
5	Data Transfer	Restricted points of data transfer	
10	Data Transfer	Sequencing multiple data transfers	

Fig. 2. Problematic Architecture Interactions

The next step in the assessment is the identification of integration elements that resolve the PAIs. This completes the design path from an identified problem to the fundamental solution. We model the basic functionality needed for integration as three integration elements: *translator, controller,* and *extender* [24,25]. These integration elements supplement the traditional architecture connectors.

A *translator* has some basic properties. It should communicate with other components independent of their identities. Input must have a uniform structure that is known by the translator's domain. Third, conversions must be represented by a total mathematical relation or composition of relations that maps the input to the output. Translators are particularly necessary in heterogeneous, COTS-based integrations, as consistently formatted data is never expected between vendors.

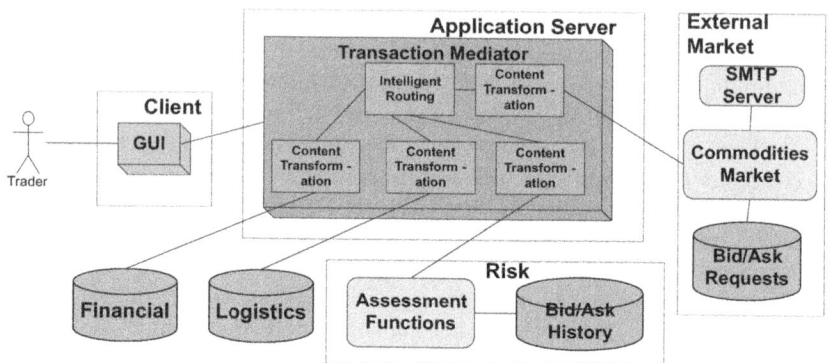

Fig. 3. The InfoTrade System Architecture

A *controller* integration element coordinates and mediates the movement of information between components using predefined decision-making processes. The decisions include determining what data to pass, from which component to accept data, and to which component data should be sent. Multiple decisions can be made within a single controller. Decisions can be based upon input data, input components, output components, or a combination of data and components.

An *extender* integration element adds those features and functionality to an integration solution to further adapt it to the application environment, embodying those behaviors not performed by a translator or controller (e.g., buffering, adding call-backs, opening files, and performing security checks). Because of the diverse behavior of extenders, each distinct action is modeled independently.

The above integration elements may be combined with each other and with simple connectors (e.g., a UNIX pipe) to form *integration architectures* as needed to resolve specific conflicts. An integration architecture, then, is defined to be the software architecture description of a solution to interoperability problems between at least two interacting component systems [11,26]. An integration architecture forms the foundation of design patterns and off-the-shelf (OTS) middleware.

The use of static, relevant architectural characteristics, standardized conflicts, and simple integration functions to resolve conflicts provides the history of design decisions. Therefore, when evidence changes, it points directly to the resulting functionality that is affected.

4   An Evolving Application

In this section, we study the requirements of a composite application called InfoTrade, a system for automated trading of commodities, like oil and gas. The drive to develop such an application comes at a time when automated stock trading is in full swing. Yet, commodities trading is just beginning to be automated. Many of the needed independent software components (some of which are COTS) are in place but only partial automated trading is being done. Much of the information before and after a trade is entered manually. Furthermore, because automated trading is limited, there is a mix of old and new styles of information and flow that must be blended.

The InfoTrade system architecture is shown in Fig. 3. The participating components include External Market, Risk, Logistics, and Financial. The External Market is comprised of a national commodities market information module, a database to house all of the bid/ask requests put to the market, and a SMTP for dynamic messaging. Risk uses a history of Bid/Ask requests to assess the financial exposure of the corporation. Logistics is a database of transportation (car, boat, plane, etc.) information, including specifications and statistics associated with transporting commodities. Financial is a database of customer billing information, as well as, corporate-wide financial information.

InfoTrade integrates COTS components essential to the execution of a commodities trade using the Transaction Mediator (Fig. 3) – an implementation of the Integration Mediator architecture [13]. This solution accommodates the different component data formats and communication methods. Within the integrated application, the Transaction Mediator is stateless, needing only the current Bid/Ask request to perform its mediation. Thus, to make a trade in this system, the user places a bid, which is routed through the Transaction Mediator. The Intelligent Router coordinates the direction of the Bid/Ask message. Content Transformers intercept the message and transform it to a format for their respective components. Risk analysis is performed only on a weekly basis when the market is closed and no bids are being placed. The Intelligent Router calls the External Market to request the current store of Bid/Ask requests, sequencing any concurrent communications such as a SMTP packet being sent. It then routes these records to Risk for financial exposure analysis. During communications to Risk and External Market, a unique Content Transformer translates incoming/outgoing requests to ensure the request data formats are correct.

With the expansion of e-commerce opportunities for service-oriented corporations, more companies desire an automated commodities facility with *real-time risk analysis*. This institutes a new composite application requirement causing the application architecture characteristics to evolve.

The real-time requirement places new demands on the Transaction Mediator, as it must retain the current Bid/Ask request to arbitrate the concurrently executing trade and the financial exposure calculation. The question becomes how can the integration solution now meet this new requirement? One alternative is to scrap the existing implementation, choosing more dynamic integration architectures such as a Broker. Another alternative is to re-write the Transaction Mediator, perhaps transitioning from its combined Java and JMS implementation to one utilizing real-time CORBA. Both of these choices go against the reuse ideals that led to the original integration.

The design decisions supported by our methodology (Sect. 3) provides a direct link from the application requirements to the integration elements that make up the integration solution. This fosters evolution by providing the developer with insight into which parts of the integration solution should be modified or replaced, as well as insight into where additional pieces of functionality are needed. The assessment method does not discount any of the alternatives, but helps to determine which – a new design, re-implementation, or evolution – is the best choice

There are many factors that contribute to the formation and, subsequent, evolution of the InfoTrade integrated application. First, it is important to look at the components in the current application. As these are COTS systems, little is known of their internal functionality. Besides their obviously dissimilar data formats, only the component-level characteristic *control structure* can be discerned. Refer to Alpha and Beta in Fig. 1 as the External Market and Risk components, respectively.

For InfoTrade to accommodate real-time risk analysis, the application itself must be characterized differently. Table 1 shows how this change affects how the application will be newly described. The component values remain the same.

Table 1. Evolving Application Characteristics

Characteristic	Original Value	Evolved Value
Control Structure	Single -Thread	Concurrent
Control Topology	Hierarchical	Arbitrary
Data Topology	Hierarchical	Arbitrary
Synchronization	Synchronous	Asynchronous

The way in which changing application characteristics shape the current integration can be seen in a comparison of these new values to the current control structure values of the components. Collidescope detects the new PAIs shown in Fig. 4.

Gamma		Beta	
Control Structure	Concurrent	Control Structure	Single Thread
4 Control Transfer		Sequencing multiple control transfers	
Gamma		**Beta**	
Data Topology	Arbitrary	Control Structure	Single Thread
3 Control Transfer		Inhibited rendezvous	
5 Data Transfer		Restricted points of data transfer	
Gamma		**Beta**	
Control Topology	Arbitrary	Control Structure	Single Thread
1 Control Transfer		Restricted points of control transfer	
3 Control Transfer		Inhibited rendezvous	
Gamma		**Alpha**	
Control Structure	Concurrent	Control Structure	Concurrent
4 Control Transfer		Sequencing multiple control transfers	

Fig. 4. The PAIs Resulting from the Evolved Application Characteristics

The stateless Transaction Mediator (depicted in Fig. 3) as initially implemented only embodies translation and control. In the new application, both are still needed. However, the Transaction Mediator now must also buffer the data being processed by Risk and External Market in order to calculate financial exposure while placing a bid. Otherwise, refusal of a trade by Risk will result in an *inhibited rendezvous* as that refusal cannot be correlated with the actual correct request to circumvent the acceptance of the trade by External Market. The PAIs in Fig. 4 reflect this problem as well as additional conflicts that the Transaction Mediator currently handles. Figure 5 shows the evolved architecture.

By using this style of analysis, a developer is more likely to ascertain the distinctive problems that are caused by changing characteristics. Moreover, a direct and minimal resolution may be achieved.

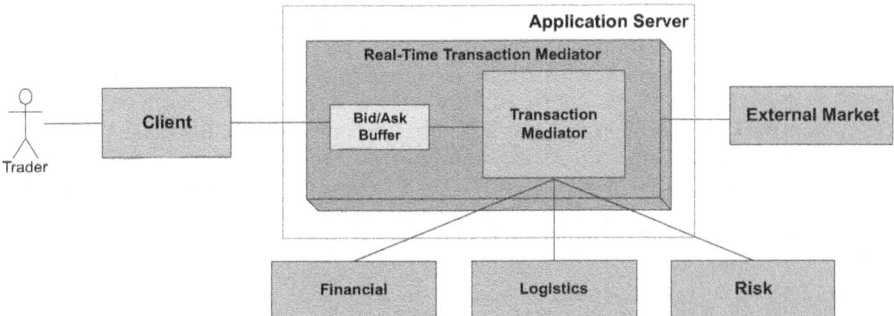

Fig. 5. The New Architecture of InfoTrade

5   Conclusions

Little attention has been paid to the evolvability of these architectures and their embedded functionality. In this paper, we show how design choices rely on the history of interoperability conflicts and resolution decisions that comprise the integration architecture. Additionally, we advocate that certain functional aspects of a pattern can be pinpointed to resolve a conflict. Combining these two facets of integration architecture design, we illustrate that often evolution is possible with minimal changes to the integration solution.

The approach we advocate has both advantages and limitations. The assessment, though a first-pass, is at a high-level of abstraction, and forms a reliable history of design information. In turn, the history is easily maintainable. Given the high-level of abstraction present in the assessment, evolutionary impacts are relatively easy to determine. However, the abstraction level restricts the depth of the assessment, as exact implementation details are not provided. Furthermore, we have not yet proven the analysis is scalable to either applications comprised of a large number of components or applications with diverse middleware products in use. We reserve these findings for future work.

References

1. Shaw, M., Garlan, D.: Software Architecture: Perspectives on an Emerging Discipline. Englewood Cliffs, NJ: Prentice Hall, (1996).
2. Abd-Allah, A.: Composing Heterogeneous Software Architectures. Ph. D. Dissertation, Computer Science, University of Southern California, (1996).
3. Garlan, D., Allen, A., Ockerbloom, J.: Architectural Mismatch, or Why it is hard to build systems out of existing parts. In, 17th International Conference on Software Engineering. Seattle, WA, (1995).
4. Shaw, M., Clements, P.: A Field Guide to Boxology: Preliminary Classification of Architectural Styles for Software Systems. In, 1st International Computer Software and Applications Conference. Washington, D.C., 6-17, (1997).
5. Allen, R., Garlan, D.: A Formal Basis for Architectural Connection. ACM Transactions on Software Engineering and Methodologies, 6(3): 213-49, (1997).
6. Garlan, D.: Higher-Order Connectors, Workshop on Compositional Software Architectures. Monterey, CA, January 6-7, (1998).
7. Keshav, R., Gamble, R.: Towards a Taxonomy of Architecture Integration Strategies. 3rd International Software Architecture Workshop, 1-2, (1998).
8. Medvidovic, N., Gamble, R., Rosenblum, D.: Towards Software Multioperability: Bridging Heterogeneous Software Interoperability Platforms. 4th International Software Architecture Workshop, (2000).
9. Mehta, N., Medvidovic, N., Phadke, S.: Towards a Taxonomy of Software Connectors. In, 22nd International Conference on Software Engineering, (2000).
10. Buschmann, F., Meunier, R., Rohnert, H., Sommerlad, P., Stal, M.: Pattern-Oriented Software Architecture: A System of Patterns. John Wiley & Sons, (1996).
11. Mularz. D.: Pattern-based integration architectures. PloP, 1994.
12. Schmidt, D.C., Stal, M., Rohnert, H., Buschmann, F.: Pattern-Oriented Software Architecture: Patterns for Concurrent and Networked Objects. Wiley & Sons, (2000).
13. Lutz, J. C.: EAI Architecture Patterns. EAI Journal, (2000).
14. Gamma, E., Helm, R., Johnson, R., Vlissides, J.: Design Patterns Elements of Reusable Object-Oriented Software. Addison-Wesley, (1995).
15. van der Hoek, A., Heimbigner, D., Wolf, A.: Capturing Architectural Configurability: Variants, Options, and Evolution. Technical Report CU-CS-895-99, Department of Computer Science, University of Colorado, Boulder, Colorado, December (1999).
16. Oreizy, P., Medvidovic, N., and Taylor, R.: Architecture-Based Runtime Software Evolution. In Proceedings of the 20th International Conference on Software Engineering, (1998), 177-186.
17. van Ommering, R., van der Linden, F., Kramer, J., Magee, J.: The Koala Component Model For Consumer Electronics Software. IEEE Computer, Vol. 33, No. 3, (2000), pp. 78-85.
18. Shaw, M., DeLine, R., Klein, D., Ross, T., Young, D., Zelesnik, G.: Abstractions For Software Architecture And Tools To Support Them. IEEE Transactions on Software Engineering 21(4), (1995), 314-335.
19. Lung, C.-H., Bot, S., Kalaichelvan, K., Kazman, R.: An Approach to Software Architecture Analysis for Evolution and Reusability. Proceedings of CASCON '97, (Toronto, ON), (1997).
20. Davis, L., Gamble, R., Payton, J., Jonsdottir, G., Underwood, D.: A Notation for Problematic Architecture Interactions. In Foundations of Software Engineering '01, (2001).

21. Kazman, R., Klein, M., Clements, P.: ATAM: Method for Architecture Evaluation. Carnegie Mellon University, (2000).
22. Payton, J., Davis, L., Underwood, D., Gamble, R.: Using XML for an Architecture Interaction Conspectus. In XML Technologies and Software Engineering (2001).
23. Davis, L., Gamble, R., Payton, J.: The Impact of Component Architectures on Interoperability. Journal of Systems and Software, (to appear 2002).
24. Keshav, R.: Architecture Integration Elements: Connectors that Form Middleware. M.S. Thesis, Dept. of Mathematical & Computer Sciences: University of Tulsa, (1999).
25. Keshav, R., Gamble, R.: Towards a Taxonomy of Architecture Integration Strategies. 3rd International Software Architecture Workshop, 1-2, (1998).
26. Payton, J., Gamble, R., Kimsen, S., Davis, L.: The Opportunity for Formal Models of Integration. In, 2nd International Conference on Information Reuse and Integration, (2000).

Issues in Developing Security Wrapper Technology for COTS Software Products

John C. Dean[1], CD and Li Li[2]

[1] National Research Council Canada, Software Engineering Group
Building M-50, Montreal Road, Ottawa, Ontario, Canada, K1A 0R6
John.Dean@nrc.ca
[2] Entrust Technologies
9 Auriga Drive, Nepean, Ontario, Canada, K2C 7Y7
Li.Li@entrust.com

Abstract. The use of Commercial Off-The-Shelf (COTS) software products as components of large-scale systems has become more and more pervasive. One of the interesting questions that has arisen is "Can you build secure applications using insecure components?" We have been investigating ways to protect data that is shared between two or more independent, insecure applications. Our initial attempts to accomplish secure data storage and transfer have been directed toward building data encryption tools that interact with various COTS products. The goal was to test our theory that security wrappers for COTS products are feasible. This paper describes a security wrapper technology that we have implemented for selected (COTS) software products. The technology focuses on interchangeability for COTS software components, portability for the wrapper, and security for communications between applications via the wrapper. By applying this security wrapper technology, one COTS software component to be wrapped can be replaced by another without significantly modifying the wrapper; the wrapper can work with a variety of operating systems; and data can be encrypted and stored temporarily or permanently.

1 Introduction

The use of COTS software products as components of large-scale systems has become more and more pervasive. Wrapper technology for these components is not new. It has been widely used but most of the current wrappers were concerned with providing data translation services and inhibiting direct access to the component. Little research has been done on the implications of securing data transmission between individual components. When security issues are considered, one of the interesting questions that has arisen is "Is it feasible to build secure applications using insecure components?" Our goal is to build a generic security wrapper for insecure COTS products, thus allowing us to implement secure systems using these wrapped products.

The wrapper project focuses on three issues: interchangeability, portability, and security. The ideal situation is that by applying our security wrapper

J. Dean and A. Gravel (Eds.): ICCBSS 2002, LNCS 2255, pp. 76–85, 2002.

technology, one COTS software component can be replaced by another, without significantly modifying the wrapper. In addition, the wrapper should be portable to a variety of operating systems and hardware platforms with minimal modification. Finally, it should provide for secure data transfer between components.

This paper describes the security wrapper technology that we have implemented for selected (COTS) software products. Discussions cover feasibility analysis, experimental solutions, results and directions for further research.

2   Background

The goal of this research was to determine if we could somehow create a security interface that would allow a system integrator to provide security services and secure data transfer between two insecure applications. This capability must be able to bypass the normal user interface because these COTS products must be invoked programmatically, that is, by another application or by the system controller software.

Given this constraint it is interesting to consider a novel point of view about the relationship between common security systems and the user. With most third party security implementations such as Entrust, PGP, etc. the user acquires a persona in the form of a "profile" that consists of, at a minimum, a security signature and a pair of encryption/decryption keys (public and private). These uniquely identify this user within the security envelope. For example, by supplying the public key to acquaintances, the user can receive and decrypt data that has been encrypted using his/her public key and sent to him/her. In addition the security signature allows the user to sign documents and forward them to a recipient. The recipient can confirm that the document actually came from the sender by verifying the signature against a certificate held by the Certifying Authority.

The problem we face in working with COTS applications is that there is normally no human user intervention in the operation of these applications when they are embedded within a larger scale system. The applications are invoked programmatically and acquire data from other applications directly. Most of the applications do not have an integrated security system for encrypting and decrypting data and this functionality must be supplied in order to ensure secure and trusted data transfer.

We proposed to develop security wrappers for COTS products that take on the role of the user within the COTS-based system. In other words the wrappers acquire the security 'persona' and perform the actions of encryption and decryption and signing data to be transferred between two cooperating COTS applications within the system. This wrapper would provide a purely programmatic interface between the COTS product and both the Certificate Authority and the other cooperating COTS products within the system. Each COTS product could acquire a security persona (a profile) by having the wrapper query the Certificate Authority to either establish a new profile or access an existing one.

These personae would then be used to allow for secure communication (data transfer) between applications via the wrappers.

In general, wrappers are software modules that are responsible for connecting individual information sources to external users. For example, in some database access wrappers for a specific system, a wrapper receives and translates instructions written in the corresponding language into executable local repository commands. In a security wrapper, the information sources to be translated are raw (decrypted) data and the external information is encrypted data. We designed this COTS security wrapper to provide a level of security in the wrapper that is not present in the COTS components. That is, the wrapper is used to add security to non-secure components. We chose several COTS software products as our elements of experiment, according to the following COTS software properties:

- it is received from the distributor and used "as is" with no changes to the source code;
- it is installed in multiple sites within different organizations; and
- the users and/or integrators do not control the evolution and maintenance of the software.[1]

We chose the following software as our COTS products: Entrust and the Entrust Java Toolkit, and a number of other commonly used desktop applications (MS Word, MS Excel, StarOffice). The platform environments for the experiments are three typical operating systems: Windows NT, Solaris UNIX, and RedHat Linux.

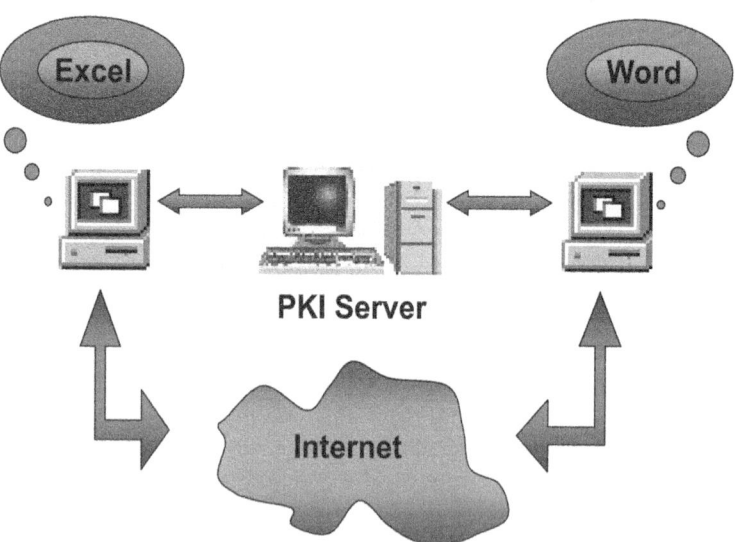

Fig. 1. Communication between distributed components

2.1   Wrapping Software Components

There are two key methods by which one can provide security for insecure COTS products. One method is to create a security layer between the application and the infrastructure support for the application. This layer might provide the interface between the application and the operating system or, for distributed systems, between the target application and the network transport. In either case the solution does not really involve isolating the product completely. Rather it involves intercepting input and output data at the infrastructure boundary and manipulating it by either encrypting or decrypting the data [2].

The second method is to provide a custom wrapper that encloses the product and isolates its interface from the user. With this method individual wrappers are responsible for encryption and decryption of data as necessary. This transfers responsibility from the platform to the wrapper itself and, in doing so, provides for the implementation of portable wrappers. We chose to investigate the individual wrapper method because it allowed us to implement our concept of the acquisition of a persona by a COTS application within the wrapper.

2.2   Entrust and Profiles

We chose to use Entrust technology because Entrust provides a Java toolkit that fits in our need for portability. The Toolkit works in conjunction with the Entrust Public Key Infrastructure architecture and the standard Java Development Kit (JDK) to form a framework for implementing Entrust security. Figure 2 shows the relationship between the various security components. The JDK supplies the class libraries used to create the wrapper infrastructure, including its interaction with the input/output functions of the current operating platform.

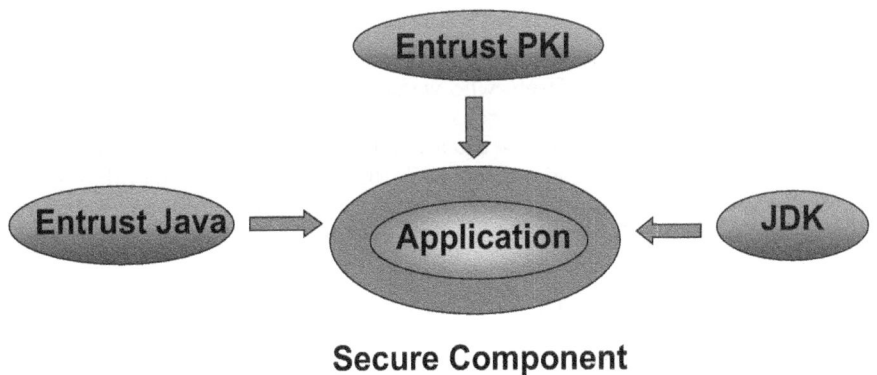

Fig. 2. Security Components

The toolkit provides a set of APIs that enables Java application to perform security-related tasks. The toolkit is implemented as a collection of functional classes. The fundamental class is the Entrust Profile. Keys and certificates that identify a certain user are stored in this class. Each Entrust Profile represents a user. When a user instantiates an Entrust Profile object that represents his or her Entrust profile, and logs on this profile, the Entrust profile can be used to perform security operations. Each profile is personalized and will merge its unique persona into the wrapper. By using individual Entrust profiles, different users will be using the same wrapper but with different persona.

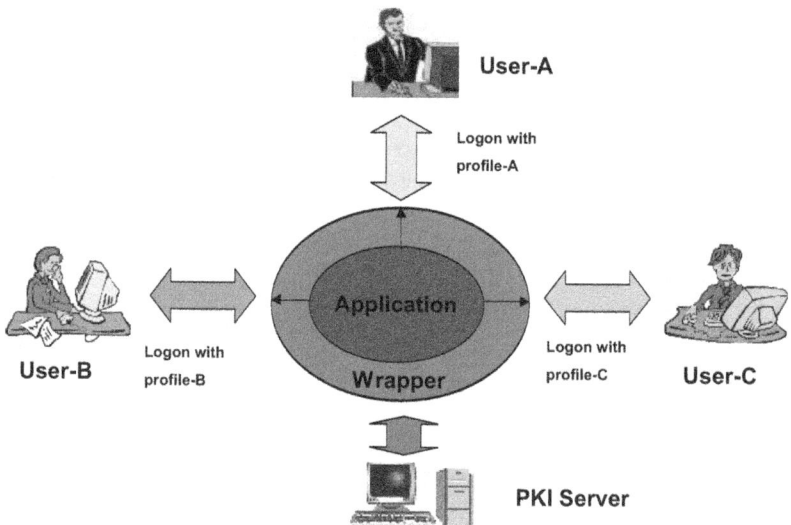

Fig. 3. Multiple persona usage

Figure 3 illustrates how these personae interact with a wrapper that wraps an individual application. Users who want to access the application must logon to the wrapper first. Each user logs on with his or her unique profile. The wrapper then validates the keys and certificate of the profile by contacting the PKI server. This ensures the keys and certificate in the profile are always updated. Note that although the Figure shows these 'users' as people they could, and in fact probably commonly would, be other applications within the COTS-based software system.

3   Implementation Criteria

Our plan was to implement a COTS security wrapper that would allow us to examine three criteria: interchangeability, portability and security. The ideal situation would be that the wrapper works with a variety of operating systems; the COTS application can be replaced inside the wrapper easily, without significantly modifying the wrapper; and that the security of data transferred between cooperating applications was highly ensured. This section will discuss the three criteria and describe the techniques employed to fulfill them.

3.1   Interchangeability

High interchangeability means that the wrapper should be able to wrap different applications with minimal changes to the wrapper code. There were two cases we needed to consider. First, we needed this capability because we recognized that the applications themselves may not be portable between operating systems. For example, Microsoft Excel does not run on the Linux operating system and therefore wee would have to substitute a competing product if we wish to use the wrapper on another platform. So, we wanted to ensure that substituting the StarOffice word processor for Corel WordPerfect was feasible. Secondly, we wanted to be able to substitute applications on the same platform as well. This would allow us to confirm the generic attributes of the wrapper. For example, we wanted to be able to substitute Microsoft Excel for Microsoft word with as little modification to the wrapper as possible.

The most important concept is that we needed to minimize the interface between the wrapper and the COTS product as much as possible. Since Microsoft Word, Microsoft Excel, StarOffice are COTS products, these components should be used on an "as is" basis. We accomplished this in our initial experiments by only allowing the COTS applications to be invoked using a command line call. This allowed us to effectively transparently substitute applications at will.

However, with every advantage gained there is a cost. The cost of implementing the wrapper in this way was that we introduced a complexity in intercepting the applications i/o calls. In addition to being platform dependent the input/output mechanisms are application-dependent as well. We implemented a 'brute-force' style algorithm to temporarily overcome this problem. Current research efforts are focused on developing a more efficient and effective solution.

3.2   Portability

Portability means that the wrapper can be transferred easily from one operating platform to another. The wrapper should be able to work with a variety of operating systems without significantly modifying the wrapper itself. This is affected by primarily the choice of programming language for implementing the wrapper. While this was could be difficult to accomplish with many programming languages, we chose to use Java which allowed us to write the code once and install it on multiple platforms. Again this approach has limitations in that the Java environment does not provide sufficient low-level access to the file system on the various platforms. As we become more dependent on operating system functionality we pay a price in portability.

We implemented two versions of the wrapper, a GUI version that allowed for direct user intervention and interaction and non- GUI version that was intended to be invoked programmatically. The GUI version was only implemented in order to allow us to demonstrate the concepts while we intended the non-GUI version to be the one most commonly used within a COTS-based system. In order to ensure that both versions exhibited the required portability we implemented the GUI component using Java Swing components, which have advantages of speed, keyboard navigation and plugable, system independent look-and-feel.

3.3 Security

The security is ensured by a dynamic method – a wrapped application acquires a persona via a profile, which is created at runtime, and uses the profile to encrypt and identify its output data to other "wrapped", trusted applications. The wrapper is password-protected. The wrapper itself does not store the password information. Entrust profile does instead. This is a significant advantage of using the Entrust profile scheme. Since each Entrust profile represents a user, the wrapper allows users to create new users or recover themselves via the Entrust PKI server. The procedure is implemented interactively with an Entrust PKI server. That way the Entrust profiles can be created or recovered at run time. Once the Entrust profile is saved locally, user can either log on to a Entrust profile online or offline. The wrapper will check the password and profile given by the user, verify that this is a valid user. Otherwise the log on attempt will be rejected and an error message will be given.

The encryption scheme is relatively straightforward. All raw data saved from the wrapped application is intercepted and encrypted transparently to the COTS application. Data files read by the wrapper for input to the wrapped COTS product are decrypted before being passed to the application. This is completely effective because the application cannot be invoked directly but only via the wrapper.

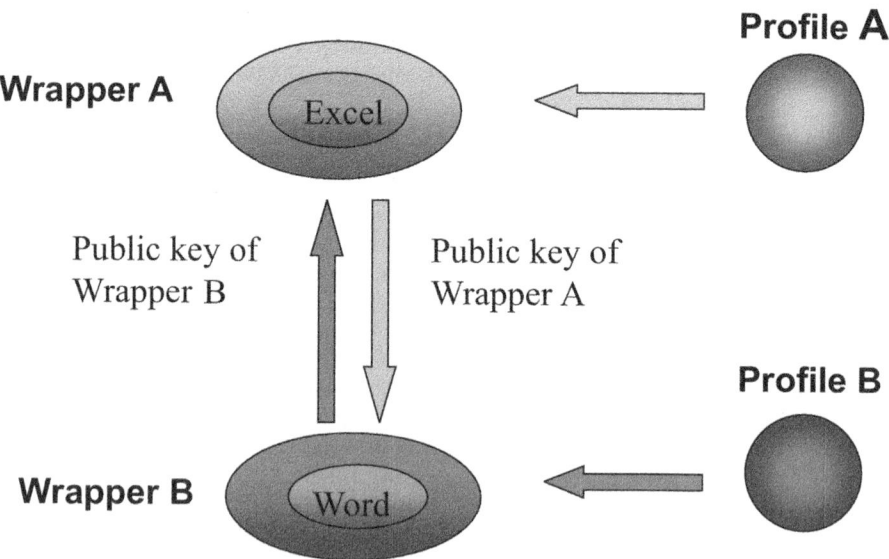

Fig. 4. Communication using different profiles

4   Experiments

We divided the experiment into three sections in order to verifying the inter-changeability, portability and security capabilities of the wrapper. This section describes some of our results to date. As this is an ongoing research effort we anticipate being able to elaborate on some of the results in the future.

4.1   Interchangeability

To wrap different components, the wrapper has to find the main characteristics of a software component in order to recognize it, memorize it, and then recall it when later use. We define the main characteristics as the application's executable file path and the file format. We enable the wrapper to read them in, save them, and apply them. To configure the wrapper, the installer has to browse the operating system to find the exact executable file to be invoked. The installer also has to know the file format of this particular software. In addition, the wrapper was constructed in such a way to allow for different command line structure on different platforms by ensuring the command string could be provided via the configuration file and not hard coding it into the wrapper code itself. In this way we were able to easily switch applications as well.

The wrapper was tested with a number of applications, notably Microsoft Word, Excel and PowerPoint on the Windows NT machine. We also tested it using the StarOffice 5.1 suite of applications on the Linux and Solaris systems. It performed flawlessly in all cases. The only modifications required were to a configuration file at installation. However we intend to further automate this capability in a future experiment.

4.2   Wrapper Portability

We choose three commonly used operating systems: Windows NT, Solaris UNIX, and RedHat Linux, to experiment with the portability of the wrapper. The wrapper was built using pure Java and Java Swing components, and no extra layer was added to the local system. The wrapper was originally developed for the Windows NT operating system and was ported later to the Linux and Solaris systems. In order to port the application we had to move the Entrust Java support files to the new platforms. This was accomplished by simply copying the files to an appropriate location on the new machine and setting the classpath to the correct value. The porting required no changes to the custom Java code, however we did need to change one configuration file in order to account for the different paths to the executable being wrapped. We stress that wrapper porta-bility will likely become an issue as we extend the call interception mechanism. We foresee that in the future there may be two components to our wrapper, a portable one and one that is platform dependent.

4.3   Security Analysis

During the implementation the application is invoked by the wrapper, simply by calling the executable file. The wrapper subsequently keeps track with the application's read and write actions by recognizing file format and timestamps. Any change made to local or remote files by the application is protected by automatic encryption and decryption within the wrapper.

There are two ways to use the Entrust profile: logging onto the profile either online or offline. The difference between online and offline may have some significance when user is due for a key rollover or a Distinguished Name change. In this case working online is also a part of the certificate verification process, and the wrapper may end up encrypting messages for users with revoked certificates or trusting signatures that user should not trust.

We enabled the wrapper to work both online or offline and, in the case of the demonstration system, allowed the user to make choices at initialization either to create a new persona or to assume an existing one. When the user chooses to create a new user, the new user ID is securely generated when users enter a one-time use reference number and authorization code via the wrapper's GUI. The wrapper provides users with a transparent and automatic way of creating their own identities. By applying the Entrust Toolkit, the wrapper provides a broad range of algorithms developed both in North America and in Europe:

- Symmetric: Triple-DES, DES, CAST, RC2 and IDEA
- Asymmetric: RSA, DSA, Diffie-Hellman and Elliptic-curve
- Hashing: SHA-1 and MD

This was not a significant issue for our non-GUI wrapper except that in that case the profile choice is pre-programmed because we do not normally expect user intervention.

There are a number of unresolved issues with the wrapper as it is currently implemented. The most significant of these is the inability of the wrapper to track and encrypt temporary files created during the operation of the wrapped application. For example, Microsoft applications create a number of buffering temporary file in which intermediate data is stored. One of the uses for this data is to enable rollback of modifications (the undo function). To be truly secure our wrapper will have to eventually account for this. Again this is a topic for future research.

5   Conclusions

We have successfully implemented a COTS security wrapper and used it to construct building a security COTS mini-system using insecure COTS components. The wrappers demonstrate that it is feasible to build a security property into the architecture of a COTS-based system, while all the components integrated remain untouched.

The wrapper functioned effectively in three areas:

- Interchangeability
- Portability
- Security

Our implementation of the wrapper allowed us to interchange COTS products at will, often quite transparently to the external system. We also were able to port the wrapper to a number of platforms with no changes to the core code and minimal changes to the configuration files. Finally we were successful in implementing encryption and decryption for all permanent input and output data.

The optional graphical interface of the wrapper is entirely separated from the implementation of the wrapper itself. It remains independent of the underlying component so that wrapper substitution is possible. The interface is also under configuration management.

This research is in a preliminary stage and it is obvious that there are a number of issues yet to be investigated. They include developing a more efficient method of intercepting the input-output data streams (possibly by hooking interrupts) and examining the communications between multiple applications. We also believe that there are significant issues in embedding multiple cooperating wrappers in an actual system. However, the evidence we have presented implies that these types of wrappers are feasible and our efforts are now being directed towards evaluating this technology further.

References

1. Tran, Tam: Interoperability and Security Support for Heterogeneous COTS. Master's thesis, United States Naval Postgraduate School Monterey Ca, (2000).
2. Badger, L, Feldman. M., Ko, C.: Secure Execution Environments, Generic Software Wrappers - DARPA/ITO Project Summary. September (2000),
   http://www.pgp.com/research/nailabs/secure-execution/wrappers-darpa.asp.
3. Mitchum, Terrence: Hypervisors for Security and Robustness. Secure Computing Corp Roseville Mn, (1999).
4. Meeson, Reginald: Analysis of Secure Wrapping Technologies. Institute for Defense Analyses Alexandria Va, (1997).
5. Dean, J.C.: Security Wrapper Technology for COTS Software Products. 13th Annual Software Technology Conference, Salt Lake City, Utah, May (2001).

A Process for COTS Software Product Evaluation

Santiago Comella-Dorda[2], John C. Dean[1], Edwin Morris[2], and
Patricia Oberndorf[2]

[1] National Research Council Canada
Building M-50 Montreal Road, Ottawa, Ontario, Canada, K1A 0R6
`John.Dean@nrc.ca`
[2] CBS Initiative, Software Engineering Institute[* * *]
Carnegie Mellon University, Pittsburgh, PA USA
`{po, ejm, scd}@sei.cmu.edu`

Abstract. The growing use of commercial products in large systems makes evaluation and selection of appropriate products an increasingly essential activity. However, many organizations struggle in their attempts to select an appropriate product for use in systems. As part of a cooperative effort, the Software Engineering Institute (SEI) and the National Research Council Canada (NRC) have defined a tailorable software product evaluation process that can support organizations in making carefully reasoned and sound product decisions. This paper describes that process.

1 Introduction

Many organizations find themselves faced with the prospect of constructing major software systems from commercial off-the-shelf (COTS) products[1]. An essential part of such an endeavor is evaluating the commercial products that are available to determine their suitability for use in the particular system. Yet, as we look at the experiences of these organizations, we find one of the hard lessons of COTS product evaluation: reasonable people doing reasonable things still have problems that are traceable to the quality of their evaluation process. Among the common evaluation mistakes we have seen are:

– Inadequate level of effort
– Neglecting to re-evaluate new versions or releases

[* * *] Special permission to use the "A Process for COTS Software Product Evaluation" (c) 2001 by Carnegie Mellon University, in *The Proceedings of ICCBSS* is granted by the Software Engineering Institute.

[1] A COTS product is a product that is sold, leased, or licensed to the general public; offered by a vendor trying to profit from it; supported and evolved by the vendor, who retains the intellectual property rights; available in multiple, identical copies; and used without modification of the internals. This definition is by design imprecise, since the COTS market continues to redefine itself. We do not intend this definition as an "acid test", but rather to provide the general essence of a COTS product.

J. Dean and A. Gravel (Eds.): ICCBSS 2002, LNCS 2255, pp. 86–96, 2002.
© Springer-Verlag Berlin Heidelberg 2002

- Use of "best of breed" lists that do not reflect the characteristics of the system
- Limited stakeholder involvement
- No hands-on experimentation

In response to these and other problems, the Software Engineering Institute (SEI) and the National Research Council Canada (NRC) have co-developed a COTS software product evaluation process that is tailorable to suit the needs of a variety of projects. This evaluation process addresses the examination of COTS products for the purpose of determining their fitness for use in a system.

2   An Evaluation Process

We have seen many cases where projects are told to pick a particular product because the vendor offered a good deal (or it was on a list, or the boss wanted it). We believe that consistently good evaluation results can only be achieved by following a high quality and consistent evaluation process. This does not mean that each evaluation activity requires a highly complex, exquisitely documented process (although sometimes they do), but if you do not follow some kind of consistent process, it is likely that the quality of your results will vary.

The high level process we describe is flexible and amenable to many specific process implementations. It consists of four basic elements:

- **P**lanning the evaluation
- **E**stablishing the criteria
- **C**ollecting the data
- **A**nalyzing the data.

The process, called PECA, begins with initial planning for an evaluation of a COTS product (or products) and concludes with a recommendation to the decision-maker. The decision itself is not considered as part of the evaluation process – the aim of the process is to provide all of the information necessary for a decision to be made. PECA is in part derived from ISO 14598 [1]. Where our experience differed from ISO 14598, we freely changed the process to fit our needs.

As illustrated in Fig. 1, the elements in the PECA process are not always executed sequentially. Evaluation events, such as a need for new criteria to distinguish products, unexpected discoveries that lead to the start of a new iteration, or inadequacy of collected data, will direct process flow through one of the process elements as needed. One of the hallmarks of the PECA process is this flexibility to accommodate the realities of COTS-based systems.

The PECA process is intended to be tailored by each organization to fit its particular needs. PECA is flexible enough to be used within many organizations and with many COTS-based development processes.

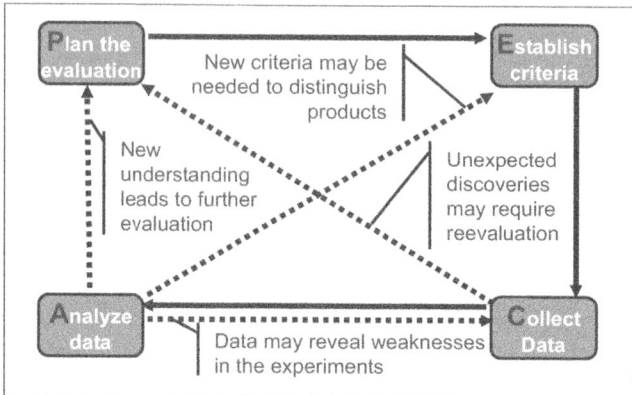

Fig. 1. The Peca Process

Finally, a successful COTS evaluation relies on more than just a process. In addition you will need to employ a set of techniques that allow you to plan, establish criteria, and collect and analyze data effectively. For example, the popular GQM technique [2] can be used to establish COTS evaluation criteria. This paper will not devote significant space to techniques. More complete coverage of techniques is available in a COTS product evaluation tutorial developed by the authors.

3   The PECA Process Examined

The main section of this paper provides detail about the four basic elements of the PECA process. As you consider these elements, keep in mind that PECA assumes a highly contextual evaluation of a COTS product. This implies that part of a PECA evaluation will be conducted in concert with evaluations of other COTS products that are also being considered for use in the system. A PECA evaluation is therefore a complex activity in which individual products are not evaluated in isolation.

Note also that PECA considers the fitness of a product for use to involve more than just meeting technical criteria. Criteria can also include such concerns as the fitness of the vendor (e.g., reputation, financial health), the technological direction of the marketplace, and the expectations placed on support staff.

This breadth relies on a wide range of inputs. Two obvious inputs are the set of products that will be considered and the system requirements (both functional and nonfunctional) that must be met. However, system requirements alone are normally not sufficient for making an appropriate choice from among the set of products. They often fail to address many important characteristics of COTS products and vendors, such as underlying technology, quality of reputation, and support services offered.

The expectations held by stakeholders are another important input. Such expectations are imperfectly captured as system requirements, yet often determine the eventual success of the COTS product in the system. In addition, the use of COTS products may introduce an entirely new set of stakeholders. Another set of inputs includes system decisions that have already been made regarding system architecture and design, other system components, and development and maintenance processes to be supported. These will constrain the COTS product selection.

3.1 Planning the Evaluation

Planning for each COTS evaluation is different, since the evaluation may involve both different types of products (from simple to extremely complex) and different system expectations placed on the product (from trivial to highly demanding).

3.1.1 Forming the Evaluation Team.
The importance of an effective team for a successful evaluation should not be underestimated. Unfortunately, there are situations where the most junior engineer, with little support from others, is assigned to evaluate products. In most cases, a lone engineer – even a senior engineer – does not have the range of skills necessary to perform a broad-based COTS evaluation. Most evaluation teams should include technical experts, domain experts, contracts personnel, business analysts, security professionals, maintenance staff, and various end users. And, as with any team, a good balance of power is important, so no single individual can bias the results toward his personal preferences.

3.1.2 Creating a Charter.
The evaluation team creates a charter that defines the scope and constraints of the evaluation. The charter includes a statement of the evaluation goals, the names and roles of the team members, a commitment statement from both the evaluators and their management, a summary of factors that limit selection, and a summary of decisions already been made.

3.1.3 Identifying Stakeholders.
The stakeholders for the entire system may have already been identified, and some may be included on the evaluation team, but each COTS evaluation entails its own, often unique, set of stakeholders. Evaluation stakeholders are those individuals or groups with vested interest in the results of a COTS evaluation or on whom the selection of a particular COTS product will have an appreciable effect. Stakeholder relevancy can be determined by the "hole" the products are trying to fill or by the constraints imposed by the products.

Evaluation stakeholders may not be a proper subset of the stakeholders who are identified for the system, since the scope of the expectations for a COTS product and vendor are sometimes different than documented expectations for the system.

As additional stakeholders are identified, some may become members of the evaluation team. However, the size of the team normally must be limited to avoid situations of broad participation with no progress. Practical experience suggests that the core working team should be limited to approximately 7-8 individuals. If there are a larger number of stakeholders, multiple sessions and management of various groups may be necessary.

3.1.4 Picking the Approach. Next, planning determines the basic characteristics of the evaluation activity. Some of the parameters of the approach selected include the depth or rigor of the evaluation, the basic strategy for selection, and the number of iterations ("filters") needed to reduce the number of candidate products.

Some evaluations must be extremely rigorous while others are successfully accomplished with far less rigor. More rigorous evaluations that yield more accurate results will be used in cases where the system risks from failed products are high, while less rigorous techniques will be used where the risk from failed products is lower. Two factors that determine the depth or rigor of an evaluation are:

— the likelihood the wrong product will be selected, given a specific level of rigor of the evaluation
— the potential impact or system risk incurred if the wrong selection is made

To identify the necessary depth of a PECA evaluation, the criticality of the component and the candidate products should be considered. There is a spectrum of criticality according to which one can select appropriate approaches to evaluation.

For situations involving low technical risk and low involvement with strategic objectives, less evaluation effort and precision is required. For the lowest possible risk, a near-random selection (pitching pennies into fishbowls) may be justifiable.

For situations involving moderate technical risk or that have a significant, but not all-pervasive impact on the strategic objectives, moderate effort and precision of evaluation are required. The evaluation can focus on the specific discriminators between the various products that indicate some useful enhanced capability.

For situations involving high technical challenge or risk or are critical strategic objectives, the greatest effort and precision is required. These situations normally involve the potential for great financial, environmental, or property damage, or the harming or loss of life. This class of COTS implementation justifies the greatest rigor in COTS evaluation. In most situations, the best approach is to employ a methodic research process to gather necessary data.

A selection strategy involves the basic algorithm that will be used to identify an appropriate product. Two common selection strategies are used: first fit and best fit. First fit can be used when the selected product must fill a well-understood core set of needs. In this case, additional "goodness" of a product is unimportant or it is not worth extra evaluation costs. First fit considers minimum requirements and answers the question, "Is it good enough"? This does not imply that the set of criteria by which products are assessed is any less stringent or complete. The only implication is that the first candidate found that meets all requirements is selected without comparison to other candidates' capabilities.

Best fit is used when there is an appreciable gain in getting more than the minimal amount of some characteristic, or when no candidates are likely to meet all requirements. For example, in some situations a minimum performance is specified, but better performance adds significant value to a product within the context of the system. Best fit answers the question, "How good is each product"?

Sometimes it is not reasonable to evaluate all candidates because the number is too large. When this is the case, there must be a way to reduce the number of candidates that are considered for in-depth (and more costly) evaluation. The solution is to develop one or more "filters", which are inexpensive ways of eliminating candidates. Factors to consider in deciding whether to use filters and how many to use include the size of the field of candidates, the availability of discriminating criteria, and the evaluation budget. Each filter by itself may represent a full iteration through the PECA process (i.e., careful planning, establishment of criteria, etc.), or it may be more appropriate to include multiple filters in a single PECA process iteration.

3.1.5 Estimating Resources & Schedule. Unfortunately, there are few specific techniques available for estimating resources and schedule for COTS evaluation. COCOTS [3] is one of the few attempts to address the costs associated with building a COTS-based system. However, the technique does not isolate the costs associated with COTS evaluation.

Fortunately, general techniques with which you are already familiar are applicable, such as expert opinion, analogy, decomposition, and cost modeling. Some of the COTS-specific factors that may affect your estimates include:

- The level of rigor required. In general, the more rigorous the evaluation, the greater the short term cost. However, rigorous evaluations may lower long-term costs in building the system by avoiding the wrong choice.
- The number of candidates being evaluated: The more candidates evaluated, the higher the overall cost.
- Your evaluators' experience and availability: Evaluation costs are often higher when evaluations are performed by experienced evaluators, as they tend to perform more rigorous evaluations. However, use of experienced evaluators can be expected to reduce costs down the road.

We have seen cases in which inadequate resources are allocated to critical COTS evaluations and other cases where excessive time and effort are spent for trivial ones. It is important that the effort expended match the importance of the product decision.

3.2   Establishing Evaluation Criteria

Evaluation criteria are the facts or standards by which the fitness of products is judged. Evaluation criteria should be derived from requirements. As noted previously, however, system requirements rarely address the specific concerns that determine whether a COTS product is viable in a particular setting. Thus, the first step in establishing evaluation criteria must be determining appropriate evaluation requirements. Evaluation criteria are then constructed from these evaluation requirements.

3.2.1   Identifying Evaluation Requirements.   There are actually two problems associated with identifying evaluation requirements. The evaluation team must determine which system requirements are legitimate requirements for the COTS product, and the team must determine any additional evaluation requirements that are not directly derived from system requirements.

Normally, a single COTS product is not expected to satisfy every system requirement. Therefore, the subset of system requirements that are applicable to the COTS products under consideration must be identified. This activity is called applicability analysis. Since COTS products are not mirror images of each other, it often occurs that different candidates will fulfill different subsets of system requirements.

Even after system requirements are analyzed for applicability, there are likely to be additional requirements on the COTS product that are not yet documented. Examples of legitimate evaluation requirements that are not always addressed by system requirements include:

- Architecture/Interface constraints – COTS product decisions are often constrained by other decisions that have already been made. These constraints become evaluation requirements. For example, if a decision has been made to use CORBA [4] as the middleware mechanism, it makes little sense to select a product that conflicts with this technology.
- Programmatic Constraints – Time, money, available expertise, and many other programmatic factors may be sources of evaluation requirements.
- Operational and Support Environment – Not all aspects of the operational and support environment are included as system requirements. For example, information about the organization that will perform maintenance on the system is frequently omitted.

Regardless of whether evaluation requirements are derived from system requirements or from additional expectations placed on COTS products, errors can arise. Some errors arise from assigning too many requirements to a particular evaluation. This can result in the elimination of suitable COTS products because they don't meet all of the requirements. An example of this is the tendency to want every "cool" capability offered in the COTS marketplace. To combat this tendency, consider the risk to the system mission should the feature be absent.

Other errors occur when the set of evaluation requirements is incomplete. This reduces the scope of the evaluation and can result in the selection of unsuitable COTS products. Insufficient understanding and oversimplification of the problem can cause these errors. An iterative approach to building evaluation requirements and evaluating products will help mitigate this risk. As you gain understanding about the problem you will inevitably identify requirements that were initially overlooked.

3.2.2   Constructing Criteria. An evaluation criterion consists of two elements. These are a capability statement and a quantification method. The capability statement is a clearly measurable statement of capability to satisfy a need. The quantification method is a means for assessing and assigning a value to the product's level of compliance with the capability statement.

Well-defined criteria exhibit a number of common characteristics. First, they are discriminating, in that they allow the evaluator to distinguish between products. Criteria that are met by most or all products don't discriminate. For example, the presence of a graphical user interface will not (normally) discriminate between modern word processors. Including criteria of such limited value also dilutes the effort spent determining product performance on discriminating criteria.

Well-defined criteria also exhibit minimal overlap. If criteria overlap, then the associated product characteristics can be factored into deliberations multiple times, which can lead to wasted effort or misleading results. Finally, well-defined criteria reflect the context of the system that is being constructed. This calls into question the value of a list of products that was approved for use by some other organization, since the criteria used by that organization are unlikely to match those that are produced specifically for the system.

3.3   Collecting Data

Collecting data involves executing the evaluation plans to determine the performance of various products against the evaluation criteria that have been developed. However, the act of collecting data will often change the basic assumptions, since COTS software is full of surprises (a few good ones and more than a few bad ones). This is one of the reasons for applying an iterative approach to building COTS-based software systems – as the evaluator learns by collecting data, this new knowledge can be reflected in new concepts about the system and COTS products and new criteria for evaluation.

Different criteria and different situations require different data collection techniques. For example, the technique applied for determining the value of a critical criterion will likely be more rigorous than that applied for determining the value of a criterion that carries with it little risk.

The specific techniques you choose will be in part determined by the degree of confidence you need in your results. Obviously, the closer the technique comes to execution of the COTS component in your specific system context, the higher the degree of confidence you can have about how the product will perform in your actual system. Different families of techniques include:

- literature review – a wide variety of techniques with the common characteristic of being based on reviewing documents. Documents include user manuals, release notes, web based reports, product history, third party evaluations, etc.
- vendor appraisals – techniques that focus on the characteristics of the vendor that provides the product. Information about the vendor may be obtained from interviews, vendor literature, formal capability evaluations, independent financial analyses (e.g., Standard & Poor's), trade journals, and customer kudos and complaints (often published on web sites).
- hands-on experiments – techniques that employ and execute the actual COTS. Hands-on techniques are an essential part of a rigorous evaluation. They are necessary to verify vendor claims and to determine interactions with other components, the feasibility of proposed architectures and designs, and performance and reliability in the system context. Hands-on techniques include product probes that investigate specific features of products, prototypes, scenario-based evaluations, benchmarks, experimental fielding, and product demonstrations in which users assume control.

Determining how a specific product (or products) stacks up against the criteria is not the only data that can be gathered while collecting data. In some situations it may not even be the most important result. For example, the improved understanding of the COTS marketplace and of the system context gained during COTS evaluation is an invaluable contribution to the development of the system. Some of the many less obvious results that should be captured during data collection include the degree of confidence in data, the system architecture and design implications of the selected product, limitations and conditions on how the product is used, and deficiencies in assessment methods, evaluation requirements or criteria.

3.4   Analyzing Results

Data collection typically produces a large number of data, facts, and checklists. This raw data must be consolidated into information that can be analyzed. Consolidation does not compare products; it simply makes sense of data. Analysis is required for reasoning about the data collected.

3.4.1   Data Consolidation.   Consolidation almost always implies some loss of detailed information. This is the price that is paid for condensing a large mass of information into some more quickly comprehensible format. A balance must be struck between the need for easy understanding (a high level of consolidation) and the risk of losing too much information. For example, weighted aggregation [5] is commonly used to condense values for all criteria into a single overall fitness score. This technique provides a quick, but often misleading comparison of products since high levels of consolidation can make two very different products appear to be virtually identical.

3.4.2   Data Analysis. Data analysis involves reasoning about the consolidated data in order to make a recommendation. Analysis is a very creative task, and the best approach is simply the application of sound and careful reasoning. There are, however, three particularly useful techniques: sensitivity analysis, gap analysis and analysis of the cost of repair.

Gap Analysis highlights the gap between the capability provided by a COTS component and that capability required for the system. A gap analysis typically uses a matrix of product performance against evaluation criteria, where individual cells contain information about how well a product fulfills the criterion, or a description of what functionality is lacking.

Sensitivity Analysis considers how the evaluation results react to changes in assumptions – for example, changes in the weighting of criteria or scoring by judges. By evaluating the sensitivity to changes in assumptions, it is possible to determine the impact of slight changes in judgments on recommendations of products.

Cost of repair [6] assumes that the evaluated products do not fully meet the system needs. Analysis of the cost of repair focuses on the implications to the system if a product is selected by considering the work that must be done to the system to repair deficits in the product. Deficit does not necessarily refer to a product flaw, but to a capability that is required in the system that the product does not demonstrate. Deficits may be repaired in many ways (e.g., by altering system architecture, adding additional functions, or modifying the requirements). Also keep in mind that a deficit may be caused by an overabundance of features as well as a paucity of features. "Cost" is not necessarily in terms of dollars; it could be in time, shifted risks, etc.

3.4.3   Making Recommendations. The goal of evaluation is to provide information to the decision-maker. The evaluators must focus their recommendations on the information that the decision-maker needs. This can vary according to the type of organization and the characteristics of the decision-maker. For example, the decision maker at a bank emphasized that the evaluation demonstrate due diligence, such that any decision could be justified to bank investors. This emphasis "flavored" both the type of data gathered and the format and content of recommendations presented to the decision maker.

There are three main outputs of the PECA process:

– The *product dossier* is a repository of documentation, discovered facts, assessment results, classifications, etc. that details all that is known about a product at a point in time. There is one product dossier for each product evaluated. For the selected product, the product dossier serves as a source of information for the team that will architect, design, and integrate the system using the product.

- The *evaluation record* is a description of the evaluation itself. Information in the evaluation record includes evaluation plans; personnel involved; details of meetings and evaluation tasks; the context in which the products were evaluated; specifics about product versions, configurations, and customizations; results of evaluation activities; rationale for decisions made; and lessons learned that might be useful for subsequent evaluations.
- The *Summary/Recommendations* document provides a synopsis of the evaluation activity and the findings, along with the message the evaluation team wants to convey to the decision-maker. It includes both an analysis of fitness and of evaluation deficiencies (e.g., need for further evaluation, confidence in results).

4   Conclusions

Some individuals believe that following any documented process is a waste, particularly when the end goal is to save time and money. Our experience in analyzing troubled programs is that too often highly informal COTS evaluation processes share the blame for the failure. The process described here is a *means* of performing COTS evaluations and not an end in itself. Expect to tailor this process for your own situation, and do not let it get in the way of getting good data and making an informed recommendation.

Regardless of the COTS evaluation process you adopt, remember that COTS evaluation is an ongoing activity. Your organization will need to evaluate new product versions and potentially identify product replacements over the life of your system. If you have a foundation of good evaluation processes and practices, along with good documentation of the characteristics of products and the rationale for decisions, you have a good start at making COTS products work for you.

References

1. International Organization for Standardization (ISO): ISO/IEC 14598-1:1999 – Information Technology – Software Product Evaluation. Geneva, Switzerland, (1999).
2. Briand, L., Morasca, S., and Basili, V.R.: Goal-Driven Definition of Product Metrics Based on Properties. CS-TR-3346, UMIACS-TR-94-106, University of Maryland, Computer Science Technical Report, December (1994), 24 pages. More information available online at: http://sel.gsfc.nasa.gov/website/exp-factory/gqm.htm.
3. Abts, Christopher M. and Boehm, Barry: COCOTS (Constructive COTS) Software Integration Cost Model: An Overview. USC Center for Software Engineering, University of Southern California, briefing. Available online at:
http://sunset.usc.edu/COCOTS/cocots.html, August (1998).
4. The Common Object Request Broker: Architecture and Specification. Version 2.0. Framingham, MA: Object Management Group, (1996). Also available online at URL: http://www.omg.org.
5. Saaty, T.: The Analytic Hierarchy Process. McGraw-Hill, New York, (1990).
6. Wallnau, K., Hissam, S. and Seacord, R.: Building Systems from Commercial Components. Addison Wesley (2001). ISBN: 0201700646.

Five Hurdles to the Successful Adoption of Component-Based COTS in a Corporate Setting

Anthony Earl

1416 West Mountain Avenue, Fort Collins, Colorado, USA
Anthony.Earl@MountainAvenue.com

Abstract. In this paper, the author reports experiences with component-based technologies that have been observed from the roles of component technology engineer, evangelist, and consultant within the corporate world. The goals are firstly to capture those observations for the interest and benefit of component vendors and secondly to offer some interest and basis for further studies that may show whether or not such experiences are commonplace. Armed with such data, there is clearly a better chance that component vendors and corporate entities can form collaborations through which each can achieve their aims.

1 Introduction

While the success of COTS software may not be exclusively linked to the successful adoption of component-based technology there are clear technical reasons why this would be a natural pairing. Component platforms are built with the expectation that users will add new pieces to their foundations that increase the effectiveness of their systems. Customers will be able to do this economically if a marketplace of components exists for that platform. Once established, this cycle can be positively reinforced. Additionally, for component writers, the platforms usually contain a set of core services that are always available and can be taken advantage of to ease the development and increase the potential interoperability of components. For example, the collection service in CORBA [1] or the transaction service in Jini [2].

However strong the positive technological cycle becomes, there is still a need for a successful economic landscape to emerge. This can only come from an economically strong customer base such as government agencies or corporate entities. If such a base of regular consumers can be found at the component-based COTS software marketplace then a self-sustaining cycle of improved software may result.

In this paper, the author reports experiences that have been observed from the roles of component technology engineer, evangelist, and consultant within the corporate world. The goals are firstly to capture those observations for the interest and benefit of component vendors and secondly to offer some interest and basis for further studies that may show whether or not such experiences are commonplace or not. Armed with such data, there is clearly a better chance that component vendors and corporate entities can form collaborations through which each can achieve their aims.

J. Dean and A. Gravel (Eds.): ICCBSS 2002, LNCS 2255, pp. 97–107, 2002.

The observations have been organized into five main hurdles that appear to the author to be the most difficult barriers for adoption in a corporate setting. The observations are informal and come from multiple corporations. They attempt to focus on the aspects of adoption that are most closely related to component technology issues while recognizing that the adoption of any new technology has its own set of commonly observed [3] issues that would also have to be addressed in attempts to overcome the problems.

The hurdles that are described are:

1. The steep learning curve for creating distributed systems and the complex development environments that they imply;
2. Partial adoption of component-based COTS is difficult and functionality overlap among COTS adds to the problem;
3. Initial demonstrations are deceivingly complete while the true cost of testing is unexpectedly high;
4. New models of interaction between the development teams and their suppliers need to be established as common practice;
5. It is harder for last ditch hacking efforts to save the project.

The observations reported herein reflect only the opinion of the author and not that of his current or previous corporate employers.

1.1 Structure

The remainder of this paper contains sections that describe the five hurdles of component-based COTS adoption along with paired sections that offer some suggestions for customers and component developers as to reasonable approaches for overcoming the issues. Concluding remarks then follow.

2 Learning Curve

With any new technology there is a level of investment that one is expected to make in order to reap the benefits that are offered. It is well-known [4] that if this investment is too great with respect to available time, cost, level of experience or skill required, or any other resource then adoption is likely to fail.

The potential benefits of being able to buy ready-written and tested components in a competitive marketplace that can be used with your own software and with components from other vendors upon a platform that itself offers useful services are clearly very attractive. It also suggests to the unwary that their software development woes could be reaching an end. After all, what could be easier than shopping for exactly what you need and "simply" plugging it in to a well-defined system embedded with fundamental services?

Fortunately for the software development industry, there are some skills that are necessary for allowing this to work anywhere near the desired manner. But is it fair to say that those skills are difficult to acquire? After all, components are abstractions of behavior with well-defined interfaces that can be accessed from other components. Surely, the skills to use them already exist within your community of object oriented developers. It cannot take a lot of effort to learn about these new interfaces and put them into effective use quickly. This point of view is typical of that found in the marketing of component-based technologies. It is also quickly shared by corporate software development managers. So why is it not observed in practice?

The convenience that component-based technology vendors offer is focussed on providing services that support users in the construction of useful components while avoiding construction of every service from the ground up. The vendors offer training in component construction along with examples and timely responses to online discussion groups. These are necessary provisions for those climbing the learning curve.

However, there are two hidden traps into which optimistic development managers in the corporate environment are apt to step. The first is that they assume there is a small conceptual leap between developing client-server applications and the truly distributed applications that are implied by modern component models [5]. Let's call this the "distributed world trap". A corollary trap is that the development and test environment that has to be set up by the team is substantially more complex than what has existed for previous projects by the same team. Let's call this the "complex environment trap". It is interesting that the former of these traps is not a direct consequence of choosing to use COTS software or even component-based approaches. The root cause is usually a desire to attempt the construction of more complex systems as the software marketplace becomes more competitive. COTS components have the tempting property that succeeding with such desires is now possible. Whether or not there is direct cause and effect between COTS component adoption and a movement towards complex distributed systems, it can be observed that the two are often found in tandem in a corporate setting. New technologies such as wireless are putting further pressure on a move towards distributed systems.

There are consequences for the "distributed world trap" upon the project team. While the team may have had weaknesses in their experiences with formal or semi-formal design techniques such as the Unified Modeling Language (UML), they were previously able to overcome those by applying the easily-understood examples from OTS books and courses. Additionally, fixes at the coding and testing stages of the project were apt to successfully repair earlier mistakes. However, moving to tackle more complex system development in this style is fraught with higher costs for mistakes and omissions at the requirements or design stages [7,8]. The "distributed world trap" creates symptoms that are often attributed to the adoption of COTS components and the steepness of its learning curve whereas they really stem from a degree of immaturity in corporate software development teams. Some of the blame may also lie with the UML tool vendors who have been slow to support uses of UML notations in methods such as Catalysis that specifically address component-based development.

There are also consequences of the "complex environment trap". Unlike the "distributed world trap", this is a direct consequence of adopting component-based technologies (although the difficulties are increased with the development of distributed components). While developers are quite familiar with a cycle of edit, compile, start-server code, start-client code and test for ordinary software development, a component-based cycle may require a more complex cycle to edit, generate interfaces, compile, deploy components, instantiate components, start client, and test. Developers also have to face the issue of what is at the root cause of the error messages they see. Are they coming from problems in the components that they have written, or bought, or from services in the component platform itself? Additionally, developers have to take on some of the responsibilities of system administrators. It is simply too inefficient to wait for a response to a system or network reconfiguration request during the search for the cause of a bug or to test a potential implementation improvement. While many developers are familiar with common system administration tasks, the use of new and specific network protocols (e.g. multicast [9]) in some distributed component technologies puts some tasks out of reach without additional training and experience.

Component platform vendors do not normally assume that people need help moving to distributed component models and setting up a reasonably easy and efficient working environment. Yet that is exactly what makes the learning experience so difficult. It is important to remember that architects, developers, and testers are also facing the learning curves associated with the components that they are assessing and adopting. They would prefer to concentrate on these than on problems with using their core component technology.

2.1   Addressing Learning Curve Issues

The previous section identified two key traps. The "distributed world trap" cannot be overcome with technology since its root cause is not technological. Education is how people are going to see how much more difficult it is to develop for a truly distributed environment than for a client server setup. One way to convince them of that is to ask them how they would solve problems that are clearly tractable in a non-distributed world when they are moved to the distributed case. Good examples of such problems are the model-view-controller pattern or the singleton pattern [10]. It is really up to them if they believe that adopting a fully distributed approach is really what they need to build their new systems. In some cases it will be, in which case they should be made aware of the necessary additional training they will need for their development teams. In some cases distribution will not be what they need and they can avoid the trap. They are still left with the option of adopting a component model to help with their work.

The second trap, that of the "complex environment", is one that development teams can explicitly ask for help for from their component technology suppliers. Those suppliers have to have example components, example development structures, and necessary test harnesses. They should be encouraged to share those with their customers. It will give their customers many solutions to real-world issues and thus have a positive impact on the adoption rate. It will also benefit the suppliers in the following manner. If most of the component technology users adopt a de facto standard development structure then the effort that has to be put into the support department can be substantially reduced as a whole swath of potential problems is eliminated.

3   All or Nothing

Component technology vendors generally offer a component model and its implementation [2]. They may also offer a set of components that provide commonly required services. A common perception of corporate decision-makers of that offering is that some useful functionality exists in some of the components that can be taken advantage of outside of the component model. They are then overcome with shock or panic that the adoption of that piece of component technology has other implications and costs. The experienced component-based developer will recognize that this behavior brings the majority of the costs associated with components while gaining only a minority of the benefits.

The consequences of this mismatch between expectations and outcome are best explained by an example. Suppose that a corporate manager is responsible for enabling several corporate software products to exchange events among one another. Imagine that manager sees a commercially available component platform that contains a suitable event service and decides to adopt that component platform with the goal of satisfying the requirement to exchange events. At this point, the manager is apt to fall into the "partial adoption trap" by basing resource and schedule estimates on simply linking together the COTS applications and the COTS event service.

The "partial adoption trap" fails to take into account that typically, component platform services are only available to components that conform to that platform's component model. The manager really had to base estimates on getting the team far enough up the learning curve to succeed with the design and implementation effort of wrapping at least part of each of the existing applications as components so that they can use the event service to exchange events.

Another observed anti-pattern of component adoption is to make use of services in the component platform for one part of the target system yet use other existing software to address some of the same responsibilities. For example, an existing piece of software may notify some clients about the health of an application while an alarm service is adopted from the component platform to issue other health warnings. This may save the cost of re-writing existing, tested code and of developing new client pieces that already respond correctly. However, the "competing responsibility trap" has increased the complexity of maintenance and evolution of the final product [11]. Under some similar circumstances, the pieces of code with competing responsibilities may actually interfere with each other and introduce intractable bugs.

3.1   Addressing the All or Nothing Issue

The "partial adoption trap" should not be interpreted to mean that traditional code cannot be effectively in conjunction with new component-based COTS software. It simply warns that developers, particularly in the corporate settings where these traps have been observed, need to be made more aware of the true costs of gradually incorporating component-based software into their development efforts. They will also have to face the issues that are associated with mixing a traditional development process and a good component-based development process [12,13]. With awareness of the trap, managers can design process and schedules that take the issues into account. That will enable them to make more realistic estimates of the benefits and costs of adopting a component-based technology. It will also encourage them to try to find opportunities to take advantage of larger percentages of a component platform and thus reduce their own development efforts.

The "competing responsibility trap" is really the responsibility of the product architect. Only they have the expertise and visibility to recognize that responsibilities are being competed for and that they should make a better decision than leaving the status quo. If they can do this early in the project then the overall cost of creating an effective solution can probably be contained to a reasonable level.

4   Costs of Formal Testing

Many corporate cultures have embedded confidence and even exhibit irrational exuberance when faced with the prospect of being able to vanquish new dragons or exterminate some software werewolves with the latest silver bullet. Forces such as time-to-market and eagerness to build reputations by grabbing the iron while it is hot work against the careful discovery and analysis of the possible problems and the costs that can accompany component-based development. Within such an environment, it is not hard to see why people can assume that it is easy to do testing. Moreover, they perceive that apparently problems can be easily solved. They are then shocked or panicked that the costs associated with fixing and extending what they bought are so high.

A somewhat entrenched corporate behavior is the reaction to a good demonstration being the conviction of managers that their support to create a shippable product from what they see is appropriate. There also seems to be belief in the illusion that purchasable software from the outside world is more reliable and robust than that which the corporate entities themselves are producing. When you combine this belief with the proceeding reaction you end up with decision-makers being liable to immediately support a product based on a simple demo of COTS components doing something close to meeting established requirements.

The "shippable demo trap" also takes advantage of people's natural assumption that the gaps left in a demo can be filled with a little time and effort on the part of the software engineers. What they don't see are the inherent design weaknesses and the forces of tight coupling working against the necessary evolution of the software that they intend to invest in.

The technical consequences of skipping the careful stages of verification and validation of 3rd-party components are just about the same as doing a poor job of testing requirements, reviewing designs, or traditional testing. Bugs are uncovered at the point where they are most costly to fix. However, the political consequences of rash decision-making in component purchases can severely impact not only the individuals concerned but also the overall future prospects for COTS component usage within the failed organization.

The costs of not testing are substantial, as described above. But the costs of effective testing are not insignificant for a couple of major reasons. Firstly, the COTS components being tested are, almost by definition, from outside the testing organization. This may mean that it takes a lot of effort to understand the principles and details with which any component can be properly tested. Secondly, should any components fail the tests, there is an investment to be made to address the situation by: working with the supplier to get a fixed version; testing other equivalent or alternative components; working out how to develop your own component that will fill the void in design of your product; or re-designing your product without this component.

4.1   Addressing the Costs of Formal Testing

The "shippable demo trap" is one that is best addressed by employing experienced managers who have seen the consequences of this trap in action. They have collected the knowledge to ask the appropriate questions and avoid a lethal leap to an inappropriate conclusion. Such a careful examination of what the demo can and cannot do could form and effective initial project plan that is realistic yet takes advantage of the lessons that have been learned during the construction of the demonstration.

Perhaps the more difficult issue for managers in this area is to attempt to balance the costs of formal testing against the costs of too little testing. One approach that may work here is to give each component a relative value within the overall solution. The impact of failure of the components with the highest values would probably cause the overall project to fail, while one might be able to live with failure of lower-valued components. These proportions can then be related to the overall value of success and failure of the project as part of a rational risk assessment just as one may do for a traditional project [14].

5   Tangled Communication Paths

Corporate entities already have a complex structure with which they face the business world of software development. Relationships that the software development teams currently have with the outside world tend to focussed through the product manager who is experienced enough to cope with typical problems that are encountered in getting requirements in from customers, functionality out to customers, and the typical issues that arise from using traditional COTS for major components such as databases and from using engineering tools such as Integrated Development Environments.

But a true component-based COTS development effort generates a much more complex relationship set with entities that are outside the corporate framework and that has a traffic level well above the currently norm and of a much greater technical content. This presents the "strangled communication trap".

A common reaction is to try to extend the current communication paths to handle the new situation. This is fraught with problems that can strangle effective communication to an extent that can kill the development effort that has to be so dependent on harmony with its suppliers and potential suppliers.

Let's look at why it is reasonable to open communication paths outside the corporate scope to many of the developers in a component-based team rather than channeling everything through the product manager. First and foremost, one of the key advantages that you hope to obtain with COTS components is that your engineering staff do not have to write or maintain anywhere near the amount of code that they have responsibility for at the moment. They are thus freed up for the possibility of effective communication with the suppliers. Secondly, your engineering staff is employed for their technical expertise and innovation. They are the ones who are most likely to see the specific values and weaknesses in particular 3rd-party offerings. Not only will technical issues remain undetected if communication is stifled but you are also likely to encounter a lack of innovation in putting the available components together in imaginative ways. With time to study the components' functionality, the engineers can learn how to get as much value from each COTS component as is possible within current and future projects. Thirdly, by exposing engineers to communication with successful COTS suppliers, it opens the possibility that they will learn the lessons of how to build effectively reusable components themselves when you need them to fill the many gaps that exist between components on the shelves.

There are a couple of problems that can be encountered in exposing engineering staff to outside communications. The personality types of many engineers act against them in their effectiveness with open communication. Such weaknesses can be addressed and it has to be remembered that those weaknesses are often less of a problem when the topics of discussion are purely technical. Another problem that is perhaps more worrisome is that so many open communication paths can make effective internal communication less effective. And a final problem to note is that the possibility of exposing proprietary secrets is increased.

5.1   Addressing Tangled Communication Paths

The previous section described the "strangled communication trap" as a consequence of attempting to extend the existing structure. Addressing the problem thus has to avoid doing that. The benefits of directly involving engineering staff was also examined. This seems like a reasonable approach so long as the associated problems can be addressed.

There are many COTS courses in effective communication and legal issues for technologists. These should be taken advantage of with team-based training so that expectations and responsibilities are made as clear as possible.

6   Hacking Gets Harder

It is no secret that the level of maturity with respect to formal software development processes and application of advanced software development techniques is far lower than many software development corporate entities would like to admit. A clear consequence is that many a project today is saved by the most experienced programmers in the team finding tricky ways to solve tricky problems. Let us look at the reasons why this "fire fighting trap" is more likely to be encountered in COTS component-based development efforts. Following that, we need to determine whether or not it is likely to be a savior as frequently.

The additional skills that are required to be successful with component-based technologies may be a double-edged sword for today's fire fighters. On the one hand, their ability to solve problems of a difficult nature will help them maintain their lead ahead of their teammates. On the other hand, the additional complexities may enable the currently "trailing" team members with a tendency to stick to more formal approaches and attention to detail to find themselves catching up and even overtaking the existing "heroes".

Opinions have been expressed earlier in this paper that there are several traps that decisions makers are liable to fall into during their initial encounters with component-based technologies. Necessary testing will be skipped, information will fail to make it to the right engineer at the right time, it will be assumed that less work is required that really is, or the impact of the learning curve will be underestimated. These are the fundamental reasons that one can expect to see more projects attempting to adopt fire fighting as an escape from the traps into which they have fallen. Will those attempts prove as successful as they are in traditional software development?

There are various arguments that can be made in answering the above question. Firstly, the nature of component models does encourage (though rarely enforces) a more formal approach to interface definition in general. Thus many of the issues that arise from misunderstanding ill-defined interfaces should be reduced overall. Similarly, the presence of a set of component technology layers between the caller and the method called can force out problems in the build environment or overall structure of the implementation more quickly than may happen in traditional projects. Each time a source of problems is removed, the value of the fire fighter is diminished. Even simple component design adds an additional level of structure to the software project that can diminish the chances of miscommunication among the development team.

However, component technology can open up new avenues of opportunity for the fire fighting hacker. For example, a common need in component-based development is to wrap an existing piece of software with a component interface. That existing software may be unintelligible to the mortal code writer and have little or no documentation. One might say it should not be used in such a state but the pressures of project success can force it to be necessary. A good hacker can help here. There are some traps in the technology of component development itself. A good example of this also comes from attempts to wrap existing code for distributed components. The existing code may have been written as a client-side cache that kept a large data structure in memory. The developer has to be aware of the circumstances that may cause that data structure to be unnecessarily stored to disc or transmitted across the network by the inadvertent use of a non-transient reference to that structure. These are the details in which hackers excel and they can still have value on a component-based project. However, their overall likelihood of putting a lagging project back on schedule with some neat trick is reduced by a COTS components approach where many of the success factors are removed from the coding internals and placed on the qualities of the overall architecture and of the effectiveness of the testing teams guaranteeing that the desired interfaces will play a correct role in the well-defined interactions in which they will participate.

6.1   Overcoming Hacking

One can generally see that the value of and need for hacking diminishes proportionally to the increase of the maturity of the software development team. If you agree that hacking is less likely to be effectively in a COTS components approach then you can take advantage of all the available literature and training to improve the maturity of the teams involved.

Additionally, the process of change towards a disciplined approach can be encouraged by setting well-defined, reasonable goals, and rewarding conscientious attempts to meet them. These rewards can effectively replace attempts to hack for attention and avoid putting problems in place for the future that would have outweighed the near-term benefits.

7   Concluding Remarks

As stated in the introduction, the observations reported here were not collected in a scientific manner. However, they have been seen in multiple corporations. They do not, from the author's perspective, exhibit any real surprises when compared with other reports of the reactions of software development teams to other pressures and technologies. Despite this, the hurdles are tough to overcome for many in the corporate sector and are accompanied by traps that many find it easy to fall into. This means that there is probably a significant amount of work to do in finding and documenting solutions and ensuring they are effectively communicated to corporate decision-makers in a form they can digest.

Although there is plenty of room for technological improvements, these are rarely the key inhibiting factors in each of the areas identified. This implies that the business and marketing people associated with COTS components need to work the hardest in addressing these issues. They could find useful partners in those organizations specializing in software process improvement since it seems clear that more mature development organizations could take the greatest benefits from adopting a COTS component-base approach.

References

1. Harkey, D., Orfali, R.: Client/Server Programming with Java and CORBA. 2nd Edition, John Wiley & Sons, John Wiley & Sons.
2. Arnold, K. (ed): The Jini(TM) Specifications. Second Edition, Addison-Wesley Pub Co., December 15, (2000).

3. Earl, A.: A Process-Based Approach to Software Engineering Technology Transfer. In Proceedings of 4th IEEE Computer Society Workshop on Software Engineering Technology Transfer, (1994).
4. Boehm, B.: Software Engineering Economics. Prentice Hall, (1981).
5. Li, S.: Professional Jini. Wrox Press Inc., August (2000).
6. Brown, A.: Large-Scale Component-Based Development. Prentice Hall PTR, December 15, (2000).
7. Tvedt, J. D.: An Extensible Model for Evaluating the Impact of Process Improvements on Software Development Cycle Time. Ph.D. dissertation, Arizona State University, May (1996).
8. Madachy, R. J.: A Software Project Dynamics Model for Process Cost Schedule and Risk Assessment. Ph.D. dissertation, University of Southern California, December (1994).
9. Oria, L.: Approaches to Multicast over Firewalls: an Analysis. HP Labs Technical Report, HPL-IRI-1999-004, April (1999).
10. Grand, M.: Patterns in Java. Volume 1, A Catalog of Reusable Design Patterns Illustrated with UML, John Wiley & Sons, September 28, (1998).
11. Brown, A. W., Wallnau, K.C.: A Framework for Systematic Evaluation of Software Technologies, in Component-Based Software Engineering. IEEE Computer Society Press, (1996).
12. Christie, A., Earl, A., Kellner, M., Riddle, W,: A Reference Model for Process Technology. In Proceedings of 5th European Workshop on Software Process Technology, Nancy, France, Springer Verlag, ISBN:3-540-61771-X, October (1996).
13. Botterill, D., Earl, A.: Using the Unified Modeling Language (UML) to Design Jiro Technology Dynamic Services. Proceedings of SPIE, Java/Jini Technologies, Vol 4521, pp. 123-133, 21-22, August (2001).
14. Clements, P., Northrop, L.: Software Product Lines: Practices and Patterns. Addison-Wesley Pub Co., August 20, (2001).

On Building Testable Software Components

Jerry Gao, Ph.D., Kamal Gupta, Shalini Gupta, and Simon Shim, Ph.D.

San Jose State University
One Washington Square, San Jose, CA 95192-0180
jerrygao@email.sjsu.edu

Abstract. Component engineering is gaining substantial interest in the software engineering community. A lot of research efforts have been devoted to the analysis and design methods for component-based software. However, only few papers address the testing of software components and component-based software. This paper focuses on how to build testable software components by increasing the testability of software components. The paper introduces the concept of *testable bean*, and proposes a new way to construct a testable bean based on a testable architecture and well-defined built-in interfaces. In addition, the paper also reports our efforts on developing a test bed to achieve automation for test beans.

1 Introduction

As the software program increases in size, it becomes very important to reduce high software cost and complexity while increasing reliability and controllability. With the advances in Internet technology, more distributed systems are being built to meet diverse application needs. Currently component engineering is gaining substantial interest in the software-engineering community. As more third-party software components are available in the commercial market, more software workshops have begun to use the component engineering approach to develop component-based programs for the distributed applications.

Although a lot of research efforts have been devoted to analysis methods and design strategies of component-based software, only a few papers address the testing of software components and component-based software [1,2,3,5,7,9, 10,11]. To build high quality software, we need good quality components and cost-effective component testing methods [11]. In the practice of component engineering, we have encountered some new problems and challenges in testing of software components and component-based software [2,3]. One of them is how to build software components with good testability. As pointed out by Jeffrey Voas [9], testability is an important indicator for component quality and reliability. To solve this problem, we must have a clear understanding about component testability, and provide new architecture models and methods to help engineers to construct testable components. In addition, we need new component test tools and technologies to support the automation of a test process for software components.

In component engineering practice, we encountered several challenges concerning testing of software components. They are:

J. Dean and A. Gravel (Eds.): ICCBSS 2002, LNCS 2255, pp. 108–121, 2002.

- What is software component testability?
- How to increase the testability of software components during component design?
- How to construct testable software components with a systematic approach?
- How to construct tools to perform component testing in a systematic way?

In this paper, we focus on design for testability of software components and a way to facilitate component testing in a systematic manner. We believe component testability is a very important factor to increase component quality and reducing testing cost. Therefore, it is essential for component developers to construct deployable, executable, testable and manageable software components.

To help people understand how to construct testable software components, we introduce a new concept, called *testable beans*. To explain this concept, we propose a new component architecture and well-defined built-in test interfaces to enhance the component testability and facilitate component testing. In addition, our application and implementation experience indicates that the research result here is very useful and practical to develop a software test tool to automate a component testing process. Our application experience suggests that this approach is one of the cost-effective ways to build highly testable components. Moreover, standardized testable beans can help us to automate a component test process for all software components.

The paper is structured as follows. In Sect. 2, we discuss the work that has been done in the past and is related to our work. In Sect. 3, we introduce a new concept, known as *testable beans*, to help engineers understand testable components in terms of supporting features, properties and capabilities for software testing. Section 4 presents a systematic approach to construct testable beans and facilitate component testing. Finally, our conclusion remarks and future work are given in Sect. 5.

2   Related Work

This section summarizes the related work on software component testing and tools. In the past years, a number of research papers have addressed component-based software testing. In addition, a few of commercial testing tools have been developed to help the automation of testing process for software components and component-based software.

David S. Rosenblum in [7] reports his effort on developing a test model for component-based software. In this paper, Rosenblum defines a formal model of test adequacy for component-based software, and proposes a systematic test adequacy criterion, which can be used to determine whether a test suite provides an adequate amount of testing for an under-test software component.

Jeffrey Voas and Keith W. Miller [9] addressed the testability issue of software components from the software reliability perspectives. They view software reliability as one of three pieces of the reliability puzzle. The pointed out that software testability analysis is useful to examine and estimate the quality of software testing. In their paper, they described an empirical analysis approach to achieve this.

Jerry Gao, et al [2,3] discussed the issues of testing and maintenance problems for software components. The paper focuses on the traceability of software components. It proposes systematic ways to increase component traceability, and reports a client-server environment to monitor the behaviors of software components in component-based software.

Yingxu Wang, Craham King, and Hakan Wickburg [10] proposed approach to construct built-in test (BIT) components for maintainable software. In this approach, a built-in test in a software component is explicitly described in software source code as member functions for enhancing software maintainability. Based on the built-in test, a software program operates in two modes: a normal mode and a maintenance mode. In the normal mode, the software program has the same behavior as the conventional system. In the maintenance mode, the built-in tests can be activated in a corresponding component as its member functions.

P.A.Stocks and D.A.Carrington in [8] focused on specification-based testing. They described a Test Template Framework (TTF) that is a structured strategy and a formal framework for Specification-based Testing (SBT). Specification-based Testing (SBT) offers a simpler, structured, and more formal approach to the development of functional tests than standard testing techniques. The strong relationship between specification and tests facilitates error detection and simplifies regression testing.

Kenneth Nagin and Alan Hartman [6] reported TCBeans Software Test Tool Kit. It is a software framework designed to assist testers in developing, executing and organizing function tests directed against Application Program Interfaces (APIs) and software protocols written in Java, C or C++. Their approach treats a test case as a reusable JavaBeans software component that can be customized and assembled off-line during code development, or dynamically at run time. The software tool can be used to load test cases and control test execution.

"JavaSpec" (http://www.sun.com) is a unit test tool for classes. It can be used to test non-GUI code of Java technology-based applications and applets through their Application Program Interfaces (APIs). Once users create a Java technology-based code test specification, JavaSpec software compiles and runs the test, and the test specification automatically drives JavaSpec software to generate a collection of test cases for every possible combination of test data.

3   Testable Software Components – Testable Beans

3.1   What Is a Testable Bean?

A testable bean is a testable software component that is not only deployable and executable, but is also testable with the support of standardized components test facilities. Unlike normal components, testable beans have the following unique requirements and features.

Requirement 1. A testable bean should be deployable and executable. A JavaBean is a typical example.

Requirement 2. A testable bean must be traceable by supporting basic component tracking capability that enables a user to monitor and track its behaviors. As defined in [3], traceable components are ones constructed with a built-in tracking mechanism for monitoring various component behaviors in a systematic manner.

Requirement 3. A testable bean must provide a consistent, well-defined and built-in interface, called test interface, to support external interactions for software testing. Although different components include diverse functional interfaces, they must include a consistent test interface to support software testing. This is very important to automate component testing, and reduce test costs on environment setting and test driver construction.

Requirement 4. A testable bean must include some program code that facilitates software testing by interacting with external testing facilities or tools to support test set-up, test execution and test validation.

To construct cost-effective testable beans, it is very important for developers to understand following design criteria:

- It is essential to minimize the programming overhead for developers.
- It is important to standardize the test interface for testable beans.
- It is suggested to prevent adding detailed testing functions inside beans.
- It is always a good idea to separate the functional code of a bean from the built-in code that facilitates the interactions between the bean and external testing facilities and tools.
- It is not good to include detailed tests inside a bean, otherwise, it is not easy to manage, reuse, and maintain tests in a flexible manner.

The test interface for a testable bean must support three basic functions. They are a) set up a test (test case and/or test data) for testing a bean, b) exercise a test for a specific function of a bean, and c) validate the test result of a test with the given expected test data and report it.

Like traditional software testing, we can include the following features in a component-testing environment:

- A test management tool, which allows testers to create, update, and maintain component tests. In addition, this tool also records the testing results from component testing.
- A component test bed, which uses component test drivers to set-up and exercise various test cases for a component.
- A component test generation tool, which helps testers to automatically generate component test cases and test data.

There are three questions regarding the design of testable beans. The first question is how to design and define a common and consistent architecture and test interface for all testable beans. The next question is how to generate testable beans in a systematic way. The final question is how to control and minimize program overheads and resources for supporting tests of testable beans.

3.2   Why Do We Need Testable Beans?

Increasing software component testability is a key to reduce software test costs and enhance software quality. Jeffery Voas, M. Miller, W. Keith in [9] define an interesting approach to measure and evaluate software testability of a program from the software reliability perspective. Their approach can be useful to check the testability of software components to help testers to find out the quality of the components. In this paper, we use the term 'testability' to indicate how well a component is structured to facilitate software testing. The major purpose of constructing testable components is to minimize testing cost and efforts.

The objectives to design and construct testable beans are summarized below.

- To provide components that are traceable, reusable, executable, deployable, and testable.
- To minimize the testing efforts by providing a plug-in-and-test environment to support component testing and component integration.
- To standardize the test interface for components so that various test tools and facilities can be integrated and used together.
- To find a systematic approach to achieve the goal of the test automation for software components.
- To provide a new way to construct software testable components with well-defined design architecture and testing interface.

There are three different systematic mechanisms to construct testable beans by adding program codes and interfaces to support and facilitate component testing and program testing.

Method 1. Framework-based testing facility – In this approach, a well-defined framework (such as a class library) is provided to component engineers to facilitate them to add program testing code into software components according to the application interfaces of the given framework. It usually is a testing facility program or a class library. Component engineers can use the facility to add their built-in testing code into components. This approach is simple and flexible to use. However, there are several drawbacks. Firstly, it requires a high programming overhead. Secondly, it relies on engineers' willingness to add the testing code due to its high overhead in programming. Moreover, this approach assumes that component source code is available. Therefore, it is difficult to deal with commercial components (COTS) because usually they do not provide any source code to clients.

Method 2. Build-in tests – This approach requires component developers to add test code and tests inside a software component as its parts. Usually, this approach needs a well-defined component built-in mechanism and coding format. Developers must follow them to add tests and built-in test functions inside components. This causes a high programming overhead during component development. The major advantage of this approach is that tests are built-in inside components. Therefore, engineers can perform component tests without any external support from testing environment and test database. It is clear that this is a good idea to include component acceptance tests inside components like COTS. The major drawback of this approach is that components consume large system resources and become more complex because they include a lot of unrelated functional features. In addition, only limited types of tests can be included inside components.

Method 3. Automatic component wrapping for testing – This approach uses a systematic way to convert a software component into a testable component by wrapping it with the program code which facilitates software testing. Like the first method, this approach usually uses a well-defined test framework to interact with test tools or detailed testing functions. Compared with the first two methods, this approach has several advantages. First, its programming overhead is low because of automatic code wrapping. Next, it separates the code (which facilitates testing) from the original source code of a component. In addition, this method can be used for in-house reusable components and commercial components (COTS).

Since each approach has its own advantages and limitations, hence, in real practice, we need to use them together to support different types of testing for a program and its components. To design and construct testable components, engineers need more guidelines on component architecture, testing interface, and supporting facilities. The basic principles of building testable components are summarized below.

- It is essential to minimize the programming efforts and overheads on supporting component testing and maintenance by providing systematic mechanisms and reusable facilities.
- It is important to standardize the test interface for testable beans so that they can be tested in a reusable test bed using a plug-in-and-play approach.
- It is always a good idea to separate the functional code of a software component from the added and built-in code that facilitates testing and maintenance operations. This implies that we should separate the normal functional interface of a component from its testing and maintenance interfaces.
- It is reasonable to control the component overhead relating to its internal support for testing and maintenance by providing some systematic method to enable and disable the related program code.

To construct testable beans, we encounter the following challenges.

- How to design and implement testable beans in a systematic way?
- What is the component architecture and test interface for testable beans?
- How to provide a testing support framework (or facility) and a component test environment to achieve component test automation?
- How to minimize the programming efforts and system overhead during the construction and execution of testable beans?
- How to provide standardized interactions between a test bean and its supporting environment?

Here we present a solution based on the concept of testable beans to solve the above problems. We focus on component architecture and the test interface for testable beans. The solution includes a) a new architecture model to construct testable beans, b) a well-structured test interface for testable beans, and c) a testing environment for supporting component tests.

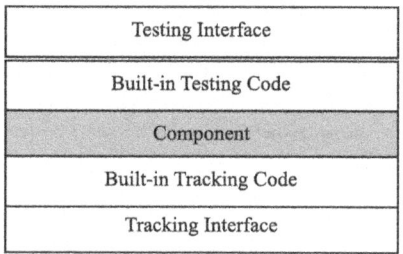

Fig. 1. Testable Bean Architecture

3.3   The Architecture Model for Testable Beans

As mentioned before, intuitively, a testable bean is a software component, which is designed to facilitate component testing. Figure 1 shows the architecture model for a testable bean. A testable bean includes the following extra parts other than its original functional parts.

- A built-in test interface that supports the external interactions for testing.
- A built-in program layer that facilitates the interactions between the testable bean and external testing facilities and supporting tools to complete various testing capabilities.
- A built-in tracking interface which supports user interactions to configure and select various tracking capability and features. The details are reported in [4].

– A built-in tracking program layer that facilitates the interactions between a
testable bean and external tracking facilities and supporting tools to complete program tracking functions. The details are reported in [4].

```
public interface IbeanTest{

public Object[] setParameters(String className,
String   methodName, TestData testData_val);

 public int runMethod(String className, String
methodName, TestData  testData_val);

 public int validateTestResult(String className,
String methodName, TestData testData_val)

}

public class TestData {

public TestData(Object[] argValueList_val, Object[]
expectedTestDataList_val)

{  Object[]   argValueList = argValueList_val;
          // Actual parameter values

Object[] expectedTestDataList =
expectedTestDataList_val;    // Expected data }

}
```

Fig. 2. Interface between the Component and the Testing Agent

This component architecture has several distinct features. First, it considers
the needs of essential testing support for a software component, such as tracking
and testing interfaces. Second, it separates the testing and tracking functional
code from normal functional parts of a component. This makes it easy to add
or remove testing and tracking code inside a component. In addition, it pro-
motes independent interfaces to support testing and maintenance of software
components.

3.4   Test Interface of A Testable Bean

As we pointed out in [2], one of the major challenges in component test automation is the fact that various components are constructed with diverse interfaces
and technologies. To deal with this issue, we have come up with an idea to design a consistent interface for components to support test interactions between
components and external tools and component users. Figure 2 shows a generic
test interface (IBeanTest) for a testable bean in Java. It includes three functions:

- Object[ ] setParameters(....), which sets up a test case and test data to exercise a given method of a Java class.
- int runMethod (....), which executes a given method of a Java class with the set-up test data.
- int validate testResult(....), which check the test results for an execution class method.

The major purpose of the interface is to define and regulate a test interface to component users and test tools for exercising various functions in a software testable component (testable bean). It plays a very important role to standardize the test interface between testable beans and component testers or external test tools.

Following this test interface, component developers and test tool vendors can provide their detailed implementation to support component testing.

4   Testable Beans and Testing Environment

To support the component testing for various testable beans, we developed a simple client-server prototype. Figure 3 shows the structure of a client-server environment for testing testable beans. This environment includes three parts: a) testable beans, b) a test agent, and c) a tracking agent.

A *Test Agent* is a multithreaded process. Each thread controls, supports, and monitors component tests for a testable bean in the environment. A test agent includes the following functional parts: a) a component test facility, which provides the detailed implementations of test functions defined in the test interface, b), a synchronous communication interface between testable beans and a test agent, c) administration and configuration GUI, and d) a linkage interface to a component test tool that generates, manages, and maintain component tests for testable beans.

In fact, the test agent can be located in the same machine as a component-based program. To deal with distributed component-based programs, we intentionally set up a client-server test environment to try our solution. We use Java RMI as a means to support the synchronous communications between a test agent and testable beans to support the test operations. Figure 4 shows the communication sequence between a client (a testable bean) and a server (test agent). First, the BeanTestAgent registers with the RMI Naming Service. After the registration, any testable bean constructed with the test interface can be supported on the network to complete the detailed test functions based on the component testing facility implemented in a test agent. The detailed test functions listed here are:

- Set up test parameters and test cases for a component function, for example *setParameter(...)*.
- Invoke a component's function with a given test case, for example, *runMethod(....)*.
- Validate test results from a test, for example, *validateTestResult(....)*.

The idea here is influenced by the concept of remote procedure call. We implement the detailed testing support function as a component test facility of a test agent. They can be shared and used by all testable components (testable beans) on the network.

A *tracking* agent is a multithreading process that controls, records, and monitors diverse component behaviors in a component-based program. A *tracking* agent consists of the following three functional parts [4].

- *Tracking Listener* is a multi-thread program that listens and receives all types of tracking events through trace message queues, and dispatches them to *tracking processor*.
- *Tracking* Processor generates program traces according to a given trace event based on its trace type, trace message and data, and stores them in the proper trace repository.
- *Tracking Configuration* provides a graphic user interface to allow a user to discover and configure various tracking features for each traceable component.

Due to the limited scope of this paper, we have focused only on test agent and testable beans. The more detailed information about Tracking Agent can be found in [4].

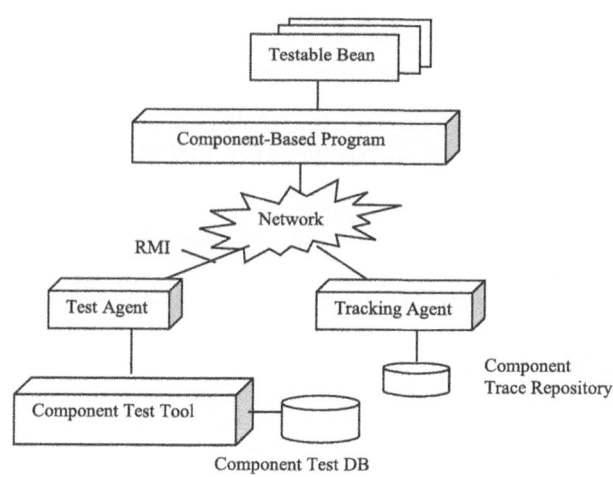

Fig. 3. Component Test Environment

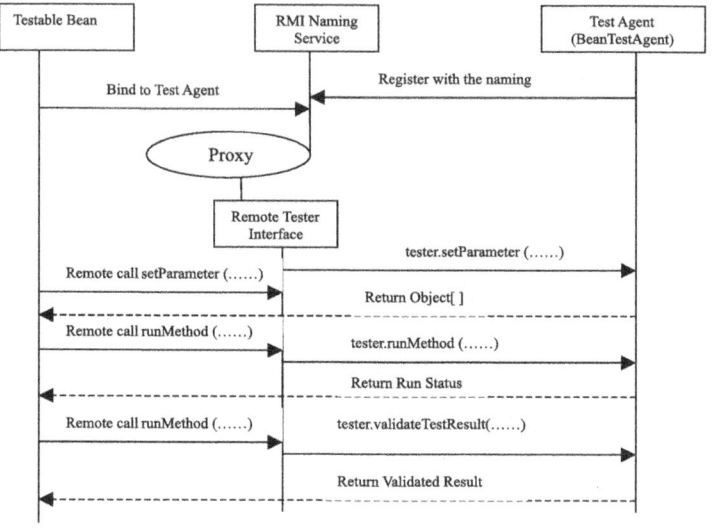

Fig. 4. Transaction Sequence between a Test Agent and a Testable Bean

4.1 Implementation

We have used Java technology and Java RMI framework to implemented a simple prototype to try our idea. We use Java JDK 1.2 to construct Java-based testable beans, and use Java RMI technology to implement the distributed communication interface between testable beans and a test agent.

A test agent is built with Java RMI-based remote interface class object, called BeanTesterImpl. It is derived from UnicastRemoteObject of the RMI technology, and provides the remote test agent enable test interface which can be accessed by testable beans on the remote machine over the network. The interface supports a binding function between a test agent and testable beans, and basic testing interaction operations, such as *setParameter(....)*, *runMethod...()*, and *validateTestResult(...)*. In addition, *getClass(Object obj)* is included to support *runMethod(...)* to determine the types of objects based on Java Reflection function. The detailed sample code and application examples can be found in [12]. The advantage of this approach is to separate the detailed implements of test interaction functions of a test agent from the interface definition. Therefore, the actual implementation work can be done by tool vendors to support a pre-defined test agent.

As shown in Fig. 5, we can construct the testable beans in two different ways:

− Build components with a test driver.
− Build components with built-in tests.

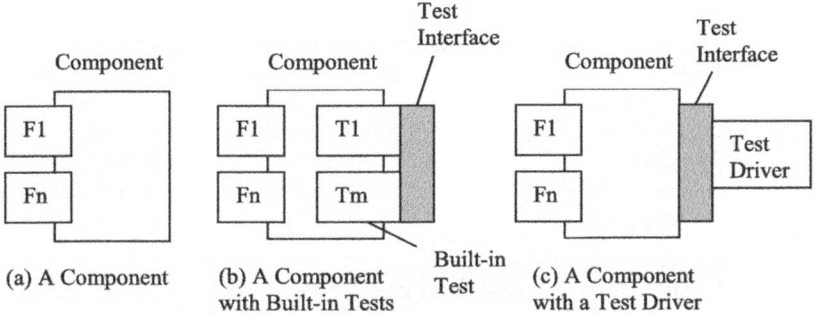

Fig. 5. Components and Testable Components

4.2   Building Component Test Drivers

In our approach, component test drivers are generated based on the presented component test interface, and test facility provided in a test agent. The basic functions of a test driver is listed below.

1. Binding to a test agent through the RMI naming service.
2. Get a test case from a test repository (or a tester via a graphic user interface).
3. Set up parameters through the remote test interface *(setParameters(...))* for exercising and different functions of a component.
4. Invoke a component method using *runMethod(...)*. The *runMethod(...)* uses Java "Reflection" to obtain the information about the classes and members of the given component. This is the technique that the JavaBeans "introspection" mechanism uses to determine the properties, events, and methods that are supported by a bean, for example. Reflection can also be used to manipulate objects in Java. We use the "Field" class to query and set the values of fields, the "Method" class to invoke methods, and "Constructor" class to create new objects.
5. Validate the test results from a test case using *validateResult(...)*. This method compares the execution result of the specified function in the given component with the expected data. A validation status is returned to indicate if the test case has been passed or not. A test record can be generated and stored in a test management tool.

More complex control structure can be added in a component test driver, such as a loop, or if then else to support the execution of one or more test cases.

4.3   Generating Built-in Test Components

For any given component, we can add built-in test scripts to make it as built-in testable components. The basic guidelines are given below.

– Add the built-in test code into a component to make it testable using the
  provided test interface and test facility.
– For each external accessible function, create and insert a test script as part of
  the component using automatic, semi-automatic or manual approach based
  on the given test interface and test facility.
– Each test script includes two parts: a) test case set-up code, which refers to
  the program code that sets up necessary parameters for a test case, and b)
  test case execution code, which refers to the program code that exercises the
  test case, and check the results.

5   Conclusions and Future Work

In this paper, we discussed the testability of software components, and introduced a new concept for software components, known as *testable beans*. The
purpose is to help engineers understand how to construct testable software components and increase component testability. We provide our solution to build
testable components with a well-defined architecture model, and standardized
well-structured component test interface. With this method we can generate
testable software components in a systematic manner. In addition, we present
our idea on how to set up a generic test environment to support testable beans.
The presented solution is applicable to both in-house components and third-
party components. Its major advantages are summarized below:

– It helps engineers to construct testable components with small programming
  overhead.
– It generates testable components with a well-structured component architecture and a consistent interface to support software testing.
– It uses a client-server structure to provide a linkage to connect to different
  component test tools.

It provides a promising approach to get started on the road to test automation
for software components in the following aspects:

– Generate testable components (or beans) in a systematic manner.
– Create a generic component test-bed to provide a plug-in-and-test environment for various software components.
– Create an independent component testing box with well-defined interfaces
  that interact with testing tools and test database to facilitate component
  testing in a more flexible way.
– Add built-in test codes inside a software component in a systematic way.

We are developing a prototype environment for supporting component test
automation. We are working on a tool to generate and test testable beans. Our
tool is partially implemented and has already successfully verified our approach
of creating a testable bean. We are extending the environment to provide a
graphic user interface and a test tool gateway. In addition, we are investigating
new models and methods to support component testing, component integration,
and component performance analysis.

References

1. Councill, William T.: Third-Party Testing and the Quality of Software Components. IEEE Software, Vol. 16 (4), IEEE Computer Society Press, (1999), 55-57.
2. Gao, Jerry Z.: Testing Component-Based Software. International Conference on Software Testing Analysis and Review (STARWEST'99). San Jose, June (1999).
3. Gao, Jerry Z.,: Component Testability and Component Testing Challenges. The Proceedings of the 3rd International Workshop on Component-based Software Engineering: Reflects and Practice, Limerick, Ireland, June (2000).
4. Gao, Jerry Z., Zhu, Eugene, Shim, Simon, and Chang, Lee: Monitoring Software Components and Component-Based Software. The Proceedings of the twenty-fourth Annual International Computer Software & Applications Conference (COMPSAC'2000), Taipei, Taiwan, October (2000), IEEE Computer Society Press (2000).
5. Freedman, Roy S.: Testability of Software Components. IEEE Transactions on Software Engineering, Vol. 17 (6), IEEE Computer Society Press (1991), 553-564.
6. Nagin, Kenneth, and Hartman, Alan: A Case Study: TCBeans/GOTCHA Software Test Tool Kit. The Twelfth International Software Quality Week 1999 (QW'99).
7. Rosenblum, David S.: Adequate Testing of Component-Based Software. Department of Information and Computer Science, University of California, Irvine, Technical Report UCI-ICS-97-34, (1997).
8. Stocks, P. A., and Carrington, D. A.: A Framework for Specification-Based Testing. IEEE Transaction on Software Engineering, Vol. 22 (11), IEEE Computer Society Press (1996), 777-794.
9. Voas, J. M. and Miller, Keith W.: Software Testability: The New Verification. IEEE Software, Vol. 12 (3), IEEE Computer Society Press (1995), 17-28.
10. Wang, Yingxu, King, Graham, and Wickburg, Hakan: A Method for Built-in Tests in Component-based Software Maintenance, Proceedings of the 3rd European Conference on Software Maintenance and Reengineering, (1998).
11. Weyuker, Elaine J.: Testing Component-Based Software: A Cautionary Tale. IEEE Software, Vol. 15 (5), IEEE Computer Society press, (1998), 54-59.
12. Gupta, Kamal and Gupta, Shalino: Design for Testability of Software Components. San Jose State University, Technical Report, (2000).

Streamlining the Acquisition Process for Large-Scale COTS Middleware Components

Ian Gorton[*] and Anna Liu

Software Architectures and Component Technologies Group
CSIRO Mathematical and Information Sciences
Locked Bag 17, North Ryde, Sydney 2113, Australia
{Ian.Gorton, Anna.Liu}@cmis.csiro.au

Abstract. CSIRO's i-MATE process is an established approach to help IT organizations in the acquisition of large-scale COTS middleware components. It aims to minimize technical risk by matching detailed application and infrastructure requirements to the capabilities of COTS middleware products. This paper describes a case study on the use of i-MATE in a project that required the selection of appropriate components in a compressed timeline and from a broad range of candidate COTS technologies. The steps and tools in i-MATE are briefly explained, along with the characteristics of COTS middleware components that make them a unique challenge in terms of acquisition and adoption. The case study project is then outlined, and the key business and technical issues explained. Finally, we describe and evaluate the enhancements made to the i-MATE approach to successfully respond to the challenges encountered.

1 Introduction

Middleware is a term that refers to a broad class of software infrastructure technologies for building distributed systems. Over the past decade, the adoption of COTS middleware products across the software industry has gathered huge momentum. It is slowly becoming a rarity to find major organizations whose business does not rely on some form of COTS middleware components. For example, the use of middleware in Fortune 500 companies is pervasive.

The two key reasons for this growth are Internet usage, and the need to integrate heterogeneous legacy systems to streamline business processes [1]. As organizations do more and more business on-line, they need to provide scalable, high-performance infrastructures to handle business transactions and provide access to core business back-end systems. The latter requires controlled and managed integration between disparate systems that were never designed to interoperate.

COTS middleware components help solve these problems [2]. They provide core software infrastructures that make it relatively straightforward to build distributed applications that are high-performance and scalable. They provide sets

---

[*] Adjunct Professor, Basser Department of Computer Science, University of Sydney, Sydney, Australia

J. Dean and A. Gravel (Eds.): ICCBSS 2002, LNCS 2255, pp. 122–131, 2002.

of services that support, for example off-the-shelf distributed transaction processing, security features, and directory and naming services. They also provide specialized components for integration with a massive variety of legacy systems, and the ability to design and deploy new business processes that integrate multiple distributed applications. There are numerous COTS middleware products available. These are based on some standard infrastructures such as CORBA or J2EE, or proprietary technologies such as COM+ or MQSeries.

This paper firstly describes the challenges that organizations face when they wish to acquire new COTS middleware technologies. A brief classification of middleware products is then given, and the steps in CSIRO's i-MATE approach are explained. i-MATE has evolved over a 2-year period and has been successfully applied in five projects with major industrial clients including the Australian Stock Exchange, the Australian Tax Office and the Defense Housing Association. These organizations all required help in the acquisition of COTS middleware technology to integrate their core business applications. Finally, we describe a case study that forced us to streamline the i-MATE process in order to meet tight deadlines and rapidly evaluate a broad range of candidate middleware products.

2   The Challenges of COTS Middleware Acquisition

COTS middleware components form the infrastructure, or *plumbing* of integrated enterprise information systems. They provide a distributed environment for deploying application level components that carry out business-specific processing.

This distinction between infrastructure level components and application level components is crucial. Application level components rely on the infrastructure components to manage their lifecycle and execution, and to provide them off-the-shelf services such as transactions and security. Hence, an application level component cannot execute outside of a suitable middleware environment. The two are extremely tightly coupled.

An important implication of this is that the behavior of application components is completely dependent upon the behavior of the infrastructure components. The two cannot be divorced in any meaningful way – the entire application's behavior is the combination of the behavior of the application and infrastructure components. This scheme is depicted in Fig. 1.

All this has profound implications upon component certification and engineering. No matter how high the quality of the application components, the COTS middleware infrastructure becomes the most crucial component in most systems. If the middleware is naively architected or implemented, has subtle errors in some services, or is simply inefficient and lacking in features, then the application components inevitably pay the price.

Interestingly, open standard COTS middleware infrastructures such as CORBA and J2EE actually exacerbate this problem. With CORBA and J2EE technologies, many vendors sell their own versions of the middleware infrastructure. These are all implemented differently, and hence behave and perform differently [3]. This means, for example, a J2EE component's performance is dependent upon the actual J2EE product that it runs on. The same component may perform very differently indeed on two different J2EE implementations [4], depending on the quality and features of the product. This of course is not the case with single-source component technologies such as COM+ or MQSeries.

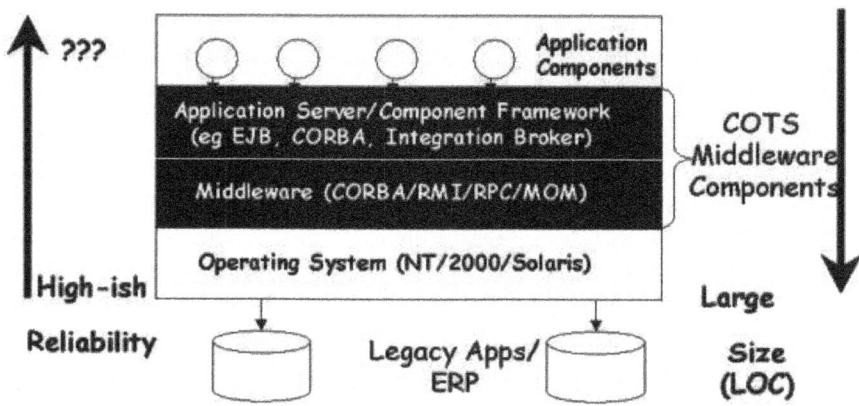

Fig. 1. Anatomy of a COTS Middleware Application

When acquiring a new COTS middleware product, most organizations do not have any pre-built application level components to run. The application components will be built when the middleware has been selected. This makes the selection of COTS middleware components absolutely crucial. If the middleware infrastructure is not 'up to the job', then the application is doomed to failure before it has even been designed.

Unfortunately, COTS middleware products are large and complex components. They will typically have well over 1000 API calls, and comprise a collection of integrated services, that are of varying levels of importance to different applications. There is rarely, if ever, a 'one size fits all' scenario in the acquisition of these technologies.

Apart from size and complexity, other issues make the acquisition of COTS middleware a challenge:

- There are numerous competing products in the middleware space. Narrowing the competition down to a manageable shortlist is a challenge.
- Vendor specifications of their COTS products are vague, and all claim superior features and functionality. This makes it difficult to do any serious comparison of the technologies at more than a very superficial level.
- Product pricing varies significantly, and rarely are acquisitions less than $500K. They are often considerably more.
- The whole middleware area is fast moving and evolving. It is often difficult to discern tested from promised functionality.

3   The i-MATE Process

CSIRO's Middleware Technology Evaluation (MTE) project commenced in 1999. Its aim is to help organizations understand, acquire, and successfully deploy large-scale enterprise information systems based on COTS middleware technologies. To this end, two main themes exist, namely:

1. **Rigorous Technology Evaluation**: This work has devised a rigorous, repeatable approach for performing qualitative and quantitative evaluations of COTS middleware components. Experiments and benchmarks are carried out in our lab, and the results are published in independent technology evaluation reports.[1] This work has so far focused on application servers and COTS message-oriented middleware (MOM) components (see Fig. 2).
2. **Middleware Technology Acquisition**: This theme focuses on working with businesses to help them evaluate and select appropriate COTS middleware components for their specific applications.

(2) has evolved over several projects [5] with major clients in to the i-MATE (Middleware Architecture and Technology Evaluation) approach. In essence, i-MATE is a specialized process for evaluating COTS middleware components, and is equivalent to the *Evaluation* set of activities defined in [6]. With i-MATE, CSIRO provides *just-in-time* technical expertise [7] and works with the business architects to match their technical and business requirements to a suitable infrastructure product.

The basic steps in i-MATE are as follows:

1. **Elaborate customer requirements**: The first step produces a document that captures the customer's requirements. It details the business and technical requirements that are specific to this application environment. Each requirement represents a single item that can be evaluated against a COTS middleware technology.
2. **Augment with generic requirements**: CSIRO has developed a knowledge base of currently around 150 generic, broadly applicable requirements for COTS middleware technologies. These are organized in categories such as message management, transaction services, and security features, and capture the key differentiating areas in middleware products. They focus across a range of functional and quality requirements, and collectively embody considerable accumulated experience from previous projects. These are merged with the application-specific requirements.
3. **Rank overall requirements**: Working with the key stakeholders, the overall set of requirements is ranked. At a coarse level, each requirement is deemed as *mandatory, desirable* or *low priority*. Within each of these 3 categories, importance weightings are assigned to give fine grain control over requirement rankings, in a fashion similar to [8].

---

[1] See http://www.cmis.csiro.au/adsat/mte.htm.

4. **Identify candidate products**: This step identifies the 3-5 COTS middleware products that are most likely to be applicable to the overall application requirements. In some cases, the customer has already identified a shortlist. In others, we use our experience to work with the customer to identify the most likely candidates.

5. **Product Evaluations**: In workshops with the key customer stakeholders and product representatives, we evaluate each of the candidate products against the overall requirements. Scores are allocated against each requirement point for each product. This involves in-depth technical discussions, and stepping through relevant application scenarios to understand precisely how the COTS middleware products actually behave. In terms of effort, this stage typically consumes the majority of the project's effort.

6. **Product Selection**: The application requirements and product scores are captured through the process in a requirement management tool based on a spreadsheet. Once complete, the tool automatically compiles summary scores based on individual requirement point scores and requirement category weightings. Summary charts are also automatically created to support reporting purposes.

At the end of this process, it is usually clear which candidate technologies are capable of satisfying the application requirements. In some cases, two or more products may be close in their overall ranking. In such circumstances, the spreadsheet tool becomes extremely useful.

In the spreadsheet, it is a simple task to modify requirement rankings to see the effect on product selection. Typical strategies involve promoting some *desirable* requirements to *mandatory*, or relaxing some *mandatory* requirements that have proven difficult to satisfy due to some technology restrictions or trade-offs. The key customer stakeholders make these decisions in order to explore a number of *what-if* scenarios.

When a requirement ranking is changed in the spreadsheet, new product rankings are automatically charted. This makes it a trivial exercise to see the effects of varying individual requirement points on product selection. In this way, a leading product can quickly be identified.

i-MATE has been successfully applied in five major projects. The focus of all these projects has been the acquisition of COTS middleware components for application integration. Hence the technology focus has been the category of middleware known as integration brokers or message brokers. These basically provide collections of specialist integration components known as adapters or connectors, a messaging-based communications infrastructure, and development tools for describing business process and message transformations that span multiple legacy systems.

Figure 2 shows how integration brokers fit in to the overall spectrum of currently available middleware technologies. Integration brokers are typically layered upon lower level middleware technologies. As concrete examples, BEA

Process Management Servers mostly proprietary	Long business processes, workflow management
Integration Servers/Brokers - mostly proprietary	Adaptors, transformation, routing, formatting
Application Servers - J2EE, CORBA/OTMs, COM+, proprietary	Transactions, naming, security, pub-sub
Transports CORBA, RMI, RPC, MOM	Data movement/exchange, basic error handling/QoS

Fig. 2. A Layered Taxonomy for COTS Middleware Technologies

System's WebLogic Process Integrator runs on top of their application server, WebLogic Server; IBM's MQSeries Integrator runs on top of MQSeries.

Consequently, a thorough understanding of integration brokers requires knowledge and experience with the underlying COTS middleware layers. In i-MATE, we are able to leverage the independent evaluations of these technologies that are published in our MTE reports. Hence the MTE reports contribute to the overall knowledge base used in i-MATE.

The unique attribute of the i-MATE approach is the inclusion of a comprehensive set of generic requirements applicable to COTS middleware technologies. This is valuable, reusable intellectual property, and saves customers from independently devising their own set. Based on these generic requirements, it is a relatively easy task to augment them with application-specific requirements. Also, once a COTS middleware product has been evaluated against the generic requirements, the evaluation scores can be reused in subsequent projects[2]. Again, we are able to reuse this knowledge, and only need to evaluate the product against the new application-specific needs.

This reuse of generic requirements and product evaluations makes it possible to apply i-MATE in relatively short project timeframes. A typical i-MATE assignment takes 3-4 weeks in elapsed time, and between 15-25 person days effort from the i-MATE team. Given the complexity of COTS middleware components and the scale of the problems they are used to solve, this is a small level of effort and cost. Importantly, it matches the compressed project schedules that are now common in Internet and e-business projects. Three-month product selection projects are rarely viable in these environments.

---

[2] Until major product changes occur.

4   Case Study

A large Australian organization has over 30 core business systems. These revolve around an Enterprise Resource Planning (ERP) system for sales and production planning, a data warehouse and a Customer Relationship Management (CRM) application. As the need for new, integrated business processes has grown, so has the number of application-specific point-to-point interfaces between applications.

At the last count, there were over 150 such interfaces, with approximately 100 new ones planned within the next year. Most of these new interfaces were being driven by the demands to open up core business systems to the Internet. This was creating major development and maintenance problems. Figure 3 gives a high-level schematic of the relationship between these systems

The organization engaged CSIRO to help them select COTS middleware components for application integration. The eventual aim is to eliminate all point-to-point interfaces and use an integration broker to manage all application integration. The integration broker will provide a single repository for the definition of message types and formats, message transformations, and business rules used in integration. The broker must also provide a high-performance, scalable and reliable infrastructure to handle large volumes of transactions for business-critical applications.

Apart from this longer-term strategic aim of eliminating point-to-point application interfaces, there were two more immediate needs for the COTS middleware technology. These are:

1. A key interface between the CRM and ERP was causing operational problems for a key business process. Due to the nature of the business, the majority of the transactions across this interface took place in a 4 hour period at the start of the week. Current loads were around 60,000 transactions in that period, and this number was growing rapidly. The middleware product was required to eliminate the problems with this interface, and provide real-time turnaround for transactions.
2. There was an increasing need for the organization to exchange information electronically with business partners. Therefore, the COTS middleware technology adopted must have features that support a wide variety of business-to-business (B2B) interface types.

In addition, due to timing and budgetary constraints, the acquisition stage of the project was scheduled for a 1-month duration. This would then be followed by a proof-of-concept stage during which the selected COTS middleware product would be tested and validated.

5   Streamlining i-MATE

At the start of the project, we began following the i-MATE process. The customer-specific requirements were quickly understood, reduced to specific requirement points and merged with the generic requirements that accompany

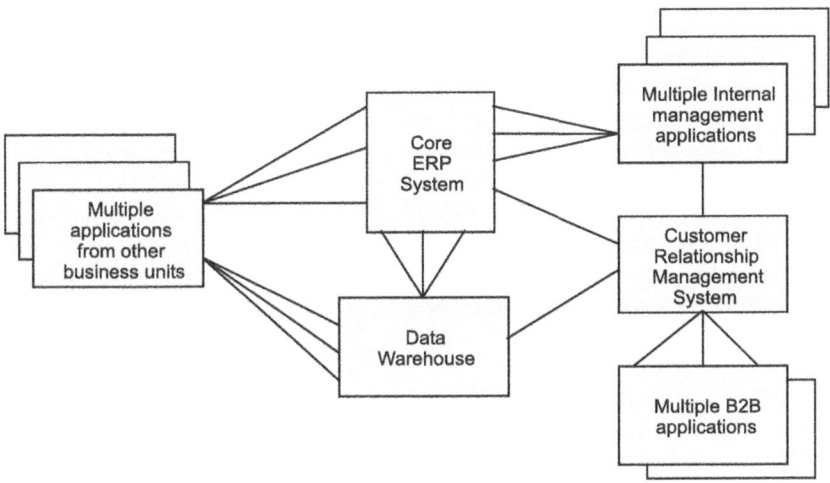

Fig. 3. Enterprise Architecture

the i-MATE process. In a series of workshops, the ranking process of the specific requirement points was commenced, and concurrently, the list of candidate technologies was drawn up.

It was at this stage where we began to encounter some problems. In past projects, i-MATE has evaluated between 3 and 5 candidate COTS middleware technologies. The product evaluations against the application requirements are time-consuming, taking at least 1 day for products that have already been evaluated in previous i-MATE projects, and typically 2-4 days for products that are new to the evaluation team.

However, for various non-technical reasons, the organization presented us with a list of 13 candidate products. This was clearly too many to fully evaluate in a one month project. As the project schedule was fixed, it was necessary to devise a strategy that allowed the number of candidate products to be reduced to a manageable size. In addition, strong justification was needed to eliminate a product, so that the organizations' upper management felt comfortable that the most appropriate technologies were being considered.

To this end, we modified step 4 of i-MATE as follows:

1. In conjunction with the customer organization's technical team, 5 key requirements were identified. These were a combination of application-specific (e.g. CRM integration components) and generic middleware (e.g. scalability) requirements.
2. The 13 candidate products were quickly categorized as *strong, weak* or *unknown* in terms of addressing these 5 key requirements. This was based on the previous experience of the i-MATE team.
3. An information gathering exercise was commenced to qualify the *weak* and *unknown* candidate products. In three cases, it was possible to eliminate a

product based on a simple non-conformance issue with regards to a platform that the organization needed support for. In 2 cases, products were eliminated because they did not have strong local organizations to support their product – this was a mandatory requirement. Finally, one product was eliminated because, in discussions with the vendor, it became clear that the product's real strengths were not in application integration.

4. Half-day workshops were organized with each of the seven remaining vendors. In these workshops, the majority of the time was spent probing on how each product could support the five key requirements. In addition, issues related to costs were broadly addressed.

The seven workshops took place during the same week. At the end of this week, we had a set of scores on how each candidate COTS product was able to address the key application requirements. Using a spreadsheet tool and weighting the five requirements in various ways, we worked through various scenarios with the customer to explore the various product strengths and weaknesses. It was clear that three of the products were considerably stronger than the others in terms of their features and underlying architectures. Consequently, these three were selected as the candidate COTS middleware products to fully evaluate in step 5 of i-MATE.

6   Evaluation

The modified *Identify Candidate Products* step of i-MATE worked extremely well. It enabled us to rapidly reduce the number of COTS middleware products to a more manageable set, and then perform relatively detailed evaluations of the remaining products against the key application requirements. This process was successful in:

1. Rapidly identifying the strongest candidates to be evaluated in more detail
2. Providing clear justification to the customer's technical and managements teams as to why certain COTS middleware products were less suitable
3. Helping identify the highest priority requirements with the client at an early stage in the process.
4. Not expanding the overall project schedule – the i-MATE process was still completed in the four-week schedule for the project.

In fact, we see step (3) above as a valuable contribution to the whole process. It helps focus the client's thinking at an early stage of the acquisition project, and brings the highest priority requirements to the fore, for primary consideration.

7   Conclusions

The i-MATE process has been developed to help with the acquisition of COTS middleware technologies. These are complex, highly technical and diverse collections of products that typically operate in business-critical environments. i-MATE's key contributions, which have formed the basis for several successful projects are:

- A pre-fabricated, reusable set of generic requirements, based upon the practical analysis in business environments of application and COTS middleware components characteristics
- A defined process for incorporating application-specific requirements
- A process and tool for weighting requirements and ranking specific COTS middleware products against the requirements
- Tool support for rapidly exploring requirement trade-offs and generating reports showing how the COTS products compare against the requirements.

This paper has described some modifications that were introduced in to the core process to enable i-MATE to cover a broader range of candidate COTS middleware products. These modifications made it possible for the i-MATE team to evaluate 13 candidate COTS middleware products, and still complete the project in a 4 week schedule. The success of these modifications demonstrates the solid core foundations of i-MATE, and its inherent flexibility and adaptability to changing business requirements during the acquisition process.

References

1. Ron Zahavi, David S. Linthicum: Enterprise Application Integration with CORBA Component and Web-Based Solutions. John Wiley and Sons, November (1999).
2. George T. Heineman (Editor), William T. Councill: Component-Based Software Engineering. Addison-Wesley, June (2001).
3. I. Gorton, A. Liu, P. Tran: The Devil is in the Detail, A Comparison of CORBA Object Transaction Services. The 6th International Conference on Object-Oriented Information Systems, 211-221, 18-20 December, (2000), London.
4. S. Ran, P. Brebner, I. Gorton: The Rigorous Evaluation of Enterprise Java Bean Technology. In 15th International Conference on Information Networking (ICOIN-15), Beppu City, Japan, Feb. (2001), IEEE.
5. Liu A.: Gathering Middleware Requirements. Proceedings of the Australian Requirements Engineering Workshop, 8-9 November, (2000).
6. Lisa Brownsword, Tricia Oberndorf, Carol A. Sledge: Developing New Processes for COTS-Based Systems. IEEE Software, Vol. 17(4), July/August (2000).
7. Kurt Wallnau, Scott Hissam, Robert Seacord: Building Systems from Commercial Components. Addison-Wesley, July (2001).
8. Patricia K. Lawlis et al: A Formal Process for Evaluating COTS Software Products. Computer, Vol. 34(5), May (2001).

Storyboard Process to Assist in Requirements Verification and Adaptation to Capabilities Inherent in COTS

Sallie Gregor, Joseph Hutson, and Colleen Oresky

SAIC, 1710 SAIC Drive, McLean, Virginia, 22102
{gregors, hutsonj, oreskyc}@saic.com

Abstract. One of the challenges of using COTS is defining which requirements and business processes can be supported with COTS products while limiting the amount of customization and integration code that is required. Limiting customization and integration code reduces risks, lowers maintenance costs, improves ability to upgrade and provides the customer more for their investment. To help customers better understand their requirements and reduce COTS customization, SAIC successfully used storyboards during the requirements phase. The storyboard process integrates "use cases" and screen captures to assist the customers in verifying and adapting their requirements to the capabilities inherent in the COTS products. An additional bonus of this process is that the screen captures also support the design phase of the user interface features. The storyboard process described in this paper was used to develop large COTS-based systems for customers who historically developed large custom software applications.

1 Introduction

Many organizations hope that using commercial-off-the-shelf (COTS) products will reduce development time, ease modernization and limit overall life cycle costs of large scale systems. COTS-based systems consist of one or more customized COTS products integrated together via special purpose integration code. To realize many of the advantages of using COTS products, system developers attempt to minimize the amount of customization and integration code that is required while addressing several unique issues:

- Overcoming customer expectations that COTS integration is Plug-and-Play. In many cases, COTS tools are not designed to interoperate with each other. Using one product may influence how other products can be integrated. Some degree of incompatibility is expected, but the goal is to minimize this as much as possible.
- Inexperience of integrators and/or users with the chosen products. This affects both architects and users during the COTS selection process.

J. Dean and A. Gravel (Eds.): ICCBSS 2002, LNCS 2255, pp. 132–141, 2002.
© Springer-Verlag Berlin Heidelberg 2002

A major challenge of COTS-based development is defining which requirements and business processes can be supported with COTS products, and what additional requirements are introduced by these COTS products. The architects work with the users to compare the requirements to the functionality of candidate COTS products prior to choosing the best combination of products. The architects must be careful not to force fit a solution that in the end will require major modifications to the COTS products or development of complex integration code. Using a product in a manner not expected by the COTS vendor will only introduce potential problems later in the development process. Ranking the requirements from absolute necessities to marginally important as well as by whether the functionality is provided by a COTS product, permits the architects and users to better evaluate those requirements that can be relaxed without substantially affecting the overall functionality of the system. When identifying those requirements that can be relaxed, the goal should be to limit the amount of customization and integration code required.

To help users better understand their requirements associated with a COTS-based solution, SAIC has successfully used storyboards during the requirements phase. Storyboards integrate "use cases" and screen captures to assist customers in verifying and adapting their requirements to the capabilities inherent in COTS products. Users gain a view of how the system will function when fully developed. It is easier for users to critique the storyboards than to try to describe what they want. They are able to iteratively refine their requirements, many of which are not understood ahead of time. The iterative process also helps to start to identify the gaps between the COTS product capabilities, and system and user expectations.

Storyboarding provides additional benefits that increase user acceptance and therefore reduces development costs due to redesign later in the development process. Creating the use cases and screen captures shots offers the next best thing to developing prototypes by allowing the system developers to gain experience with the COTS products as soon as possible. In addition, the storyboards provide the foundation for the design of the user interface. While reviewing the storyboards, users and architects verify that buttons are in consistent places on all screens, that the same operation occurs on all screens when you click on text or a button, and that the field placements are logical. The developers use the storyboards to begin system implementation.

The remainder of this paper describes the storyboard process as applied to the development of large COTS-based systems for customers who historically developed large custom software applications. The paper describes what makes up a storyboard and the advantages of using storyboarding during COTS-based development.

2   Storyboard Components

Storyboards take advantage of use case modeling and screen captures to combine traditional requirements products into a single product that provide a clear, unambiguous understanding of the system to be developed. Use cases alone do not tie the requirements to specific COTS implementation potential. Screen captures alone do not provide a clear understanding of the relationship between the various screens and the function of the set of screens. The storyboard does both. Usually, use cases are developed and presented to the customer as a text product (describing each step of a process), a Unified Modeling Language diagram, or a combination of the two. Use case development is very important for capturing the business processes and defining the requirements. Use cases may show a good understanding of the customer's requirements, however presenting them to the customer can be very tedious and often not well received by the users. They typically prove an understanding of the problem, but fall short in providing a vision of meeting these requirements. Screen captures of real and mock-up application windows are frequently used to show the customer how the application will look. This is good for clarifying the screens appearance, but even with notes by each button or menu describing their functionality, it is hard to visualize the business process. Particularly when business processes must be adapted to effectively use the COTS products, the individual screen captures do little to portray the steps required to perform the mission.

SAIC's storyboards combines use cases and screen captures on a large poster size graphic that accurately conveys what the user will see and how functions will be performed. Although SAIC developed its storyboards using MS Power Point, they can be developed in any drawing package that supports the combination of imported pictures and text in large format. Storyboards can be viewed conceptually as a combination of two layers of information. Storyboards start with a use case describing a function to be performed as shown in the top layer of Fig. 1. Screen captures are taken of each screen state for each use case step as illustrated in the second layer of Fig. 1. In some cases actual screens based on the COTS products were used. When new screens need to be developed, they can often be developed using GUI building tools such as VisualCafé®, JBuilder®, or VisualAge® for JAVA screens. These screens can later be given to developers to integrate with working code. When a needed screen state cannot be created from an actual screen capture without actually developing needed functionality, other screen captures can be enhanced with drawing tools to get the desired effect.

The screen captures are placed on the storyboard starting with one showing the use case precondition state. Each use case step is placed in a text box on the storyboard with arrows pointing to effected items (buttons pressed, output displayed, windows opened, etc.) as illustrated by the third layer of Fig. 1. Additional text is provided to clarify the processes being performed and alternatives available to the user. Additional notes are added to highlight features that are not current requirements but may be of interest to the user. These may be additional features inherent in the COTS product or areas which require additional knowledge or experience with the COTS product to fully understand and assess the implementation issues.

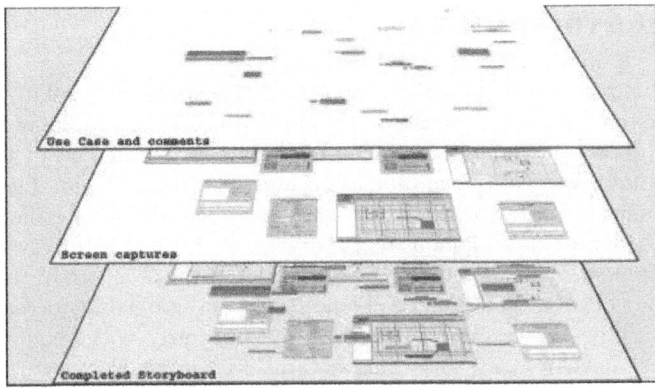

Fig. 1. Storyboard Construction

A single storyboard is used to display one or more use cases showcasing either a common theme or a continuous thread. The text boxes for each use case are displayed using a different color to clearly show where one use case ends and another begins. An example of completed storyboard is shown in Fig. 2.

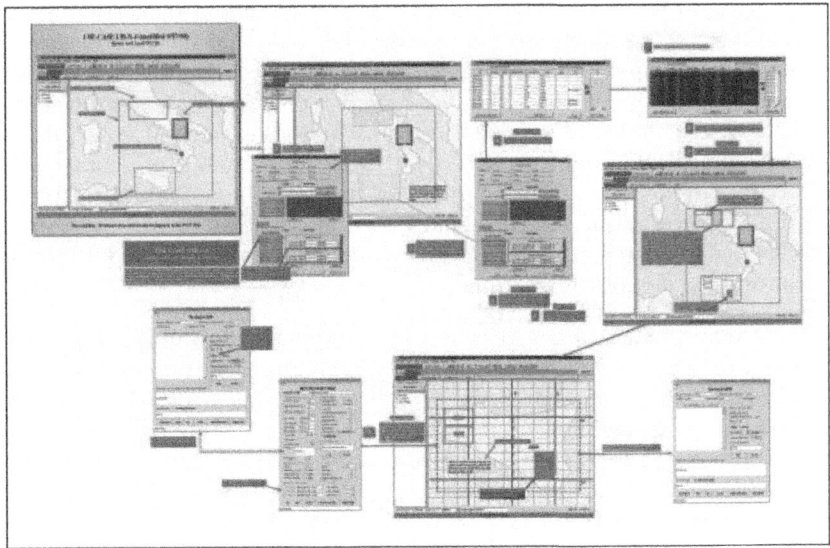

Fig. 2. Single Use Case Storyboard Example

3   Storyboard Process

Storyboards captures user decisions and actions as they relate and interface to the system. The goal of the storyboard process is to align user interface and user interaction requirements to the capabilities inherent in the COTS products, thus minimizing customization and integration code. The storyboard development can be used iteratively and incrementally with either a structured or object oriented development methodology, and it can be integrated into existing development processes. One notable aspect of the storyboard process is the concurrency of several steps that in traditional development processes[1] are executed sequentially. Our process is executed concurrently with requirements analysis, use case development, and architecture level design. If concurrency is not part of the development process then the storyboard process could be thought of as a subprocess of the requirements analysis phase. With frequent product upgrades and technology refreshes, this process can be applied to each iteration of change, however the major advantage to the storyboard will only be realized if the change is significant to the business process. This process description is relevant to software development within an integrated system development program and does not have much influence in the hardware development portion. Additionally the storyboard process does not address the ability to predict system performance other than how the COTS components will interact.

As with any process, the first step is to develop a plan (Fig. 3). This plan identifies the resources, both personnel and tools, and the schedule for the storyboard development and peer reviews. The tools used for storyboard development should be the same tools the development team uses for system development. The tools include a design tool, such as Together ControlCenter, an integrated development environment, such as Visual Café®, and a presentation tool, such as MS power point. Storyboards also require a large-scale color plotter. Electronic projection of the storyboard was not effective in presenting the "story" (flow). A large-scale plot of the storyboard was more effective in presenting the concepts and capturing comments.

The storyboard plan identifies the storyboards to be developed or in some cases, only the topical areas for the storyboards. Selection of storyboards to be developed should be based on areas of key business decisions, automation of user functions, and change from legacy systems. Distinguish between those storyboards that support requirements analysis and those that support the interface design. All storyboards support interface design, but not all storyboards provide significant support to requirements analysis. Concentrate on the storyboards that support requirements analysis because they clarify the interpretation of the requirements or clarify true requirements from legacy implementation. Since the storyboard plan is used to document which storyboards will be developed,

---

[1] Traditional development process within either spiral or waterfall model refers to the following sequence of steps; requirements analysis, architecture definition, design, code, and test.

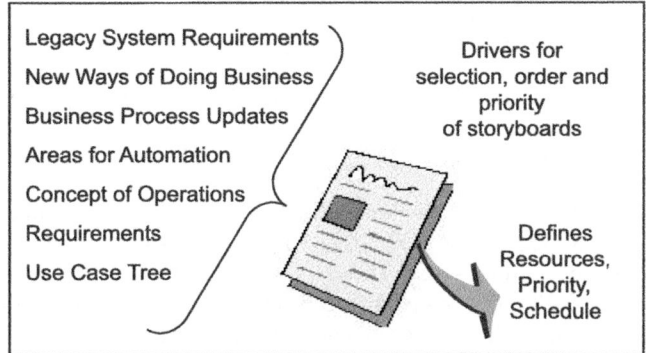

Fig. 3. Storyboard plan captures what is to be developed, when and with what resources

it also assists in the coordination between the storyboard team and both the requirements and use case teams.

The plan also captures the development sequence of storyboards. The first storyboard should be the primary functional thread. This lets the storyboard team get a baseline and initiates the users into the process. Early introduction of the COTS technology and products is a key advantage of storyboards. For this reason, one of the first storyboards should demonstrate how technology addresses one of the users' biggest headaches such as tedious tasks that can be automated, or a bottleneck task that through the use of new technology productivity can be eased. The remaining order should be based on several factors such as development schedule, change from legacy system and areas where the business processes change dramatically. For instance, automation is a key candidate where the business process for the user changes significantly. The plan should propose that a storyboard be done for each major functional thread of the system, in addition to the areas with considerable changes.

The storyboard plan should also include metrics for evaluating usefulness of the process to support future estimates and progress reporting. The metrics should include resources spent and a measure of the complexity of the storyboards.

Once the plan is in place, the storyboard team can be assembled. The best composition is a small team consisting of one requirements engineer, one software developer, and one Subject Matter Expert (SME) per major application. The actual size of the team should be driven by the size and scope of the system to be developed. The SME is usually a user of the system and represents the users' needs. Caution should be exercised when selecting the SME. Some SME's don't embrace change and are not interested in having the current business process modified. If the available SME is resistant to change, then the challenge is deciphering what functions really need to be done versus those implemented by the current system. For this case an extra requirements engineer may be required to assist in extracting true requirements versus legacy implementation.

The following description summarizes the specific storyboard process activities. As illustrated in Fig. 4, the process activities are organized into requirements identification, use case modeling, COTS identification and storyboard creation.

The purpose of requirements identification is to determine which requirements are candidates for COTS technologies. This is done via three major activities: allocate requirements, perform requirements analysis and develop concept of operations. The first steps are to filter out user interface and user interaction requirements and develop a concept of operations. The concept of operations provides an abstract description of the scenarios for the various users functions and provides an understanding of how the user would use the capability. The concept of operations can drive the definition of the types of screen, commands and reports needed by the user. It can also describe types of messages that are displayed, acknowledged or logged. A survey of the current process assists in both the concept of operations development and the requirements analysis.

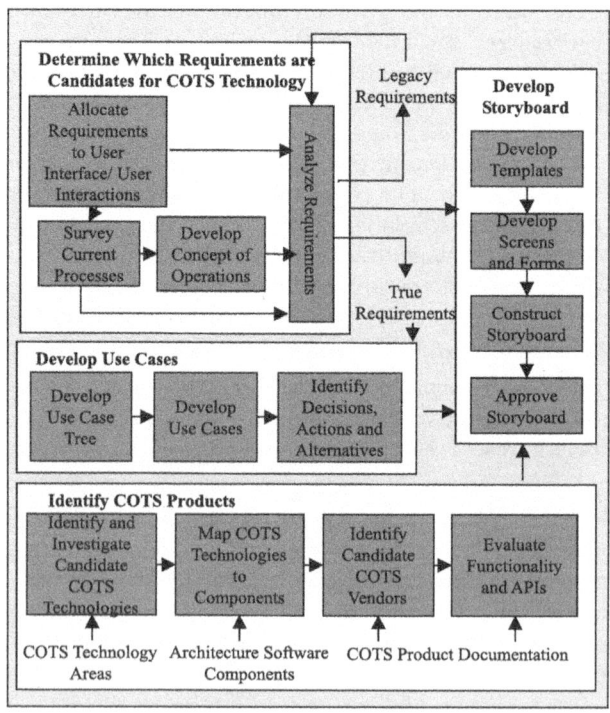

Fig. 4. Storyboard Process

Key to requirements analysis is the evaluation of true user requirements versus legacy system requirements. This is an important step for implementation of capabilities inherent in the COTS technology. We found this to be one of the biggest challenges. A close interaction with a SME or user representative assisted in accomplishing an understanding of the underlying requirements associated with the function being performed.

The purpose of use case modeling is to describe the sequences that actors (users) follow when performing a function. The first part of use case modeling is to develop a use case tree that covers the requirements scope. The use case tree provides a hierarchical organization to manage the complexity of a typical set of requirements. It identifies all use cases and their relationship to each other. In the use case tree, each use case is linked to both the preceding use cases and the branches of various courses of action resulting from invoking different decisions. Use cases support the identification of command structures, menu formats, display formats, input forms, and report formats, as applicable. The development of use cases support other aspects of the software effort and only a subset are used for storyboarding. The use cases that support user interface and user interaction requirements can be identified within a use case tree.

In order to determine which COTS technologies can satisfy the requirements, the candidate COTS technologies need to be identified and mapped to requirements. This mapping to requirements is done through the software components identified by the architecture level design. The software components are decomposed to a level where major candidates for COTS products can be identified and incorporated into the design. Requirements analysis and architecture level design need to be adequately completed to understand roles and interfaces for the candidate COTS technologies. Candidate COTS technologies are then mapped to software components based on a review of which COTS technologies can meet the requirements.

To assist in evaluating COTS technologies, documentation is obtained for candidate COTS products. It is worth noting that in general, we found that this documentation provided limited visibility into how the product actually works and dependencies it may have on other products. Experience with the products was the best way to evaluate a product's functionality and application programming interfaces (APIs). This evaluation involves comparing APIs to determine what components of a COTS product can be accessed and how it is implemented. The evaluation also needs to address how much of the business process the product addresses. We found that products that have extensive flexibility require a proportional amount of additional effort to implement a solution, but on the other hand can be made to address a larger portion of the business process.

It is also important to identify and evaluate the candidate COTS technology history and maturity. Because smaller vendors are trying to establish themselves in the market, they tend to accommodate change requests more readily than larger vendors. The big draw back is that the larger vendor tends to define the trends. In addition, the small vendors may lack the resources to complete what they promise in the timeframe required.

The evaluation of COTS products can be very complex and time consuming. All the factors discussed above contribute to the trade off between cost, schedule and resources. It is important to record all assumptions and rationale used during the evaluation. Support from a COTS technology lab can be beneficial during this evaluation process. The evaluation process needs to be carefully managed to ensure it does not consume all resources. The requirements database should be updated to show the requirement(s) with associated components that are either partially or fully implemented by each COTS product.

The construction of the actual storyboards begins with developing the user screens based on the use case descriptions. The specific steps of the use case determine the actual forms or screens on the storyboard. The layout of the screens intertwined with the use case step descriptions is tailored to the specific storyboard. Screen and form templates encourage uniform ways of performing similar functions. For instance, we used the same basic form for the various query responses. This provided standards for similar actions. The storyboard introduces the users to the application appearance and allows them to become familiar with the look and feel of the application. Peer review within the storyboard team of the storyboards prior to a customer review has two major advantages: it keeps all team members up to date and it allows them all an opportunity to provide comments and insights.

Sign-off on a storyboard from a user representative and customer is crucial to the success of a COTS-based solution. The sign-off is accomplished through a storyboard review. The customer and users (often not the same people) are involved in sign-off of the user interface requirements captured in the storyboards. The storyboards should represent at least the 80% solution to make the review productive. During reviews, we found that it was easier for the user to comment on the business process illustrated in the storyboard than to create it from scratch. In the group forum, the full spectrum of users was represented, and the storyboard helped the users communicate among themselves as well as with the storyboard team. This method of user involvement supports the concept of designing for the user from the beginning. The major advantage is that the storyboards illustrate how the end product can be used effectively and efficiently by the users. Redesign later in the development process and support costs are also reduced. Upon completion of a review, all user comments must be addressed and if necessary, another review is held. The final step of the process is to place approved storyboards under developmental configuration control for use by the design team.

4   Advantages of Using Storyboards

Although users and developers use the storyboards differently, the storyboards provide a means for all to communicate requirements more clearly and concisely. It is easier for the users to critique the storyboards, pointing out what they like and do not like, discussing screen layout and presentation, and identifying gaps in the requirement, than to clearly explain what they want or need. A picture is worth a thousand words especially when there is a language or cultural barrier. While creating the storyboards, the developers become more familiar with the technical aspects of the selected COTS products. In addition, the developers use the screen captures to insure user interface consistency and functionality. Working together, users and developers can better evaluate the pros and cons of using various COTS products, document the "true" requirements and select the best combination of COTS to satisfy these requirements.

The storyboards also provide an excellent means for managing user expectations and overcoming the myth that COTS integration is Plug-and-Play. The users see first hand what the COTS products provide so they can better understand how the end product will function. This allows them to better understand how current business processes are still being accomplished but in a different manner. Users provide input in defining any new procedures, which encourages "buy-in" to the changes because they are involved in the decision making process. When several COTS products are required, the storyboards provide a tool for the developers to explain to the users how integration may be cumbersome or require a substantial amount of code to integrate the products together. Using the storyboards, the developers help the users to understand that modifying some of the requirements may not greatly affect system functionality, while overall system development risk and time may be substantially reduced because less customization and integration code is required.

As part of the storyboard creation process, skeletons of a prototype are developed so that representative screen images can be captured. In addition to providing the users a preliminary view of how the system will function, the development team gains experience using the COTS products so they can better evaluate how difficult it will be to use the COTS products. In addition, gaps in the COTS products can be more easily identified and when products are being force fit to the solution. The developers also gain initial exposure to the available programming interfaces to help scope the customization effort. Using all this information, the developers are better able to select the best combination of COTS products and create a realistic development schedule based on how much time will be required to implement a solution, and the level of difficulty of customization and integration of the selected COTS products.

5   Conclusion

Improved communication throughout the entire system development process is the major advantage of the use of storyboards during the requirements phase of a COTS-based development effort. SAIC experienced tremendous success in using storyboards to achieve user approval of minimally customized COTS implementations by taking advantage of a large percentage of the capabilities inherent in the COTS products while still meeting the users' needs. Definition, clarification and adaptation of requirements is more easily achieved by presenting them in a realistic manner through the storyboards. This process was so successful that SAIC's customers wanted the storyboards as deliverables! They paint a compelling story. We highly recommend this process to help insure the successful completion of a COTS-based development effort.

Realizing the Potential for COTS Utilization: A Work in Progress

Rhoda Shaller Hornstein[1] and John K. Willoughby[2]

[1] National Aeronautics and Space Administration
Washington DC 20546, USA
rhoda.hornstein@hq.nasa.gov
[2] The Kendall Group, Inc.
Castlerock, CO 80104, USA
jkwilloughby1@earthlink.net

Abstract. For over a decade, the U.S. Government has been empha-
sizing its preference for using commercial-off-the-shelf (COTS) products
as a way to reduce program costs and accelerate schedules. The results
of this initiative have been mixed, with many programs reporting fewer
benefits from COTS usage than its advocates had forecast. This paper
explores the reasons for the unfulfilled potential of COTS utilization and
presents some new considerations for addressing the COTS challenges.
Between 1992 and 1996, a NASA Task Force called the COST LESS
Team developed recommendations for a combined technical architecture
and electronic-commerce marketplace strategy for reducing the cost and
cycle time of systems for space programs, while improving their quality and responsiveness to customer needs. COTS buying was a central,
but not exclusive, feature. The strategy involves a comprehensive reengineering of the entire buy/sell process and the relationships between
government program management and the supply chain. In addition to
using COTS products, the strategy includes: (1) aggregating demand
across organizational and program boundaries that traditionally are un-
coordinated, (2) determining fundamental reusable components that may
not be recognized as similar in today's organizational framework, (3)
influencing the design and creation of products available from the supply chain, and (4) revamping the mechanisms for matching the buyers
and sellers, i.e., marketplace modernization. Each of these features for a
COTS acquisition strategy is discussed in detail. Case summaries are presented which demonstrate that implementing these features will enhance
the advantages of using COTS and remove some of the impediments that
have limited its early successes. Specific recommendations are offered to
realize the full potential for COTS utilization through incorporation with
re-engineered processes.

1   COTS Track Record to Date

For more than a decade, NASA, DoD and many other Government agencies
have been increasing their emphasis on using commercial-off-the-shelf products

(COTS) as a preferred approach to implementing new systems. This is contrasted to a traditional approach of building software specifically to satisfy a unique set of requirements. The definition of true COTS software is not universally accepted [1]. However, we adopt here the pragmatic description from Basili and Boehm [2] that COTS software is provided by a vendor who:

- controls its evolution,
- often denies access of the buyer to its source code, and
- supplies it to a significant set of different users called collectively its "installed base".

The advantages of using COTS software have been promised as reduced cost, faster implementation, maximum reuse of existing technology, and less complex maintenance due to upgrades provided by the vendors. Enough time has passed using the COTS approach to allow the reporting of actual benefits versus the promises of a decade ago. The reviews are mixed. Many system developers have reported savings and functional successes. Clearly many of these success stories have been reported by the vendors themselves. Others [3,4,5,6] have documented disadvantages associated with the approach. Among the problems reported are:

- Licensing and intellectual property procurement delays
- Recurring maintenance fees
- Reliability problems
- Scaling problems
- Efficiency of execution
- Dependence on vendor
- Synchronization of upgrades
- Integration challenges and cost overruns
- Incomplete capture of all requirements
- Incompatibility with standards
- Functionality misrepresented by vendor.

In spite of the difficulties reported, the benefits have been sufficiently great to virtually assure the continuation of the COTS usage trend [7,8]. It remains then for the products and the processes for using them to be perfected. Most of the reported shortcomings of the COTS usage experience to date appear to be correctable. They result, the authors contend, from inserting COTS utilization into a supply/demand framework that is itself flawed; it is a vestige of the practice of building unique systems.

2   COTS as an Element of a Larger Framework

During 1992-1996, NASA's COST LESS team (including its predecessor teams) laid the groundwork for a radical redesign of the costly processes used by the

Agency's Strategic Enterprises to build and buy space mission systems. The redesigned processes, when institutionalized, provide an exit path from engineering one-of-a-kind, complex systems and acquiring them through large consolidated contracts. Movement along this exit path may be tracked by the extent to which NASA lets go of what has become familiar and redirects its freed up assets to premier research and development.

The COST LESS team was initially commissioned to advise how NASA's space communications program could be conducted faster, better, and cheaper. Having demonstrated ingenuity as a catalyst for change within a major program, the team's scope and membership were broadened to encompass the NASA family. The new team, composed of self-directed, volunteer representatives from government, industry and academia, was endorsed in 1994, by NASA Administrator Daniel S. Goldin as a cross-cutting, strategic agent for "faster, better, cheaper" change [9].

With this endorsement, the COST LESS team set out to challenge established traditions. Two traditions were selected based on a previous finding that unnecessary uniqueness and complexity are linked with increased costs and schedules. The first tradition was custom building and custom-buying space mission systems around original or unique requirements. The second tradition was accepting the resultant complexities as inevitable and accommodating them with extensive chain-of-command reviews and controls. The team undertook these challenges to realize "breakthrough" results of the kind offered by reengineering experts [10]. The team viewed breakthrough as the action of breaking through an obstruction. The obstructions were "stovepipe" or insular management behaviors within organizational boundaries, discipline walls, funding partitions, functional decompositions, and life cycle phases. Experience had shown that rewarding these obstructionist behaviors disincentivized the discovery of fundamental similarities across the groups, and produced mission-peculiar, project-unique, and organization-specific systems when not merited. Further, this collective shortcoming in acknowledging similarities was a major source of unnecessary complexity that generated unnecessary duplications, e.g., building and buying custom systems to perform comparable functions, or reviewing and controlling the building and buying of these custom systems.

The COST LESS team entered into candid collaborations with decision-makers and joined in pre-competitive research with colleagues, who were dispersed across the diverse boundaries (e.g., organizational, discipline, functional, geographic, and political) the results were intended to transcend. Following an international workshop in May 1995, the story of FRED began to unfold [11,12]. FRED presents a bold alternative to the status quo, and demonstrates technical and business ingenuity to create a robust and adaptable marketplace that anticipates, meets and exceeds customer needs [13]. The marketplace paradigm offers NASA an opportunity to reduce dramatically the cost of success and to position itself, not merely to survive, but to thrive, in a continuing constrained fiscal environment.

3   COTS Strategies as Seen from the Demand Side of the Market

The utility of COTS products can be enhanced by a change in the requirements and design processes for new systems. Several authors [4,14] have noted that the traditional process of defining requirements and then matching COTS products to them leads to limited COTS utilization and surely ineffective COTS exploitation. The COST LESS team recognized that to fully exploit COTS offerings, aggregation of the demand for specific functionality would have to be many times greater than it is today. This aggregation cannot simply result from increased sizes of contracts and a consolidation of program boundaries. Rather, it requires the recognition that unnecessary segmentation of the demand marketplace be eliminated by recognizing similarities in needs that cross organizational and mission type boundaries. For example, familiar partitions of the demand marketplace such as manned vs. unmanned missions, flight segments vs. ground segments, aircraft vs. spacecraft distinctions, large vs. small satellites programs create specialty requirements taxonomies that are artificial. Specificity that is unneeded creates complexity that is also unneeded. Communities of practitioners develop in alignment with these classification schemes and recognition of the similarities in requirements across these boundaries tends to diminish.

A key finding of the COST LESS team [11] was that the numerous and seemingly diverse systems used in space mission operations can be represented by only two functional categories, namely Information Handling and Resource Management & Control. Figure 1 displays the two functional categories of space mission operations and the next level of the taxonomy. Information Handling includes all activities that transfer, store, retrieve, transform, and analyze data. Resource Management & Control includes all activities that plan and command a mission. The importance of this straight-forward (non complex) abstraction lies in the fact that none of the typical organizational decompositions common in NASA's current operational practices is imposed at the top levels. The typical dichotomy of spacecraft and ground systems is not imposed, nor is the usual split of science (payload) versus platform (spacecraft) systems. Lead-time and mission-phase distinctions, such as long-range planning versus real-time planning, launch operations versus on-orbit operations, primary mission versus extended operations, and cruise phase versus encounter phase for interplanetary missions, are also not imposed. Not even the customary distinctions between human and robotic space flight are present in the top levels of the functional breakdown. This is not to say that specialized requirements that depend on the characteristics or stage of a mission are unnecessary, but rather to point out that imposing specializations too high in a functional breakdown is a major cause of unnecessary complexity and duplication. The imposition of specialization too high in a decomposition of tasks or functions creates activities that add no value.

A comparison among the activities at the second level of decomposition reveals the prominence of decision-making in the Resource Management & Control category. Engineers know how to perform the mechanics of manipulating data and converting them to information. Once it has been determined what data are to be moved, stored, etc., the systems to perform these Information Handling

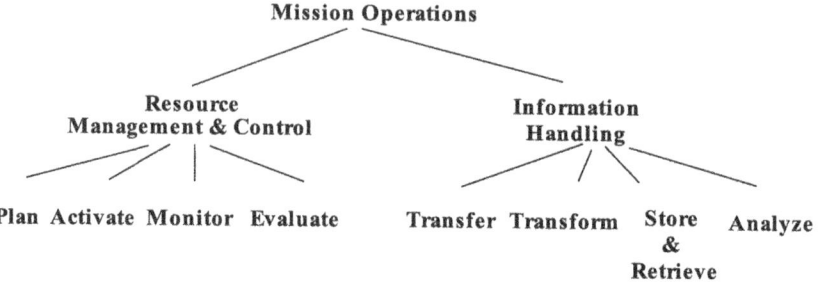

Fig. 1. Space Mission Operations Decomposition

functions can, to a large extent, be mechanized. The need for direct human involvement in routine Information Handling tasks is almost non-existent using current technology. If operational difficulties occur, humans are used to help diagnose the problems and to assign alternate resources that reestablish routine operations. However, these diagnostic functions fall more naturally into the Resource Management & Control category. In that category, we find planning, scheduling, status monitoring, trouble shooting (cause determination), and command & control. All of these functions require some degree of experiential knowledge, technical judgment, and other forms of intelligence that current practice is beginning to address with autonomous systems.

The natural separation of decision-oriented tasks from the more engineering-oriented or mechanizable tasks is useful in recognizing the nature of the fundamental functions for space mission operations. This notion of fundamental functionalities is critical to defining and implementing the reusable technology components envisioned for FRED, i.e., the fundamental building blocks that are applicable or reusable in environments that, at first glance, seem to be dissimilar. In other words, the building blocks represent the most basic units of human and robotic space system construction and may be used to satisfy a wide range of space mission needs.

To maximize the utilization of COTS, the aggregation of requirements from the marketplace must be accomplished by designing from the fundamental functional components. This dictates that the standard practice of defining requirements from a perspective of domain and organizational peculiarity must yield to a much higher level of abstraction. Sponsorship of activities to develop domain-independent functional taxonomies as a first step for supporting, and hence aggregating, requirements should be a priority if the full benefits of COTS utilization are to be realized.

Creating reusability in subsystems and components is a principal goal of several organizations working on standards. In theory, the emergence of standards will aggregate the demand for components that comply. This positive influence on the demand side of the supply-demand marketplace has been demonstrated. There is little doubt that initiatives to develop standards is justified and should be encouraged. Perhaps the greatest benefit from efforts to develop is the process that is required. Participants from various related specialties are asked to submit and/or review candidates for the standards. The compromises required for concurrence by the standards participants create the abstractions needed to avoid over-specialization and domain peculiarities that are unnecessary.

There are characteristics of the standards development processes as we have known them historically that impede a timely transition to COTS utilization. Typically the processes take years to produce results, are staffed with participants who have full time responsibilities elsewhere, and who may have difficulty delivering approval from the management of the organizations they represent. A review of the standards activities shows a segmentation of specialties, which already may omit some generalities that could be obtained by thinking across stovepipes. Standards that emerge from separate communications and computer science orientations, for example, could produce encoding regimes that are less general than necessary. Or standards that apply to planning that do not include command and control will tend to be less robust than they might have been with more cross-discipline thinking such as that represented by the top-level taxonomy started in Fig. 1.

To create the most reusable components for system synthesis, and thereby aggregate a the largest demand for potential COTS products, the priority for a large-scale engineering effort to identify reusable components must be elevated within NASA, the DoD and other large-scale buyer development organizations. Currently, Program Managers are encouraged (by policy) to buy COTS, but they are not adequately incentivized to design around COTS buying. Their failure to use COTS more extensively can be defended by the fact that COTS component availability for synthesizing their systems is inadequate. If, on the other hand, they had available to them a large set of well-specified reusable components, they could be more effectively motivated to use these components in there system designs. Obviously, if the same fundamental components appeared in many procurements, the motivation for the supply side of the COTS marketplace would be established.

4   COTS Strategies as Seen from the Supply Side of the Market

Non-traditional aerospace companies and high-technology product developers have not responded regularly to NASA's business opportunity announcements to custom-build and/or operate space mission systems around organization-specific requirements. Typifying an entrepreneurial bias in lieu of government contractor status, these companies do not consider such opportunities as attractive as offering a product line that would be useful and applicable to a sizeable and varied class of potential customers, which could include NASA [13]. The prerequisite for developing a multiple-use, and hence cross-cutting, product line is, in fact, the identification of fundamental functionalities that transcend seemingly dissimilar customer environments. As a class, entrepreneurial product vendors are well-suited for abstracting requirements obtained from multiple sources, conceptualizing generalized components or modules as potential products, arranging the financing necessary for bringing the products to market, and organizing the after-sales support for these products. Thus FRED conforms to skills that are already prevalent and well-honed in the product supplier marketplace. Four examples of entrepreneurial prowess are profiled in [15]. The focus is on *reusable productization*, a type of technology investment/transfer initiative that produces readily commercial solutions from space systems R&D.

As NASA (as well as other public sector agencies) becomes proficient in expressing its demands as customer needs and expectations, the entrepreneurial suppliers will gain entry into previously restricted markets. This new "demand pull" adventure may appear to NASA as a new kind of "technology push", financed by the entrepreneurial private sector – technology to reduce unnecessary uniqueness and complexity, resulting in "faster, better, cheaper" commercial, reusable, and cross-cutting product lines [13]. To the entrepreneurial private sector, NASA will appear to have matured in its ability to discern similarities across its Strategic Enterprises.

Entrepreneurial prowess by the sellers and marketplace savvy by the buyers are required to create a commercial, reusable and cross-cutting supply chain. In order to assure an abundant supply of appropriate component options, NASA must learn to take full advantage of the market feedback to which vendors respond. Vendors hear an expressed need for a product and are willing to compete with each other to fill that need. NASA can shape its supply chain or reusable components if it: (1) capably expresses its future needs, (2) makes its needs (at least at the component level) conform as much as possible to those of other high technology organizations, thereby creating the largest potential market for the product vendors, (3) rejects products that are unsatisfactory, (4) participates in an open marketplace where matchmaking between demand and supply is facilitated, and the buy/sell transaction is not unduly complicated, and (5) masters the skill of price, schedule and performance analysis vs. cost/schedule/performance estimating.

5   Revamping the Marketplace

Current technology using the internet to create marketplaces provides a nearly perfect environment for transitioning to a COTS buying/selling environment. This is not simply because the buy/sell transactions can be mechanized more easily using the internet than can the traditional cost-based labor-type contacts typical of the one-of-a-kind systems implementations of the past. More importantly, the demand-pull from the buyers to the sellers can be facilitated using the many communications opportunities of the internet. Suppose, for example, that NASA had successfully developed its design and specification for a robust set of fundamental reusable components. Publication of the specifications for these reusable components would be simple to provide to the supply community at large. Suppliers, or potential suppliers, would have blueprints for new products at their fingertips. The process that entrepreneurs have traditionally used to seek out what is needed and to determine what will sell has been mostly ad hoc and almost accidental in nature. NASA's needs have been published program-by-program. Only those who have seen across some of the traditional stovepipes and who have been abstractionists by inclination have been able to develop products with some generality. There has never been a source of NASA's needs that was abstracted well enough to define a financially rewarding sales prospect for the product-oriented supplier. As a result, large aerospace companies have supplied talented laborers who can build on the job as opposed to products that can be purchased, maintained and backed by customer service policies.

Catalogues, bulletin boards, FAQ's, live Q&A sessions conducted on the internet – all of these mechanisms can simplify and define a product world for NASA if it chooses to make the culture shift and take full advantages of the benefits of COTS buying.

In the authors' views, NASA and other large-scale buying agencies do not fully appreciate how responsive the supply chain would be to their needs. This belief is predicated on the assumption that the needs are expressed in terms of selling opportunities for adequate multiples of a product. The suppliers, we believe, are more than willing to invest the R&D financing needed to fill a market niche that is unfilled, provided that the costs of that R&D can be amortized over a large enough market. For NASA (the buyer) to create such a market, the fundamental reusable components must be defined carefully.

Normal market forces usually evolve the fundamental reusable components over time. De facto standards emerge in the marketplace, often without any conscientious effort by a standards group to create them. However, the time constants for this evolution are usually measured in decades. Clearly, for an agency that is always creating new programs, the economic evolution time constants must be shortened. The technology of the internet can take many years off of the normal evolution by providing the mechanisms for the buyer to seek, and the supplier to respond. But the buyer must promise the prospect of adequate sales volumes. Hence the need for the development of the fundamental reusable components as described in the FRED concept.

6   Summary

The COTS experience has been mixed. Fortunately, the benefits have been sufficient to justify the continuation of the priority on this approach to implementing systems. The negatives, we contend, are a result of not creating a culture in which COTS implementation approaches can flourish and reach their potential for saving substantial implementation time and cost. The first need is to increase the demand for COTS products by designing components that are sufficiently abstracted to be useful in many more applications than result from one-of-a-kind system designs. A commitment is needed to defining the most general set of reusable components across organizational, discipline, and mission orientation boundaries. This will take an effort that is far larger and higher priority than that given to defining standards, for example. Next, modern communication and marketing techniques must be exploited to bring the demand side and the supply side of the buy/sell relationship together. Normal product evolution timelines must be shortened by communicating the needed product components to the potential product suppliers. Internet-related technologies make this challenge easy to meet, once the fundamental product components are defined.

The vision of the NASA COST LESS team was (and remains) to create the demand pull, the supply chain availability, and the renovated marketplace necessary to achieve much greater benefits from COTS than we have achieved after a decade of emphasis on utilizing COTS from within the traditional culture of satisfying unique requirements for every new system.

References

1. Carney, D., Long, F.: What Do You Mean by COTS? Finally, a Useful Answer. IEEE Software, March/April (2000), 83-86.
2. Basili, V., Boehm, B.: COTS-Based Systems Top 10 List. Software Management, May (2001), 91-93.
3. Boehm, B., Abts,C.,: COTS Integration: Plug and Pray?. Management, January, (1999), 135-138.
4. McKinney, D.: Impact of Commercial Off-The-Shelf (COTS) Software on the Interface Between Systems and Software Engineering. ICSE, Los Angeles, CA, USA, (1999), 627-628.
5. Fernandez, R.: Applications Abound. Satellite Software, August 10, (2000).
6. National Journal Group, Inc.: Buyers Beware. Government Executive, June 1, (1999).
7. Voas, J..: Can Generic Software Be Saved? IEEE Software, (1999), 94-95.
8. Fernandez, R.: A Challenging Market of Opportunity. Satellite Software, September 10, (1999).
9. COST LESS Team: Dialogue with NASA Senior Management. Washington, DC, USA, (1994) (available on video).
10. Hammer, M., Champy, J.: Reengineering the Corporation. Haper Collins Publishers, Inc., New York, NY, USA, (1993).
11. Hornstein, R.S., et. al.: Reengineering the Space Operations Infrastructure: A Progress Report From NASA's COST LESS Team for Mission Operations. AIAA 95-3583, Space Programs and Technologies Conference, Huntsville, AL, USA, (1995).
12. Hornstein, R.S., et. al.: On-Board Autonomous Systems: Cost Remedy for Small Satellites or Sacred Cow?. IAA-95-IAA.11.2.04, 46th International Astronautical Congress, Oslow, Norway, (1995).
13. Hornstein, R.S., Willoughby, J.: Combining Technical and Business Ingenuity to Create a Robust and Adaptable Marketplace that Anticipates, Meets and Exceeds Customer Needs. International Space University-New Space Markets, Strasbourg, France, (1997).
14. Hornstein, R.S., Willoughby, J.: Development and Commercialization of Dual-Use (and Reuse) Technology: A Case Study. Technology Commercialization and Economic Growth. Washington, DC, USA, (1995).
15. Hornstein, R.S., et. al.: From Space Systems R&D to Commercial Products: Technology Transfer Initiatives to Benefit Small Satellite Missions. IAA-97-IAA.11.2.09, 48th International Astronautical Congress, Turin, Italy (1997).

Rethinking Process Guidance for Selecting Software Components

N.A.M. Maiden[1], H. Kim[1], and Cornelius Ncube[2]

[1] Centre for HCI Design, City University
Northampton Square, London, EC1V 0HB, UK
{N.A.M.Maiden, hkim}@soi.city.ac.uk
[2] Institute for Technological Innovation, Zayed University (Dubai)
P.O. Box 19282, Dubai, UAE
Cornelius.Ncube@zu.ac.ae

Abstract. This paper reports the results of ongoing research into compo-nent-based software engineering (CBSE) in the European banking sector as part of the EU-funded BANKSEC project. The importance of complex non-functional requirements such as dependability and security presents new challenges for CBSE. The paper presents BANKSEC's vision of an integrated software tool that will provide process advice for component procurement teams who are tackling these new problems. The basis for this process guidance is a situation meta-model that enables the software tool to infer properties about the current status of the selection process and recommend process guidance relevant to this situation.

1 Introduction

The European Union's Framework V programme is funding a series of new research initiatives in component-based software engineering (CBSE). BANKSEC (www.atc.gr/banksec) is a 24-month research project that is investigating component-based dependable systems for the European banking sector. Dependable systems such as internet banking generate new research challenges for CBSE, in particular how to select components that, when implemented in an architecture, satisfy complex non-functional requirements such as security and reliability. This paper reports a synthesis of the author's previous research into COTS software package selection with research thinking in CBSE and requirements engineering to propose new processes for selecting software components for such dependable systems.

Component-based software engineering provides new opportunities for the efficient development of secure and dependable banking systems. However, new techniques are needed for specifying dependability requirements for components, for developing trusted application frameworks that can accommodate non-trusted components, and for designing and developing the necessary software and process infrastructure for component selection and integration. Indeed, the need

J. Dean and A. Gravel (Eds.): ICCBSS 2002, LNCS 2255, pp. 151–164, 2002.

to handle dependability requirements and application frameworks imposes new requirements and constraints on the component selection process itself. One of the main objectives of BANKSEC is to tailor processes that will assist European banks to build systems that meet these non-functional requirements using components. We are researching and implementing a process-driven software environment for component selection and validating it in banking applications such as corporate lending support. To achieve this we have integrated previous research in PORE [4], a method for COTS software package selection, with models of non-functional requirements [10] and component specification languages to deliver innovative processes to European banks.

The remainder of the paper is in 3 parts. Section 2 elaborates the vision for BANKSEC's component selection process, and the need for situated process guidance for procurement teams. Section 3 presents BANKSEC's situation meta-model to provide a formal basis for modelling stakeholder requirements and candidate components, and for triggering process guidance for procurement teams. Finally, Sect. 4 outlines some of the significant research challenges still to be overcome in this project, and describes future research to deliver the component procurement process.

2   BANKSEC's Component Selection Process

This section describes the baseline and drivers for the research results presented in the paper.

2.1   Previous Research on PORE

BANKSEC's component selection process is an extension of PORE, a method for selecting commercial off-the-shelf (COTS) software packages [4]. PORE integrated techniques from requirements engineering, knowledge engineering, multi-criteria decision-making and features analysis to guide the selection of COTS packages. It proposed a concurrent development process, in which stakeholder requirements acquisition and COTS package selection occur at the same time to support the team to make decisions about which packages to select and which packages to reject. The stakeholder requirements are used explicitly to select and reject packages. However at the same time differences in the remaining candidate packages are used to guide further requirements acquisition, thus focusing the team's effort on the most important information about requirements and software packages for decision-making at any time [7].

Another feature of PORE was the use of situated process guidance for the procurement team [6]. Rather than prescribe a process to follow in all procurement activities, PORE recommends different techniques for acquiring information, modelling and reasoning with this information, and for using it to make decisions based on the specific situation encountered by the team. The assumption was that most procurement teams face different information and resource shortages, and the process guidance must take these differences into account to be effective.

2.2 Advancing PORE in BANKSEC

The original PORE method needs several enhancements to deliver the
BANKSEC component procurement process:

– BANKSEC supports selection of software components rather than software
  packages. Software components are not always interactive, so user-led walk-
  throughs will not always be effective for component evaluation. Software
  components also depend on other components to execute, and therefore cannot be evaluated in isolation;
– BANKSEC supports selection of multiple component to meet the stakeholder
  requirements, so it must support the analysis of different compositions of
  these components, expressed in terms of different candidate architectures;
– PORE is a research prototype method and software tool, so BANKSEC
  partners will work together to produce an industrial-strength decision support tool for component procurement teams. In particular we will have to
  revise, tighten and evaluate the situation model before further research on
  processes, techniques and software tools can continue. Indeed, the situation
  model is the foundation for process guidance in BANKSEC;
– BANKSEC bank partners have specific and interesting requirements for the
  component selection process, so features of the PORE method need to be
  specialised to meet these requirements.

These enhancements are drivers for the research in BANKSEC reported in
this paper.

2.3 BANKSEC's Component Procurement Process

Central to BANKSEC's vision for effective component procurement is a decision-
making software tool that advises procurement teams throughout the process.
The tool provides process guidance for procurement teams during a concurrent
systems development process, in which stakeholder requirements, the system
architecture and solution components are all determined at the same time. During this process stakeholder requirements inform the architecture design and
component selection, and the designed architecture and selected components
both generate and constraint current stakeholder requirements. Although specific process guidance about requirements and component acquisition, modelling
and decision-making is driven by the current procurement situation, BANKSEC
also provides a higher-level procurement process that is goal-driven, prescriptive
and common to all procurement processes. This section outlines that process, as
the basis for describing the situation model in Sect. 3.

BANKSEC prescribes 4 essential goals for any component selection process.
These goals are to reject candidate components according to non-compliance
with different types of customer requirements:

1. Simple customer requirements – high-level services and functions, requirements on the supplier or procurement contract, basic features of the software
   component such as price and source, adherence to international standards;

2. Simple customer requirements that require access to the software component through demonstration or use – lower-level services and functions, demonstrable attributes of the software component such as interface features, simple dependencies between customer requirements and component features;
3. Simple customer requirements that are demonstrable through short-term trial use of the software component – non-functional requirements such as performance, throughput, usability and training (where appropriate);
4. More complex customer requirements with dependencies to other requirements and legacy systems – non-functional requirements that require more extensive trial use, such as maintenance and reliability requirements, and inter-dependencies with other software components, systems and legacy systems.

The rationale for this decision-making sequence is a simple and pragmatic one – to make the right and most simple decision at the most appropriate time in the procurement process using reliable information that is available to the component procurement team. As such the sequence relies on a set of assumptions – that information about components that enables the team to determine compliance with simple customer requirements is more readily available than the information needed to assess compliance with complex, interdependent non-functional requirements. The sequence is similar to the decision-making process in the original PORE method, but it has been refined and improved in the light of the PORE trials and further research into decision-making methods in BANKSEC.

Furthermore, BANKSEC prescribes 4 processes to achieve the 4 decision-making goals listed above:

1. Acquire information about customer requirements, software components, suppliers and procurement contracts;
2. Analyse acquired information for completeness and correctness;
3. Use this information to make decisions about component-requirement compliance;
4. Reject one or more candidate products as non-compliant with customer requirements

Unlike the high-level decision-making objectives, the order in which these 4 processes are undertaken is situation-driven, that is the order is determined by the current state of customer requirements and compliance mappings between these requirements and component features.

Figure 1 shows a graphical depiction of a route map of BANKSEC's high-level processes. The achievement of each essential goal is a broad sequence, in which the first process is acquisition of information from stakeholders and the last is selection of one or more candidate components, but the sequence of the intervening processes is not predetermined and each process can be repeated many times.

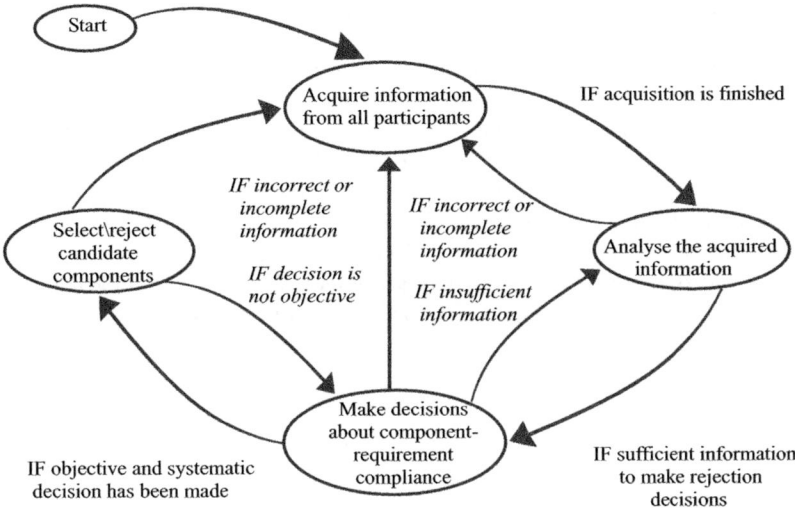

Fig. 1. BANKSEC's high-level process for making decisions about component selection and rejection

2.4   Situated Process Guidance

Previous research into CBSE processes in PORE revealed the importance of situated process guidance for component procurement teams [1,4,5]. In spite of the increasing use of components for systems development, there is still little prescriptive guidance available on how to acquire requirements for components, how to select components compliant with these requirements, or how to interleave requirements acquisition and components selection to provide the most effective process guidance.

In most CBSE processes it is difficult to prescribe sequences of lower-level processes to achieve higher-level goals, let alone what are the best techniques to use to achieve them. For example, information about customer requirements, components, suppliers, and procurement contracts is often not available in the order in which it is needed, so the sequence of the acquisition, analysis and decision-making processes cannot be preordained. Furthermore, information acquisition and software selection processes are often interwoven, in that the successful completion of one process often depends on the successful completion of the other. Therefore, BANKSEC also guides the procurement team using information about current context, or situation. It builds on PORE to recommend technique(s) to use to undertake processes by inferring general properties about the state of the customer requirements and their compliance to candidate components. It also recommends the content focus for applying each technique based on inferences about specific requirements and their compliance to components.

3   BANKSEC's Situation Model

During component procurement a large number of situations may arise at any point in the process and many techniques from different disciplines are available to achieve each situation. BANKSEC provides a situation model for process guidance through this complex space of situations and techniques. In BANKSEC a situation is modelled in three parts as shown in Fig. 2. We use the industry standard Unified Modelling Language (UML) [9]. The first part models the current state of the customer's requirements. The second part models compliance associations between customer requirements and component features. The third part models specific features of software components.

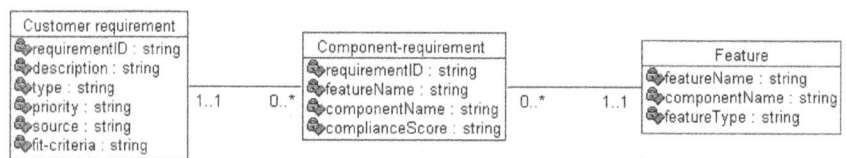

Fig. 2. The basic structure of the situation model, and the relationships between customer requirements, software components and compliance associations between requirements and component features.

This situation model enables BANKSEC to provide process guidance at two levels. At the first level, it recommends techniques(s) to use to undertake the process by inferring general properties about the current situation, expressed in term of the current model of customer requirements, (component) features and compliance associations. At the second level, BANKSEC recommends the content focus, that is specific customer requirements, components and component features to which these techniques can be applied. To infer the existence of a situation, a set of situation rules infer properties of the model of customer requirements, component features and compliance associations. The next section describes the 3 meta-models that constitute the larger situation meta-model.

3.1   The Situation Meta-model

Each meta-model is also represented in turn using the industry standard Unified Modelling Language (UML) [9]. Each meta-model is comprised of various meta-concepts and meta-links between them. The first meta-model is the component meta-model shown in Fig. 3.

Central to the meta-model is the concept of **feature**. A feature is distinctive or characteristic element of a software component. Typical examples of features of an e-mail component include Address book, Dictionary, Auto reminder, Auto spell check, Sending/Receiving new mail, etc. Features can be classified as essential features and non-essential auxiliary features. Essential features are features that are commonly possessed by components within a domain. We also enable the procurement team to model generic features that are identified during domain analysis. In contrast, auxiliary features add some extra values to the component. A feature can be specialised to a **function**, an **action** or a **component**, as all are distinctive features that are useful in the component selection process. For example, components perform functions. Likewise agents, either a component or users of the system including that component, undertake observable actions as a result of that component. Sometimes procurement teams are familiar with components, so the presence of that component in a candidate architecture is sufficient to indicate compliance with one or more requirements. Each of these specialisations of a feature is described in more detail.

Functions are modes by which the component fulfils its purpose. They are the services and capabilities provided by the component, and represent one of the more common and distinctive classes of component feature. Functions define the behaviour of the component and the fundamental processes or transformations that the component performs on inputs to produce outputs. The behaviour of a component can be mathematically characterised as a function.

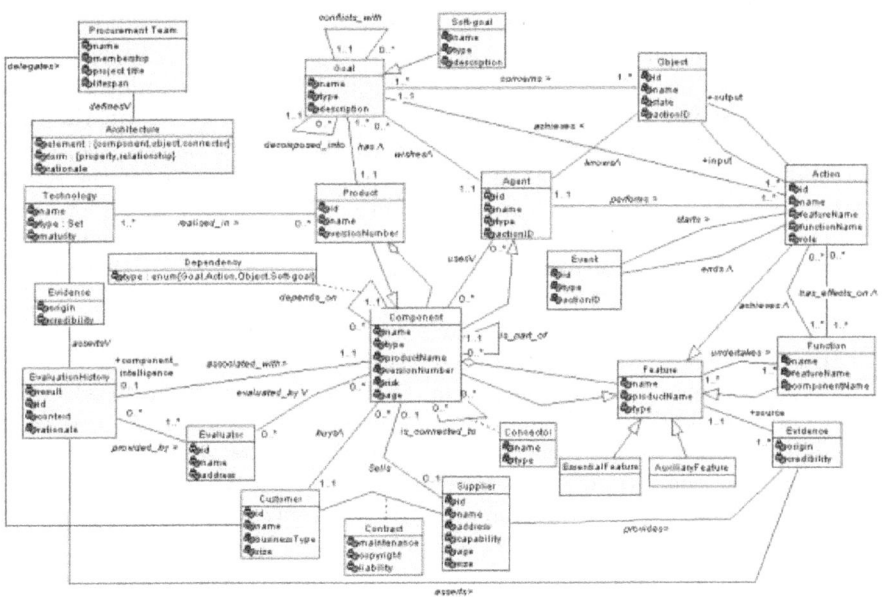

Fig. 3. BANKSEC's component meta-model

An **action** is an observable process achievable through the use of the component. Each action can be cognitive, physical, system-driven or communicative. Each action can involve one or more agents. In a requirement engineering tool, an example of an action is *Create* requirement or *Copy* requirement. An **object** is something of interest that is manipulated in the domain. Object instances can evolve from state to state through the application of actions. An **agent** performs or processes actions [2]. Each agent has certain features that determine its capabilities to perform the desired actions. Each agent is either a human agent or a software component, thus enabling the procurement team to model the system boundaries (degree of automation) of systems that include components. The attribute *type* expresses this classification.

We define a **component** as an encapsulated, distributable and executable piece of software that provides and receives services through well-defined services [8]. A component has the following attributes:

- **Type** indicates the basic type of component, from large interactive software solutions down to EJB (Enterprise JavaBean) components and DCOM (Distributed Component Object Model) components;
- **VersionNumber** indicates the version or release number of a component;
- Each component has a certain degree of **Risk** attached to it.

A component has meta-attributes and meta-classes associated with it. The **technology** is an abstract concept that is realised by each component. For example, web-browsing technologies are realised by various web browsers such as Netscape Communicator and Microsoft Internet Explorer. The meta-class **Evidence** specifies information obtained during a component procurement process that is the basis for component evaluation. It has 2 attributes: **origin** and **credibility**. An **evaluator** is a person or organisation that has used the component, and customers may contact these evaluators for advice. As information that is provided by vendors can be incorrect and misleading, obtaining information and advice from the people who have hands-on experience of a component can support component procurement. Component evaluators record **Evaluation histories** that include the results of the evaluation, the contexts and situations in which the evaluation took place, and the rationale behind which the particular results have been produced. Evaluation histories can act as a medium for "intelligence" about components. Finally, **Contracts** are used in terms of compensation arrangements used in different procurement situations. There are different interests and risks between buyers and sellers. Although there are many variations, the 2 basic compensation schemes used in contracts are fixed-price and cost-reimbursement. Under a fixed-price contract, the buyer pays the seller a fixed sum for the goods or services agreed upon. Because the price is fixed, the seller assumes the risk. Under a cost-type contract, risk is shared because the buyer agrees to reimburse the seller's allowable costs plus profit.

The meta-model specifies both **components** and **products**. BANKSEC uses the concept of a product for 2 purposes. For the first purpose, a product models a predefined configuration of software components that can be purchased as a software product, for example Microsoft Office is a composition of smaller, well-defined components such as Microsoft Word and Microsoft Excel. The second purpose of the product concept is to model candidate architectures that are developed by the procurement team to compose candidate components together in different configurations as the set of selected components grows. To handle the full range of procurement situations, the relationship between a **product** and **component** is best expressed as a *composite pattern* in a recursive fashion, and expressed as such in the product meta-model diagram (see the aggregation and inheritance relationships between them shown in Fig. 3). One invariant of the relationship between a component and a product is that a product always consists of one or more components, whereas the opposite is never true.

Finally the meta-model enables the procurement team to model important dependencies between software components within and between products. The need to model complex dependencies between components was highlighted in [4]. We have extended Mylopoulos and Yu's I* Framework [10] for modelling goal dependencies to software components. In the meta-model, we have identified various dependency relationships between products and/or components (see the association, depends-on). Here we attempt to refine this dependency using I* Framework [3,10]. The original I* Framework was for modelling the dependencies between agents (or actors). Because in our product meta-model, Component and Product are defined as subclasses of Agent, the framework can be used to describe the dependencies between components/products with minor changes. Dependencies between components constitute a transitive closure relation. Suppose there are 3 components, **Component A**, **Component B**, and **Component C**. Between these, there exist two dependency relations, i.e., (Component A, Component B) and (Component B, Component C). In this example, Component A depends not just on Component B, but also on Component C since the Component C's effect on Component B can affect the operation of Component A. Usually the communication between components is done through their well-defined interfaces, preventing other components from accessing the implementation details. This facilitates an easy substitution of a component with another during its evolution. As in object orientation, the characteristics of high cohesion and low coupling are desirable for components in CBSE. It is obvious that components depending on other many components will be very much difficult to install and maintain. Further they are likely to cause various problems related to the system integration.

Figure 4 shows the requirement meta-model. The key concept of the requirement meta-model is, not surprisingly, the requirement. One requirement can be decomposed into 0 or more use cases, and a requirement can constrain behaviour specified in use cases in the form of events. Each requirement can be either of system, supplier or contractual requirement type. System requirements can be further refined as functional and non-functional requirements. The value of the attribute, *priority* could be *low*, *medium*, or *high*. In requirement acquisition and analysis, it is important to know where the specific requirements came from. The attribute *source* captures this information. To check whether a specific requirement was satisfied in the final component, every requirement has an attribute **FitCriteria**.

To reject components that do not satisfy customer requirements, we need to evaluate the fitness of the component features against requirements. The

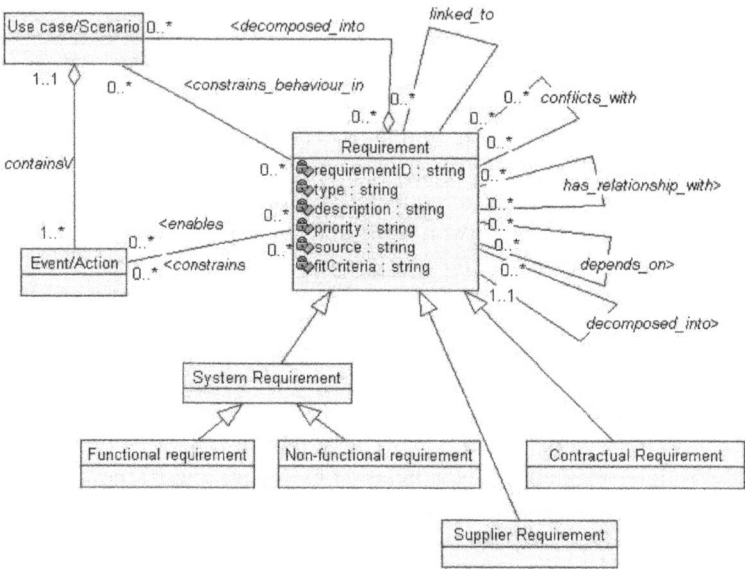

Fig. 4. The requirement meta-model

component-requirement compliance meta-model enables the procurement team to model and express mappings that indicate the compliance of one or more features of a software component to one or more customer requirements, as shown in Fig. 5. Each instance of a component-requirement compliance mapping carries information about the degree of fit of the component's feature with one or more requirements.

3.2   Inferring Properties of the Meta-model

To infer the existence of a situation state to trigger such a process, a set of semi-formal situation rules infer properties about customer requirements, component features and compliance associations between these features and the requirements. These inferences are made possible through formal instantiation of BANKSEC's situation meta-model. The following 3 rules are an example of a formal instantiation of the situation model to determine if there are any requirement-component feature compliance mapping relationships:

Rule 1. To determine components that have features that are mapped to customer requirements:

$(\forall c : Component, cf : ComponentFeature, essReq : EssentialRequirements)$
$[Compliant(c) \Leftrightarrow (\exists cf : ComponentFeature)(cf \in c) \wedge MappedTo(cf, essReq)]$

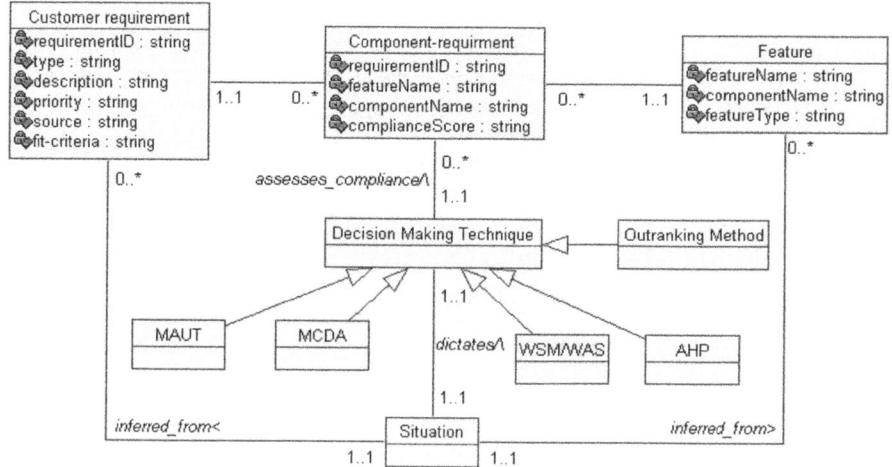

Keys:
MAUT: Multi-Attribute Utility Theory
MCDA: Multi-Criteria Decision Aid
WSM: Weighted Score Method
WAS: Weighted Average Sum
AHP: Analytical Hierarchy Process

Fig. 5. The component-requirement compliance meta-model

Rule 2. To determine requirements that have no compliance mapping to any component feature:

$(\forall req : Requirement, cf : ProductFeature)[Mapping(req, cf) \Rightarrow$
$ComplianceMapping(req, cf) \wedge (\exists req : Requirement)\neg Mapping(req, pf) \Rightarrow$
$\neg ComplianceMapping(req)]$

Rule 3. To determine when a component feature has no compliance mapping to customer requirement:

$(\forall cf : ComponentFeature, req : Requirement)[Mapping(cf, req) \Rightarrow$
$ComplianceMapping\ (cf, req) \wedge (\exists cf : ComponentFeature)\neg Mapping(cf, req) \Rightarrow$
$\neg ComplianceMapping(cf)]$

The situation rules determine from the situation model that there are no compliance mappings and infers the situation '*no (component-requirement compliance)*'. Based on this situation, the techniques {*compliance-checklist, compliance-walkthrough*} are recommended. Table 1 shows the process chunk to be processed.

After processing the process chunk, some essential functional requirements are selected to check for compliance. For each selected requirement, the degree of component-requirement compliance required based on stakeholder requirements is defined. Those components which do not meet essential customer requirements are then rejected. The following rule is used to determine the current situation:

Table 1. Chunk: Record requirement-component feature compliance rationale

Name	Record requirement-component feature compliance rationale.
Goal	Determine component-requirement compliance.
Situation	No component-requirement compliance relationship
Information	Situation model
Techniques	The C-PORE process requires a minimum set of compliance mappings between requirements and component features before effective decisions about component selection and rejection can be made. For this task, C-PORE recommends the techniques, compliance-checklist and compliance-walkthrough.
Weakness	The use of these tool-based features will depend on the effective use of BANKSEC's C-PORE software tool.

$$(\forall cc : SetOf[CandidateComponents], essReq : SetOf[EssentialRequirements])$$
$$[Reject(c) \Leftrightarrow (\exists c : Component)(c \in cc) \land \neg Compliant(c, essReq)]$$

The rule infers the situation '*small decision space*'. That is, the number of requirements, candidate products, product features and compliance relations are small enough to be amenable to decision analysis. The set of techniques {*Analytic-Hierarchy-Process, Outranking, MCDA*} is recommended, the process goal, '*reject one or more non-compliant components*' is determined. The chunk detailed in Table 2 is processed:

Table 2. Chunk: Determine component-requirement compliance mapping

Name	Determine component-requirement compliance mapping.
Goal	Reject non-compliant candidate components
Situation	Small decision space
Information	Situation model
Techniques	The C-PORE process requires a minimum set of compliance mappings between requirements and component features before effective decisions about component selection and rejection can be made. For this, the C-PORE recommends to use combination of decision-making techniques. The recommended ones are, the AHP, Outranking and MCDA.

As well as testing the compliance, it also necessary to apply syntactic rules to determine whether all customer requirements without compliance mappings have been considered, and to determine whether candidate components and component features without compliance mappings have also been considered. Therefore the C-PORE software product will be equipped with software functions to test for clerical oversights in component-requirement-compliance definition. |
| Weakness | |

This iterative nature of the C-PORE process makes it possible all components could be rejected. When this happens, the situation rules infer the situation '*all components eliminated*', and the relevant process advice is given.

4   Future Research in BANKSEC

This paper reports ongoing research in BANKSEC. Although we have made considerable progress in the first 7 months of the project, there remain a number of intellectual and technical challenges to overcome:

- The situation meta-model needs more rigorous evaluation by our BANKSEC project partners with a larger number of banking and financial software components. The current version of the meta-model is complex, requires a considerable learning curve to use, and is not used in its entirety when modelling component instances. One likely result of these evaluations will be a simpler version of the meta-model that is tailored to the skills, knowledge and preferences of our banking partners;
- The more complex the situation meta-model, the larger the set of possible situations that can arise, and hence the greater the need for a comprehensive and designed set of rules for inferring situation properties from instantiations of the meta-model. Although we are looking to simplify the situation meta-model, tests will still be needed with the prototype rule set to determine the likelihood and nature of omissions in the rules, and consequences for the perceived level of process support for procurement teams in our 2 partner banks;
- The situation meta-model has yet to be evaluated for complex compliance associations between non-functional requirements, such as dependability and security, and candidate components and component architectures to meet goals (3) and (4) of the BANKSEC process. One difficulty is that 'non-functional' features of software components are difficult to define, and often emerge from the composition of an architecture that includes that component. We are curently planning several paper-based case studies with our banking partners to evaluate the effectiveness of the situation meta-model for modelling and selecting with real non-functional requirements for banking systems.

Our development of a situation meta-model mirrors research to develop component specification languages. A workshop at ICSE2000 revealed that most important characteristics are not specific to software components. This has profound implications for software product description languages – these languages need to describe more than the software components, for example they need to describe the wider system architecture, the system environment, previous implementations and the customer development process related to the software component.

References

1. C. Ben Achour and C. Ncube: Engineering the PORE Method for COTS Selection and Implementation with the MAP Process Meta-Model. In 6th International Workshop on Requirements Engineering: Foundation for Software Quality (REFSQ'2000), Stockholm, Sweden, June (2000).
2. Robert Darimont and Axel Van Lamsweerde: Formal refinement patterns for goal-driven requirements elaboration. In Proceedings of the 4th ACM SIGSOFT Symposium on the Foundations of Software Engineering, volume 21(6) of ACM Software Engineering Notes, 179-190, New York, October 16-18 (1996). ACM Press.
3. Alexis Gizikis: I* tutorial. CORA-2 Project Report, Centre for HCI Design, City University London, (2000).
4. Neil A. Maiden and Cornelius Ncube: Acquiring COTS software selection requirement. IEEE Software, 15(2), 46-56, (1998).
5. C. Ncube and N.A.M. Maiden: Guidance for Parallel Requirements Acquisition and COTS Software Selection. In Proceedings of 4th International Symposium on Requirements Engineering, 133-141, IEEE Computer Society Press, (1999).
6. C. Ncube and N.A.M. Maiden: PORE: Procurement Oriented Requirements Engineering Method for the Component-Based Systems Engineering Development Paradigm. In Proceedings of the 2nd International Workshop on Component-Based Software Engineering (held in conjunction with ICSE'99), Los Angels, USA, May (1999).
7. Cornelius Ncube: A Requirements Engineering Method for COTS-Based Systems Development. PhD Thesis, City University London, UK, (2000).
8. Jim Q. Ning: A component Model Proposal. In Proceedings of the 2nd International Workshop on Component-Based Software Engineering (held in conjunction with ICSE'99), Los Angels, May (1999).
9. Object Management Group, Inc.: OMG Unified Modelling Language Specification. Version 1.3, June (1999).
10. Eric Yu.: A Framework for Process Modelling and Reengineering. PhD thesis, Departement of Computer Science, University of Toronto, Canada, (1994).

Definition and Classification of COTS: A Proposal

Maurizio Morisio[1] and Marco Torchiano[2]

[1] Dip.Automatica e Informatica, Politecnico di Torino
C.so Duca degli Abuzzi, 24, I-10129 Torino, Italy
morisio@polito.it
[2] Computer and Information Science Department (IDI)
Norwegian Univ of. Science and Technology (NTNU)
O. S. Bragstads plass 2B, N-7491 Trondheim, Norway
Marco.Torchiano@idi.ntnu.no

Abstract COTS based development impacts several issues in software development. New techniques have been proposed, or existing ones have been adapted. Several approaches have been proposed for effort and size estimation, product selection, and architectural mismatches identification. But a fundamental question must be clarified before: what is a COTS product? According to the literature a COTS seems to be anything from an operating system to a UI widget. It appears obvious that a finer level of granularity is required if we want to acquire a deeper insight in COTS related issues. This paper proposes a COTS classification scheme, which is as inclusive as possible. It is intended to provide both researchers and practitioners a tool to characterize more precisely their work. The next research step will be validating, by speculation first and empirically later, the influence of COTS classes on issues in COTS based development.

1 Introduction

In the last decade the use of Commercial Off-The-Shelf (COTS) products as parts of larger systems has grown steadily. The recent Open Source Software (OSS) tide adds an important new feature in the COTS market. Now it becomes more and more common to be able to find a COTS OSS product suitable for a project.

Using one or more COTS products has effects on nearly all activities and products of the software process: architecture and design, effort and cost estimation, validation and testing, and reliability. A growing body of research is dedicated to explore these areas. However, both in research papers and in informal discussions, one question remains un-answered: what is a COTS product? The definitions found in the literature are usually very broad, covering a large variety of products. As a result, researchers and practitioners use the same word with different meanings. Some of these definitions are discussed in Sect. 2 Existing COTS definitions.

We argue that COTS has to remain a term with broad coverage. But inside this class of software products a number of subclasses have to be identified. A

J. Dean and A. Gravel (Eds.): ICCBSS 2002, LNCS 2255, pp. 165–175, 2002.

recent paper [2] confirms this view, stating that assessment and tailoring efforts vary significantly by COTS product classes.

From a syntactical perspective, the acronym COTS is an adjective, thus it should be used together with a noun; for the sake of readability we will sometimes use the acronym by itself as a noun, in these cases COTS should be read as COTS product.

This paper presents the findings of the first phase of our research. Our research plan is the following:

Phase 1. General-purpose classification framework

- Identify key, recurring attributes of COTS products, using a broad definition of COTS (basically, product not developed by the developer of the final system). Here the research method is a literature search [21] and the use of any formal or informal knowledge available.
- Identify a set of attributes to describe COTS and structure them.
- Select a number of COTS products, characterize them under the attributes identified. Analyze the resulting clustering, define classes of COTS products.

Phase 2. COTS definition

- Review, if needed, the definition of COTS to be used in the study.

Phase 3. Links with the Software Process

- Using the COTS classes identified in Phase 1, and any available knowledge, state hypothesis of relationships between COTS classes and activities, products, attributes of COTS based software processes (e.g. cost models, selection methods, architectures, testing and validation techniques, etc.).

Phase 4.

- Validate empirically the hypothesis defined in Phase 3

This paper presents initial results of Phase 1 of the research. It is organized as follows:

Section 2: survey of existing COTS definitions
Section 3: proposal of a characterization framework
Section 4. application of the characterization framework

2   Existing COTS Definitions

In this section we present a survey of proposals available in the literature, directly or indirectly linked to the problem of classification and definition of COTS products.

We divided the literature related to COTS products into four parts: (1) definitions of COTS products, (2) classification of COTS-based systems, (3) attributes of COTS products, and (4) comparison of COTS products and components.

2.1 COTS Definitions

Oberndorf. In [11] the term COTS product is defined on the basis of the 'Federal Acquisition Regulations'. It is defined as something that one can buy, ready-made, from some manufacturer's virtual store shelf (e.g., through a catalogue or from a price list). It carries with it a sense of getting, at a reasonable cost, something that already does the job. The main characteristics of COTS are: (1) it exists a priori, (2) it is available to the general public or (3) it can be bought (or leased or licensed).

The meaning of the term "commercial" is a product customarily used for general purposes and has been sold, leased, or licensed (or offered for sale, lease or license) to the general public. As for the term "off-the-shelf", it can mean that the item is not to be developed by the user, but already exists.

Vigder. The work of Vigder and colleagues, presented in [14,15], provides a different definition of COTS products. They are pre-existing software products; sold in many copies with minimal changes; whose customers have no control over specification, schedule and evolution; access to source code as well as internal documentation is usually unavailable; complete and correct behavioral specifications are not available.

SEI. According to the perspective of the SEI, presented in a recent work [5], a COTS product is: sold, leased, or licensed to the general public; offered by a vendor trying to profit from it; supported and evolved by the vendor, who retains the intellectual property rights; available in multiple, identical copies; and used without source code modification.

Basili and Boehm. Recently Basili and Boehm [2] proposed another definition of COTS. According to their definition, COTS software has the following characteristics: (1) the buyer has no access to the source code, (2) the vendor controls its development, and (3) it has a nontrivial installed base (that is, more than one customer; more than a few copies). This definition does not include some kind of products like special purpose software, special version of commercial software, and open source software.

The category of products addressed by such definition presents some specific non-technical problems, related to the quick turnaround (every 8-9 month) [2] of product releases. In addition, marketplace consideration adds further variability: in the COTS products market there are no widely agreed upon standards [16] mainly due to marketing strategies aimed at obtaining vendor lock-in. Variability and marketing strategies suggest that there will never be a single unified marketplace of standardized COTS products [18].

2.2 COTS-Based Systems

Carney. In [6] Carney takes the point of view of the delivered system, instead of the part: he identifies three types of COTS systems as a function of the number of COTS used and their influence on the final system: turnkey systems are built around a (suite of) commercial product(s); intermediate systems are built around one COTS but integrate other components; integrated systems are built by integrating several COTS, all on the same level of importance.

Wallnau et al. A similar classification of COTS-based systems is proposed in [17], with the concepts of COTS-solution systems (one substantial product (suite) is tailored to provide a "turnkey" solution) and COTS-intensive systems (many integrated products provide system functionality).

2.3   COTS Products Attributes

Carney and Long. Carney and Long [7] propose two attributes to characterize COTS, origin and modifiability, and provide some examples.

There is no discussion of cost and property issues, which seems to be sometimes mixed with the origin axis, while in our opinion it should be discussed separately. No distinction can be found between what needs to be modified in order to make a product work and what can be modified in order to better integrate it into the delivered system.

COCOTS. A classification of COTS products could be derived from the CO-COTS models [1]. Some cost drivers could be used to identify COTS products categories: product maturity, supplier willingness to extend product, product interface complexity, supplier product support, supplier provided training and documentation. Most of these attributes are related to the supplier and market conditions and not to technology.

Yakimovich. Several researches addressed the integration problem of COTS products; in particular the work by Yakimovich et al. [20] proposes a set of criteria for classifying software architectures in order to estimate the integration effort. The same characteristics are used to classify both the components and the systems.

Egyed et al. A methodology for evaluating the architectural impact of software components is proposed in [8]. Such a method allows the selection of both the components and of a suitable architectural style. The key point is the identification of architectural mismatches.

2.4   Components

Component is a term now widely used, and probably as ambiguous as COTS. The relationship with COTS is strong, but COTS and components should be considered as two different concepts.

A lot of definitions of component can be found in the literature. A simple and compact definition is the following: "binary units of independent production, acquisition and deployment" [13]. But also looser definitions can be found: "a physical, replaceable part of a system that packages implementation and provides the realization of a set of interfaces. A component represents a physical piece of implementation of a system, including software code (source, binary or executable) or equivalents such as scripts or command files" [12].

In summary we can say that COTS products and components are two sets with a non-empty intersection but both need a neater definition.

3 COTS Characterization Framework

In Table 1 we propose a characterization framework for COTS. We propose a number of attributes and possible values to characterize a COTS product. A COTS product is described by a single value on each attribute. We designed the attribute framework so that each attribute has only one value. Multiple values or "don't care" are not possible. Different COTS products with the same set of values belong to the same class.

The attributes we propose are either already defined in literature, or new. The contribution we want to make is both in organizing the existing attributes in a consistent framework, and in proposing new ones. The attributes are grouped into four categories:

- Source: where the product comes from
- Customization: how much the product can or should be customized
- Bundle: in what form the component is delivered, both to the integrator and to the customer of the system
- Role: what is the intrinsic role the product can assume in the final system

All of the attributes we propose are of ordinal type, except those in the role category, which are of nominal type.

3.1 Source

3.1.1 Origin. We adopt here the definitions proposed in [7]. The possible values we propose for this attribute are: *in-house, existing external, externally developed, special version of commercial, independent commercial*. We consider as commercial a product that is generally available to the public. So are open source and free software products.

3.1.2 Cost and Property. The COTS can be obtained for a price or free. Obtaining the COTS could mean acquiring the source code or the executable code. The possible values we propose for this attribute are: *acquisition*, ownership of the product (including source code) is transferred to the buyer; *license*, a use

Table 1. COTS characterization attributes

Category	Attribute	Possible Values
Source	Origin (from [7])	In-house < existing external < externally developed < special version of commercial < independent commercial
	Cost & Property	Acquisition < license < free
Customization	Required Modification (from [7])	Minimal < parameterization < customization < internal revision < extensive rework
	Possible Modification	None or minimal < parameterization < customization < programming < source code
	Interface	None < documentation < API < OO interface < contract with protocol
Bundle	Packaging	Source code < static library < dynamic library < binary component < stand-alone program
	Delivered	Non delivered < partly < totally
	Size	Small < medium < large < huge
Role	Functionality	Horizontal, vertical
	Architectural level	OS, middleware, support, core, UI

license fee is required to use the product; *free*, no fee is required. Related legal / commercial issues are liability for defects contained in the COTS, responsibility for maintenance, and export restrictions.

3.2   Customization

Carney and Long [6] consider the modifiability attribute. We have split it into required and possible modification.

3.2.1   Required Modification. This attribute corresponds to the modifiability dimension proposed in [7]. It has five possible values: *extensive reworking, internal code revision, customization, parameterization, minimal*. The first two of them assume access to code, the second two imply some mechanism built into the COTS to modify its functionality, the last indicate almost no modification.

3.2.2   Possible Modification. This attribute refers to the internal possible customization of the COTS product. Such kind of modification is not required by the COTS to deliver its basic functionality. As an example, the open source web server Apache typically requires only simple parameterization, although its source code is accessible making any in-depth modification possible. The possible values of this attribute are: *source code*, code is available and can be modified; *programming*, a complete set of API or interfaces is provided possibly together with a scripting language; *customization*, it is possible to define macros or configuration files; *parameterization*, parameters can be defined for the product; *none or minimal*, the product cannot be modified.

3.2.3 Interface. An important factor, which impacts integration and glue-ware is represented by the interface provided by the COTS product. The possible values for this attribute are: *none*, no documented interface is provided and reverse engineering could be required; *documentation*, there is some documentation of the interfaces provided (e.g. syntax of the configuration files or protocols); *API*, a function level APIs are provided; *interface*, an object-oriented interface is formally defined by means of some standard IDL; *contract*, a contract is defined, that is both a set of interfaces and a protocol for using such interfaces.

This attribute could be very useful also in providing a better definition of component; putting a threshold on this attribute (e.g. interface) you can say if a product is a component or not.

3.3 Bundle

3.3.1 Packaging. The COTS can be packaged in different ways. Possible values for this attribute are: *source code, statically linkable binary library, dynamically linkable library, binary component, stand-alone executable program*. Packaging is the form in which the COTS product is used. A standalone program does not preclude access to the source code.

3.3.2 Delivered. Considering the product delivered to a customer or user, a COTS product can be integrated in it or not. If we consider a project developed in C, the C compiler is not part of the delivered system. However, some tools usually associated with the C compiler (e.g. the library of I/O functions) are probably integrated in the final product. Possible values for this attribute are: *non-delivered, partly, completely*.

3.3.3 Size. An important factor is the size of the COTS, we propose a simple classification in 4 groups ranging from small, like UI widgets, to huge, like the Oracle 8 DBMS or the Windows NT operating system. The approach we adopt is based essentially on the size of the COTS product (the figures in MB are indicative): *small* means less than 0.5 MB, *medium* means from 0.5MB to 2MB, *large* means from 2MB to 20MB, huge means more than 20MB.

An alternative measure is based on the number of use cases supported by the product [9]. While this method has the potentiality to become a good measure of the computational size of software products, it has several drawbacks. The size and complexity of each use case may vary greatly and thus the measure of the size could be inaccurate. Besides, use cases for COTS products usually are not available.

3.4 Role

3.4.1 Type of Functionality. COTS offer a variety of functions, however they can be classified in two broad categories. *horizontal*, the functionality is not specific to a domain, but can be reused across many different application domains (e.g DBMSs, GUIs, networking protocols, web browsers); *vertical*, the functionality is specific to a domain, and can be reused only in the domain (e.g. financial applications, accounting, Enterprise Resource Planning, manufacturing, health care management, and satellite control). Horizontal COTS have been available on the market for a long time, experience and know how about them are usually widely available. As a result, using horizontal COTS is usually less risky and more common than using vertical COTS.

3.4.2   Architectural Level. This attribute is somewhat similar to the previous one, but it refers to a generic layered computing architecture. The levels we propose are: *Operating System; Middleware*, software which enable communication and integration; *Support*, elements that cover a well defined and standardized role in the architecture but do not provide vertical functionality; *Core*, products which provide domain specific functionalities; *User Interface*, highly reusable user interface components.

4   Application

We have defined the attributes in **Table 1** with an exhaustive approach, including all attributes that, by speculation, could be relevant to characterize and distinguish COTS products. **Table 2** shows that the proposed attributes are able to discriminate products that any practitioner considers as COTS, but also as very different from one another, not only in terms of the functionality offered, such as operating system, file sharing utility, or user interface widget. For lack of space we limit the list to three products.

However, some attributes could be useless to characterize certain COTS products, or the number of attributes could be too high for any practical use. We need to discriminate the necessary and sufficient attributes.

Table 2. Attribute values for two COTS products

	COTS Product		
Attribute	**MS Windows NT**	**Samba**	**MS Chart Control**
Origin	Indep. Comm.	Indep. Comm	Indep. Comm.
Cost & Property	License	Free	License
Required Modification	Parameterization	Parameterization	Minimal
Possible Modification	Programming	Source code	Programming
Interface	API	API	Contract
Packaging	Standalone	Standalone	Binary Component
Delivered	Completely	Completely	Completely
Size	Huge	Large	Small
Functionality	Horizontal	Horizontal	Horizontal
Architectural Level	OS	Middleware	UI

4.1 Hypotheses

We identified a set of hypotheses about the possible impact of the attribute values on the development process of the delivered system. An overview of these hypotheses is presented in Table 3.

Table 3. Attribute impact

Attribute		Impact on the process
Source	Origin	ease of change, availability of certification, control on product customization, marketplace competition
Source	Cost & Property	acquisition and maintenance costs
Customization	Required Modification	customization cost, comprehension effort, integration effort
Customization	Possible Modification	adaptability, ease of integration
Customization	Interface	ease of integration, language/middleware lock-in, architectural contstraints and mismatches
Bundle	Packaging	porting and adaptation effort, configuration management, platform constraints
Bundle	Delivered	redistribution issues (both legal and commercial)
Bundle	Size	learnability, setup effort
Role	Functionality	reusability across projects, availability of required functionality
Role	Architectural level	the choice of the product can be dictated by external factors, different integration problems

5 Conclusions

Based on the attributes we presented and the definition found in the literature we propose the following definition of COTS products:

- Origin >= special version of commercial
- Cost & Property >= license
- Required modification =< customization
- Possible modification >= parameterization
- Interface >= API
- Packaging >= static library
- Delivered = totally
- Size >= medium
- Functionality = vertical
- Architectural level in { support, core }

The main contributions of this work are:

- a survey of current COTS definitions
- the proposal of a new COTS definition: as a result COTS remains a broad term but we identified a set of attributes that can discriminate different COTS products
- a set of hypotheses about the impact of the defined attributes on the COTS based development process

Both the attributes we identified and the impact hypotheses we formulated are not definitive. They are to be considered as statements to set an initial framework and stimulate discussion.

We plan to revise the attribute list and validate the hypotheses about its impact onto the development process.

References

1. Abst, C., Boehm, B., Clark, E.: COCOTS: A COTS Software Integration Lifecycle Cost Model - Model Overview and Preliminary Data Collection Findings. Technical report USC-CSE-2000-501, USC Center for Software Engineering, (2000).
2. Victor Basili and Barry Boehm: COTS-Based Systems Top 10 List. IEEE Computer 34(5), May (2001), 91-93.
3. P.Brereton, D.Budgen: Component-Based Systems: A Classification of Issues. IEEE Computer Vol. 33, No. 11, November (2000), 54-62.
4. Brownsword, L., Carney, D., Oberndorf, T.: The Opportunities and Complexities of Applying Commercial-Off-the-Shelf Components. SEI Interactive, 6/98, (1998), avail. at http://interactive.sei.cmu.edu/Features/1998/June/Applying_COTS/Applying_COTS.htm.
5. Brownsword, L., Oberndorf, T., Sledge, C.: Developing New Processes for COTS-Based Systems. IEEE Software July/August (2000), 48-55.
6. Carney, D.: Assembling Large Systems from COTS Components: Opportunities, Cautions, and Complexities. SEI Monographs on Use of Commercial Software in Government Systems, Software Engineering Institute, Pittsburgh, USA, June (1997).
7. Carney, D., Long, F.: What Do You Mean by COTS?. IEEE Software, March/April (2000), 83-86.
8. Egyed, A.; Medvidovic, N.; Gacek, C.: Component-based perspective on software mismatch detection. In IEE Proceedings-Software, Volume: 147 Issue: 6, December (2000).
9. Tsagias, M. and Kitchenham, B.A.: An Evaluation of the Business Object Approach to Software Development. The Journal of Systems and Software 52,(2000), 149-156.
10. Morisio M., Seaman C., Parra A., Basili V., Kraft S., Condon S.: Investigating and Improving a COTS-Based Software Development Process. 22nd International Conference on Software Engineering, Limerick, Ireland, June (2000).
11. Oberndorf, T.: COTS and Open Systems - An Overview. (1997), available at http://www.sei.cmu.edu/str/descriptions/cots.html#ndi.

12. OMG: Unified Modeling Language Specification. Version 1.3, June (1999).
13. Szyperski C.: Component Software Beyond Object Oriented Programming. Addison-Wesley, (1998).
14. Vigder, M., Gentleman, M. and Dean, J.: COTS Software Integration: State of the Art. Technical Report NRC No. 39190, (1996).
15. Vigder, M., Dean, D.: An Architectural Approach to Building Systems from COTS Software Components. In Proceedings of the 1997 Center for Advanced Studies Conference (CASCON 97), Toronto, Ontario, 10-13 November (1997), available at http://seg.iit.nrc/English/abstracts/NRC40221abs.html.
16. Voas, J.: Faster, better, cheaper. IEEE Software, May/June (2001), 96-97.
17. Wallnau, K., Carney, D. and Pollak, B.: How COTS Software Affects the Design of COTS-Intensive Systems. SEI Interactive, 6/98, (1998). Available online at http;//interactive.sei.cmu.edu/Features/1998/june/cots_software/Cots_Software.htm.
18. Wallnau, K.: On Software Components and Commercial ('COTS') Software. In Proceedings of 1999 International Workshop on Component-Based Software Engineering, Los Angeles, CA, USA, May 17-18, (1999).
19. Wang, H., Wang, C.: Open Source Software Adoption: A Status Report. IEEE Software, March/April (2001).
20. Yakimovich, D., Bieman, J.M., Basili, V.R.: Software Architecture Classification for Estimating the Cost of COTS Integration. Proceedings of the 21st International Conference on Software Engineering, Los Angeles, USA, (1999), 296-302.
21. Zelkowitz, M., Wallace, D.: Experimental Models for Validating Technology. In IEEE Computer 31(5), May (1998), 23-31.

The Limitations of Current Decision-Making Techniques in the Procurement of COTS Software Components

Cornelius Ncube[1] and John C. Dean[2]

[1] Institute for Technological Innovation (ITI)
Zayed University, P.O. Box 19282, Dubai, United Arab Emirates
Cornelius.Ncube@zu.ac.ae
[2] Sotfware Engineering Group, Institute for Information Technology
National Research Council Canada, K1A 0R6
John.Dean@nrc.ca

Abstract. The fundamentals of good decision-making are, first, a clear understanding of the decision itself and second the availability of properly focused information to support the decision. Decision-making techniques help with both these problems. However, the techniques should be thought of as aids to decision-making and not the substitutes for it. Numerous decision-making techniques have been proposed as effective methods of ranking software products for selection for use as components in large-scale systems. Many of these techniques have been developed and successfully applied in other arenas and have been either used directly or adapted to be applied to COTS product evaluation and selection. This paper will show that many of these techniques are not valid when applied in this manner. We will describe an alternate requirements-driven technique that could be more effective.

1 Introduction

One of the critical issues for the COTS-based development process is COTS component assessment and decision-making. In order to select or recommend a suitable required component, the evaluated alternatives must be ranked according to their perceived relative importance to meet the customer's requirements. Decision-making techniques have been used for this purpose. As in other activities, decision making in COTS selection may occur under conditions of (1) Certainty; (2) Risk – where each action has several possible outcomes for which the probabilities are known; and (3) Uncertainty – where each action has several possible outcomes for which the probabilities are not known' [3].

Therefore, making a decision that does not help to achieve the goal of selecting the required component can lead to long lasting user disappointments. Decision-making in component evaluation is a very complex process that combines probability judgments that may be affected by the evaluator's beliefs and underlying preferences. Figure 1 depicts the principles of decision-making in

J. Dean and A. Gravel (Eds.): ICCBSS 2002, LNCS 2255, pp. 176–187, 2002.
© Springer-Verlag Berlin Heidelberg 2002

COTS component evaluation and selection that the decision-makers usually have to contend with, represented as a hierarchy of three levels taken from Saaty [12]. At the first level is the main goal for the decision making process (e.g. selecting a suitable component among the alternatives). At the second level there are some criteria for selecting the component. The suitable component will be judged by these criteria. At the third level are the actual alternative candidate components in which the criteria will be applied to achieve the main goal. The figure clearly shows how complex decision-making becomes if there are many components to compare and criteria to apply to each component.

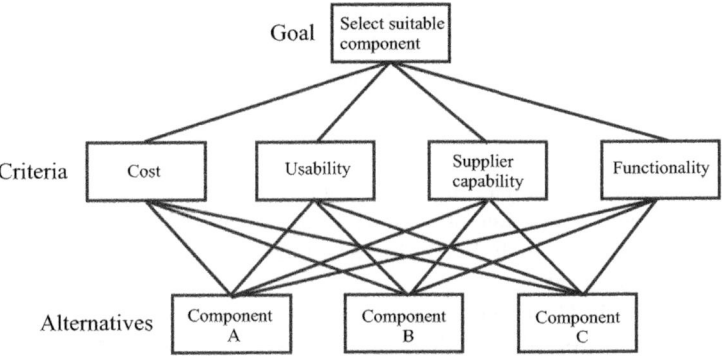

Fig. 1. Principles of a decision-making problem

2   General Difficulties with Current Decision-Making Techniques

Some factors that give rise to problems in evaluating and assessing COTS software are:

- that there is a large number of component attributes or features that have to be considered;
- that various combinations of hardware platforms, operating systems and application software need to be considered;
- that there is rapid technological changes in all aspects of computing, the business environment and the needs of the users;
- that most users lack the technical expertise or time to develop criteria, measurements and testing procedures for performance assessments and to conduct the actual evaluations;
- that there are considerable variations in performance between the attributes of each component and across the components for each attribute.

Mistree & Allen [4] further suggest that characteristics of decisions for selecting COTS software are governed by decision characteristics such as the following:

1. Selection decisions are invariably multileveled and multidimensional in nature;
2. Decisions involve information that comes from different sources;
3. Decisions are governed by multiple measures of merit and performance;
4. All the information required to make a decision may not be available;
5. Some of the information used in making a decision may be hard, that is, based on scientific principles and some information may be soft, that is, based on the selectors judgment and experience;
6. The problem for which a decision is being made is invariably loosely defined and open and is characterized by the lack of a singular, unique solution. The decisions are less than optimal and represent satisfying solutions, that is, not the 'best' but 'good enough',

Tkach & Simonovic [5], furthermore suggest that selecting the best COTS product from a number of potential alternatives is a complex decision making process that may include conflicting quantitative, qualitative criteria and multiple decision-makers. Currently, a number of decision-making techniques that can be used in COTS component evaluation and assessment are available in the market. However, almost all of these techniques are found not to be suitable for assessing software components due to their fundamental underlying assumptions in their judgment value system. Most currently existing traditional decision-making approaches rely on compensatory models such as the linear weighted score model which sums the weighted ratings of the component's capability attributes to arrive at a single score for each component. The end result is either an aggregate total score for the component or a group of scores representing various attributes of the component. However, aggregate total scores tend to mask individual attributes of the component that may represent particular strengths or weaknesses in a component. These models are problematic in that they can permit very good performance on one attribute to offset poor performance on another.

3   Current Proposed Decision-Making Techniques

The techniques summarized below all attempt to consolidate the evaluation results or rank the alternatives in one way or another. The following sections give brief discussions of four such decision-making techniques.

3.1   The Multi-attribute Utility Theory (MAUT)

The MAUT decision-making model deals with choosing among a set of alternatives which are described in terms of their attributes [10]. A typical multi-attribute decision problem is choosing among COTS software components described by such attributes as cost, usability, functionality, size, portability, supplier capability, etc. To deal with the multi-attribute situations, the MAUT technique requires information about:

- the decision-makers preference among values of a given attribute (i.e. how much does s/he prefer a commercial database over a proprietary database), and;
- the decision-maker's preference across attributes (i.e. how much important is the database than cost). A marginal value function is associated with each criterion and a global value function is computed in an additive or multiplicative form.

The MAUT technique asks the decision-maker for an assessment on the strength of preferences. The decision may be reduced to a number of independent attributes that involve making trade-offs between different goals or criteria. MAUT uses a reductionist approach to a problem and it is up to the decision-maker to split the problem into a number of dimensions that are perceived to be independent. This independence is essential for MAUT because without it, certain attributes could be over represented in the final result. This is the fundamental weakness of the method.

3.2   The Multi-criteria Decision Aid (MCDA)

The MCDA approach is in the category of the utility theory. Morisio et al [11] proposes the following advantages for using MCDA in COTS component evaluation and selection:

- the MCDA approach makes explicit reference to the decision process so as to take into account the different actors involved in the process, their different objectives and the partiality of the information provided;
- the MCDA approach allows handling judgments based on qualitative, partial information and the subjective nature of the problem of evaluating and selecting software components. This is done by adopting appropriate specific techniques to help in the decision making process (including multi-attribute utility theory, multi-objective interactive techniques and out-ranking technique) and provide the evaluator with both formal and substantial reasons for any choice;
- the MCDA approach combines strictness (non-redundancy of the set of criteria, appropriateness of the aggregation procedure, etc) with flexibility, different problem statements, different aggregation techniques, custom evaluation attributes and measures.

With MCDA, a list of criteria that the component should meet is established first, then scores are assigned to each criterion based on its relative importance in the decision. Each alternative is then given a number of scores according to how it fully meets the criterion. For the scores, a scale of 1 to 5, or 1 to 7, etc can be used. An example is shown in Table 1.

In the example, component A is rated 25 out of 30 points for the "cost" criterion, while component C is rated a little less favourable. Once all the alternatives have been assigned their points for each criterion, all points for each alternative are added together and the alternative with the highest total is the one chosen. In the example, this would be component A. The main weakness of the method is that if the criteria set is large, it quickly becomes very complicated.

Table 1. A list of criteria that the component should meet and scores assigned to each criterion

Criteria	Possible Points	Component A	Component B	Component C
Cost	30	25	20	15
Functionality	40	35	10	20
Supplier	20	15	5	10
Usability	10	5	3	2
Total	100	80	38	47

3.3   Weighted Score Method (WSM) or Weighted Average Sum (WAS)

The WSM/WAS is an aggregation technique and the most commonly used technique in many decision-making situations. Its 'weights' are trade-offs between the criteria; i.e. they are ratios between the scales of each criterion. 'Criteria are defined and each criterion is assigned a weight or a score' [9].

The scales themselves represent preferences relative to each attribute. The WSM/WAS technique is a fully compensatory model in that each preference relative to a criterion can be totally compensated for by a countervailing preference on another criterion. This trade-off between criteria may result in any big difference that may exist being compensated for, so that an indifferent situation is created instead of the actual incomparability situation [11]. This scenario is one of the many weaknesses of this technique. Although weighting methods seem very diverse, they all have the following characteristics:

- a set of available alternatives with specified attributes and attribute values;
- a process for comparing attributes by obtaining numerical scalings of attribute values (intra-attribute preferences) and numerical weights across attributes (inter-attribute preferences);
- an objective function for aggregating the preferences into a single number for each alternative;
- a rule for choosing or rating the alternatives on the basis of the highest weight.

Table 2 below shows an example application of the WSM and its limitations. The criteria weights were assigned using a scoring method by assigning a value of between 1 and 5 to each criterion. The overall score of each alternative was calculated using the following formula [9]:

$$score_a = \sum_{j=1}^{n}(weight_j * score_{aj}) \tag{1}$$

Where:

a=alternative
n=number of criteria
j=criteria

The problem with the method is in assigning the scores. For example, the security and compatibility could be interpreted as twice as important as ease of use, whereas in reality this might not be the case.

However, WSM/WAS techniques have additional serious limitations that are often ignored when they are applied in COTS component evaluation and assessment [9]:

- As the Weighted Score Method produces real numbers as results, these results can easily be interpreted as if they represent the true differences between the alternatives. In actual fact, the resulting scores only represent relative ranking of the alternatives and the differences in their value does not give any indication of their relative superiority;
- Assigning weights for the criteria is very difficult when the number of criteria is large. If the number of attributes is large, it is very difficult to mentally cope with the dependencies between individual attributes. Assigning scores instead of weights is even more limiting because it effectively sets predetermined lower and upper limits to the weights that can be assigned to the criteria;
- It is very difficult to define a set of criteria and their weights so that they are either independent from each other or if they overlap, their weights are adjusted to compensate for the overlap.

Table 2. Example of the weighted score method

Criteria	Weight Score	Component A	Component B	Component C
Ease of use	2	3	3	3
Compatibility	4	1	5	2
Cost	3	3	5	1
Functionality	5	4	4	3
Security	4	1	2	5
Supplier	5	2	5	3
Score		53	94	67

3.4   The Analytical Hierarchy Process (AHP)

The AHP [12] is a multiple criteria decision-making technique that is based on the idea of decomposing a multiple criteria decision-making problem into a hierarchy. The decisional goal is decomposed into a hierarchy of goals and ratio comparisons are performed on a fixed ratio scale. The overall priorities are computed using an eigenvalue technique on the comparison matrix. The factors are arranged in a hierarchic structure descending from an overall goal to criteria, sub-criteria and alternatives in successive levels as shown in Fig. 1. At each level of the hierarchy, the relative importance of each component attribute is assessed by comparing them in pairs. The rankings obtained through the paired comparisons between the alternatives are converted to normalised rankings using the eigenvalue method, i.e. the relative rankings of alternatives are presented in ratio scale values which total to one as shown in the Priority Vector column of Table 3. The technique suggests that comparing criteria in pairs result in more reliable comparison results and that in this way, it is possible to avoid the problem of having to assign absolute values to alternatives, but only their relative preferences or values are compared. A typical application of the AHP method is shown in Table 3. Functionality is shown to have the highest total score and priority vector and therefore ranked more important.

Table 3. An example of applying the AHP method

Level 1 Priority Vector

	Cost	Functionality	Usability	Technical	Supplier	Total Scores	Priority Vector
Cost	1	4	5	4	6	20	0.339
Functionality	0.25	1	7	7	7	22.25	0.377
Usability	0.2	0.143	1	5	3	9.343	0.158
Technical	0.25	0.143	0.2	1	4	5.593	0.095
Supplier	0.167	0.143	0.333	0.25	1	1.893	0.032
						59.079	1

However, the AHP technique has some fundamental drawbacks when applied to COTS component evaluation. One of its main problems is that it assumes total independence between the component attributes, i.e. in order to do a pair-wise comparison, the technique assumes that the component attributes/features are independent of each other and this is rarely the case with software requirements. Also, especially for large complex systems, it is difficult to apply the AHP technique as its calculation model involves a very high number of pair-wise comparisons. The large number of individual assessments is also one of its main weaknesses. Even if the overall duration of the assessment sessions are not very long, the repetitive assessments cause tiredness and boredom. Furthermore, the assumption that there should be complete comparability and the imposition of the ratio scales at all levels of the hierarchy is very demanding [9].

4   Limitations of the Current Decision-Making Techniques

As Tkach & Simonovic [5] state, most current decision-making techniques are characterized by a great diversity with three main groups: out-ranking techniques, multi-attribute utility techniques, and mathematical programming techniques. Out raking techniques require pair-wise or global comparisons among alternatives, which is not practical when the number of alternatives is large. Multi-attribute utility techniques rely on linear additive or simple multiplicative models for aggregating single criterion evaluations. They are not appropriate for the analysis of complex software systems. Mathematical programming techniques, on the other hand, are used in continuous context. They identify solutions that are closest to the ideal solution as determined by some measure of distance. The solutions identified to be closest to the ideal solutions are called compromise solutions and constitute the compromise set. The ideal solution is one that provides the extreme value for each of the criteria considered in the analysis. The distance from the ideal solution for each alternative is measured by the distance metric. This value, which is calculated for each alternative solution, is a function of the criteria values themselves, the relative importance of the various criteria to the decision makers, and the importance of the maximal deviation from the ideal solution.

Therefore the selection of a decision-making technique for COTS evaluation and assessment should be done with care. Current decision-making techniques do not adopt a requirement-driven approach to component selection decisions and are therefore inadequate and not suitable for the COTS based decision-process. The fundamental criticism of these techniques is their underlying theory and their value judgment system, i.e. where the values come from.

For example, the idea of producing a single number from the individual scores (e.g. by some arithmetic combination formula such as weighted ranking) is misleading because many different combinations of numbers can produce the same aggregate score. Furthermore, certain features may attract higher average scores than others because an assessor may understand them better and be more able to recognize support in the component. There are also deeper reasons concerning the nature of the ordinal scales that are usually used to assess component features. For instance, a score of 4 is not necessarily twice as good as a score of 2.

5   An Alternative Approach

There is an alternative approach that one can consider that is requirements-driven and that mitigates the loss of detail encountered when employing a weighted aggregation approach. The approach applies the principles of gap analysis to evaluation and allows selection based on the cost of bridging the gap. This requires a novel viewpoint where we examine products, not for the purposes of eliminating them should they not meet the requirements, but for the purpose to attempting to determine what capabilities the products lack in terms of the requirements context. We then analyze these capability deficiencies to determine the cost of implementing supplemental functionality for each product or product set under evaluation. These are the fulfillment costs and there will be a set of these for each evaluation that we undertake. The fulfillment costs are used as a basis for selection of an appropriate product set.

5.1   Gap Analysis

Gap Analysis is a technique adapted for our purposes from environmental GAP analysis. The Dictionary of Business [1] defines gap analysis is "A methodical tabulation of all the known requirements of consumers in a particular category of products, together with a cross-listing of all the features provided by existing products to satisfy these requirements." In order to apply gap analysis to COTS product selection we still need to assess a product's capabilities against requirements. The determination of the gap requires that we highlight and record those capabilities that are not fulfilled by the product under consideration. This can be accomplished by constructing a 2-dimensional matrix of requirements versus products. The cells of the matrix would contain information about the gap. Figure 2 shows a simple example of such a matrix.

Product Requirement	P1	P2	P3
R1	Limited Java support	Complete solution	Complete solution
R2	In accurate math	Precision only to 2 decimals	No Math engine
R3	10%<required reliability	No reliability figures available	Complete solution
R4	Complete solution	Vendor out of country	Vendor Canadian
R5	Complete solution	Linux platform required	Windows only

Fig. 2. A Gap Analysis Evaluation Matrix example

One matrix would be required for each evaluation conducted and, in a large scale system employing multiple COTS products, the number of evaluations, and thus the number of matrices derived, could be significant. However for each individual evaluation it is assumed that the number of competing products examined in detail would be in the range of three to five so that the internal complexity of the matrices is not a factor. A further assumption is made that the evaluations can be conducted relatively independently. The implication of this assumption is that the system requirements have been stated in such a way as to minimize overlap.

There are three potential results that might be obtained during an evaluation. The first is the trivial case in which the capabilities of the product and the requirements match exactly as shown in Fig. 3(a).The second is the case where the product partially fulfills the requirements and does not provide any inherent capabilities that exceed the requirements as in Fig. 3(b). The third case is where the product fulfills some or all of the requirements but also incorporates capabilities that fall outside the boundaries of the original system needs as shown in Fig. 3(c).

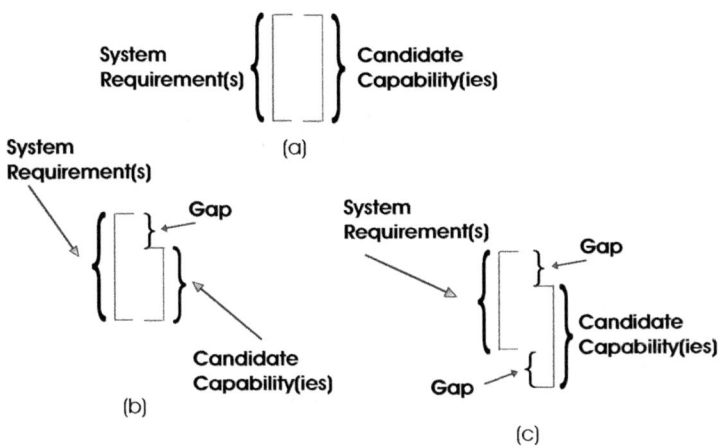

Fig. 3. Gap analysis results

5.2   Fulfillment Cost Calculations

Once the gaps between product and system requirements have been determined a further step is required to establish the cost of reducing the gap to an acceptable solution. At this point there are a number of strategies that could be followed, all of which depend on the parameters and nature of the gap. These strategies can be derived from Fig. 3 as well.

In the trivial case of an exact match between requirements and products capabilities the cost of gap reduction is zero. In the case where a product does not fully meet a requirement and that requirement is firm, i.e. it cannot be restated or relaxed, then the strategy which must be followed is to determine the cost of adding functionality to account for the product's deficiencies with respect to the requirement. In a COTS-based system this must be accomplished without modifying the COTS product itself. Thus we are restricted to the strategy of implementing a custom code solution to the deficiencies.

A third case occurs when the product does not fully meet a requirement but that requirement is less rigid. In this case one might negotiate a change in the requirement so that the product's capabilities and the requirement match more closely. The most common situation would be that a combination of requirements adjustment and adding functionality is required to meet the deficiency. The cost of employing this product would be calculated from both the cost of negotiation as well as the cost of custom code implementation.

A final case is the situation where the product's capabilities fall outside the boundaries established by the known requirements. Here we have the situation where we either accept the excess capability, (i.e. the capability is a benefit), and provide it as a part of the system, or we must attempt to inhibit access to that capability (i.e. the capability is a liability) from within the system. There are, of course, various degrees of acceptance or rejection that can be negotiated as with the previous case. The costs here are calculated from the cost of custom coding, the cost of adding beneficial functionality and the cost of restating the requirements.

If we consider the matrix shown of Fig. 2 we can visualize a transformation of the information contained in individual cells into a fulfillment cost for each product-requirement pair.

5.3   Aggregation

There remains the issue of aggregation of the results of the cost calculations. Gap analysis leads to the creation of multiple matrices corresponding to the number of evaluations performed. Each of these matrices is transformed into a fulfillment cost matrix during the fulfillment cost determination. For each matrix we can find a preferred product There is a final step required to select the optimal combination of these products with which to construct the system. This problem has already been described by Briand [2] as a operational research optimization problem. The goal is to find the optimal path through the matrix series based on selecting the most suitable product from each matrix.

6   Conclusions

Therefore, the concluding view of this paper is that most of the current decision-making techniques available are not adequate for component-based evaluations and assessments due to their underlying assumptions and their judgement value systems. There is a need for new requirements-driven decision-making techniques for the component-based development paradigm. The alternative paradigm presented here provides the appropriate relationship between requirements and products in the system context has the potential to provide accurate recommendations for product selection. It can be adapted to systems of varying complexity and size.

Research into fulfillment cost determination is currently underway.

References

1. Dictionary of Business, Oxford University Press, © Market House Books Ltd (1996).
2. Briand, L.C.: COTS evaluation and selection. Proc. International Conference on Software Maintenance, Bethesda, Nov. (1998) IEEE Comput. Soc, Los Alamitos, pp 222-223.

3. Nand K. Jha: Decision-Based Design Value Design. Position paper, Decision Based Design Open Workshop (1997).
4. Farrokh Mistree and Janet K. Allen: Optimization in Decision-Based Design. Position Paper, Decision-Based Design Workshop, Orlando, Florida, April (1997).
5. Robert J. Tkach & Slobodan P. Simonovic: A New Approach to Multi-Criteria Decision. Journal of Geographic Information and Decision Analysis, vol. 1, no. 1, pp. 25-43.
6. Anderson, E. E.: A Heuristic for Software Evaluation and Selection. Software Practice and Experience, vol 19(8), August (1989).
7. Fenton, N.: Out Ranking Method for Multi-Criteria Decision Aid: with emphasis on its role in systems dependability assessment. Centre for Software Reliability, City University, London, UK (1994).
8. Frair, L.: Student Peer Evaluations Using the AHP Method. Foundation Coalition, Department of Industrial Engineering, University of Alabama Tuscaloosa, (1995).
9. Kontio, J.: A Case Study in Applying a Systematic Method for COTS Selection. Proceedings of the 18th International Conference on Software Engineering, IEEE Computer Society Press, (1996).
10. MacCrimmon, R. K.: Proceedings of Multiple Criteria Decision Making. University of South Carolina, October 26-27, (1972).
11. Morisio, M. and Tsoukias, A.: A Methodology for the Evaluation and Selection of Software Products. Dipartimento di Automatica e Informatica, Politicnico di Torino, Italy, (1997).
12. Saaty, L.T.: The Analytic Hierarchy Process (AHP): How to make a decision. European Journal of Operational Research, 48, (1990), 9-26.

COTS-Based System Engineering: The Linguistics Approach

Nguyen Thanh Quang[1] and Isabelle Comyn-Wattiau[2]

[1] Programme Doctoral ESSEC
ESSEC Business School, France
[2] University of Cergy-Pontoise and ESSEC, France
{nguyentq, wattiau}@essec.fr

Abstract. As software systems become more and more complex and software artifacts developed by third party emerge frequently, the move towards COTS-based system engineering is a natural maturation process of software engineering. However, current requirements engineering methods for COTS-based systems have proven to be less successful than expected. The paper is an attempt to identify key properties of existing COTS software and other software components. We suggest a systematic approach which examines COTS-related issues under three linguistic levels: lexicon, syntax, and semantics. The driving force behind this approach by analogy is to outline a new requirements engineering method for COTS-based systems.

1 Introduction

The shift from custom development towards using Commercial off-the-shelf (COTS) software as components in building a variety of large-scale software-intensive systems aims essentially at reducing development costs and time. This new paradigm raises many challenges for both research and industrial communities. Using COTS software components for building software systems supposes requirements engineering process to be performed in a much more flexible way than with traditional methods. However, current requirements engineering methods for COTS-based systems have proven to be less successful than expected [13].

According to [14,15], there are two broad approaches when matching high-level requirements with low-level COTS capabilities: component-driven and requirements-driven. Both handle the requirements definition process in an ad hoc manner, only taking either requirements or components as the starting point for eliciting requirements. However, COTS capabilities and requirements are equally important within the COTS context. Moreover, both approaches suffer from the lack of a mechanism to consider selected COTS components in their system context. We believe that the requirements engineering for COTS-based systems is a much more complex process involving many factors. Thus it justifies the need to look for an improved methodology that should be able to:

J. Dean and A. Gravel (Eds.): ICCBSS 2002, LNCS 2255, pp. 188–198, 2002.
© Springer-Verlag Berlin Heidelberg 2002

- Propose a model for COTS characterization and classification that makes connection with system requirements.
- Lead to a better understanding of the roles of system requirements, system architecture, and COTS/components and their inextricable relationships in COTS-based system development and evolution.
- Encapsulate the complexity of the COTS-based requirements process and propose a better method for COTS requirements engineering.

To deal with these problems, we propose an analogy-based solution framework to examine COTS-based systems under three linguistic levels: lexicon, syntax, and semantics. The following section justifies the analogy between linguistics and COTS-based system engineering. In the remainder of the paper, we illustrate how this analogy can help in dealing with some of the problems above. Section 3 presents three models of COTS/components according to the three linguistic layers. Section 4 discusses in more detail strengths as well as weaknesses of current approaches for COTS-based system requirements engineering and sketches a new method for it. Some conclusions and perspectives are drawn in the final section.

2 An Analogy between COTS-Based System Engineering and Linguistics

In searching for improved solutions to COTS problems, we have found a strong analogy between COTS-based systems engineering and linguistics, which provides us with a new vision into COTS-related problems. In linguistics, experts usually examine five major components of language: phonetics, phonology, morphology, syntax, and semantics [1]. The first four components deal primarily with the form of linguistic elements while semantics deals with the meaning of these elements. In the COTS context, we can ignore the phonetics and phonology components. By following the "conquer-and-divide" principle, we describe COTS software using three layers: lexicon, syntax, and semantics. This separation of concerns enables us to divide complex problems into layers of smaller and easier-to-resolve problems and makes logical links between these layers. Since morphology studies the basic linguistic units, the morphemes, and the way in which they combine into words, we group this component with lexical aspects into the lexicon layer. The syntax and semantics layers correspond to the syntax and semantics components, respectively. In languages, words are used as is and there is generally no question on why a word has such writing or spelling. For instance, the word "cat" is used to represent a kind of domestic animal, and we accept "cat" as is without further wondering why this word is made up of three letters "c", "a", and "t". The situation is similar in COTS-based systems: we use COTS components on an as-is basis since any access to the internal codes of COTS products is not recommended. COTS software components are acquired and incorporated into our system to provide the required functionality.

The syntax concerns how words can be put together to form correct phrases and sentences and determines what structural role each word plays in a sentence [1]. In COTS-based systems, we define the architecture as an overall design structure of systems and we consider techniques for integration of COTS components as building blocks into these systems. The semantics layer deals with the meaning of individual morphemes and different linguistic constructions. This layer of linguistics corresponds to requirements engineering, and within the COTS context, may be useful in determining what requirements a combination of COTS software and other components might satisfy.

Linguistics and COTS-based system engineering also share at least three important properties : modularity, evolvability, and flexibility. A lexical structure is composed of sub-structures which, in turn, are composed of other sub-structures and basic lexical elements (morphemes). A living language continually undergoes changes: sound change, lexical change, morphological change, syntactic change, and semantic change. The flexibility in languages is related to the fact that we generally may not have only one fixed structure but several grammatical structures to express an idea. A COTS-based system shares all these properties.

In system theory, a system can be viewed under three recognized angles: structure, functionality, and evolution [6]. The structure angle describes what components or sub-systems a system is composed of (to be); the functionality angle expresses what a system has to do to fulfill certain requirements (to do); and the evolution angle captures all changes to the system (to become). Since structure is similar to lexicon and syntax and functionality is similar to semantics, the structure-functionality side can be divided and mapped into three layers: lexicon, syntax, and semantics (see Fig. 1). The evolution angle is considered to be similar to ongoing changes of languages. The complex nature of evolution goes beyond the scope of this paper.

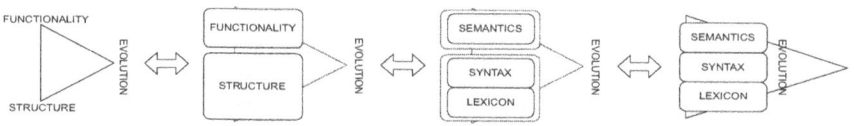

Fig. 1. Analogy between COTS-based system engineering and linguistics

For a long time, theoretical and applied research has made use of natural languages in many areas of software and system engineering. However, in COTS-based software system engineering, to the best of our knowledge, there is no research work that applies linguistics to COTS-related issues. Few papers address some linguistic aspects but do not explicitly study the logical links between these aspects [3,7,11,12].

Table 1 illustrates the analogy between COTS-based system engineering and linguistics by listing some of their similar elements under the three linguistic levels.

Table 1. Comparison between COTS-based system engineering and linguistics

Levels	Linguistics	COTS-Based System Engineering
Lexicon	- Lexicology, lexicography - Morphemes, words, phrases, sentences - Linking words - Morphology	- COTS classification and characterization - COTS components, COTS packages, COTS-based systems - Connectors/ glue code/ middleware - COTS wrapping, customization
Syntax	- Sentence structures and construction - Spell checking, neologism	- Architectural styles, system topology, system integration - COTS testing and certification
Semantics	- Meaning - Styles (stylistics) - Pragmatism - Synonymy	- Functional requirements - Non-functional requirements - Component use contexts - Requirements matching

Hence which contributions could linguistics approach bring to COTS-based system engineering? We think this approach by analogy allows us to get a new insight into COTS-based systems along with applicable or adaptable methods and solutions. In order to achieve that goal, each COTS component is regarded as a basic software unit having three linguistic elements (see Fig. 2). Each linguistic element will be described in more details in a respective meta-model. These models enable us to determine how the three linguistic aspects of COTS are interrelated.

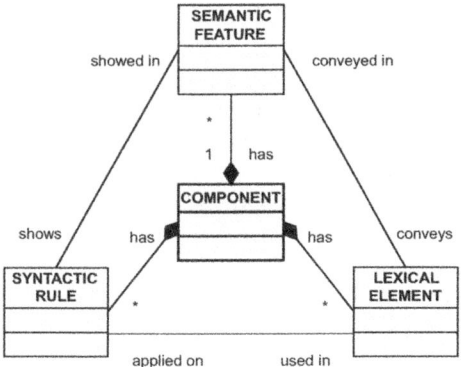

Fig. 2. COTS/components meta-meta-model

3   Three Linguistic Models of COTS Software

This section describes the COTS software using three linguistic models: lexicon, syntax, and semantics.

3.1   Lexicon Model

At the lexicon layer, words are classified into different parts of speech and have many variations to be used in different structures. Fig. 3 describes a COTS-based software system comprising COTS products, legacy parts, custom items, and connectors. At this lexical level, we do not separate communication components (connectors) from computational components. Moreover, to cope with concrete as well as abstract concepts, lexical elements are composed of different levels of abstraction. COTS components have various levels of abstractions which are grouped into three relevant dimensions: instantiation, granularity and genericity. Each dimension of abstraction consists of several levels of abstraction on which perform two groups of functions: forward functions and reverse functions (see Table 2 and Fig. 3).

Table 2. Table of abstraction levels of COTS/components

Dimension	Abstraction levels	Transformation functions
Instantiation	run-time instance, executable, source code, conceptual model	instantiation/ compilation/ execution – reverse engineering
Granularity	atomic, composite	composition/ integration – decomposition/ disintegration
Genericity	specific, generic	specialization – generalization

The visible externals of a COTS component are captured at the component signature and component interfaces or ports. The ports are means by which a component interacts and cooperates with other software components. There are two kinds of ports: imports to receive services from other components and exports to send services to other components. The services may be properties, operations, or events.

The characterization of software components is essential to have a better understanding of COTS/components and to enable us to define a classification framework of COTS software and other software components. However, the elaboration of such a classification framework goes beyond the scope of this paper.

3.2   Syntax Model

Let us consider a sentence which composes of the four basic English words "the", "cat", "mouse", "kill". The role of a word may vary depending on its order in the sentence. In "the cat kills the mouse", the word "cat" plays the role of a

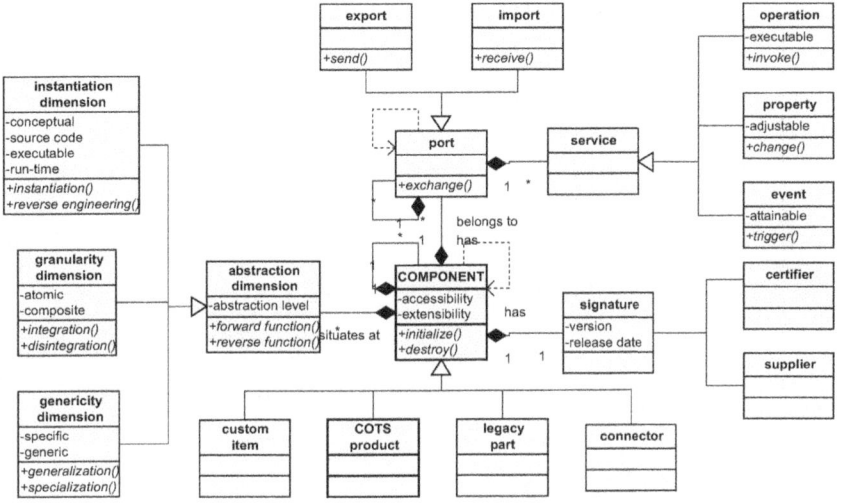

Fig. 3. Lexicon meta-model for COTS/components

subject while "mouse" plays the role of an object although they both fall into the noun category at the lexicon layer. At the syntax layer, we have to define rules specifying how to assemble COTS software into correct combinations. In current English grammar, these following grammatically correct combinations of the words can be produced: "the cat kills the mouse", "the mouse kills the cat", "the cats kill the mice", etc. Notice that some words are adapted (e.g. kill, mouse) to cope with grammar rules. In the same way, some COTS products need to be customized at assemble-time or run-time through component properties or operations or by means of wrappers. Components interact and cooperate with each other through their ports (see Fig. 4). Computational components are linked together by communication components (glue code, connectors) into a whole functional system. These connectors are supported by underlying middleware technologies (CORBA, JavaBeans, DCOM, etc.) as well as communication protocols and other integration techniques. Architecture is a collection of connectors and sub-architectures. A sub-architecture is a set of connectors and roles played by various COTS/ components. This description is part of Architecture Description Languages (ADL) [10] which describe the overall structure of a COTS-based software system and define rules and properties for integration.

3.3 Semantics Model

At the semantics layer, we are interested firstly in what meanings separate words convey. Semantic information such as COTS functionality, non-functionality, usage profile [16], usage context, etc. have to be integrated into COTS components under the form of meta-data, for example CORBA or Java Interface Definition Languages (IDL) specify contracts between components [7] (see Fig. 5). In order

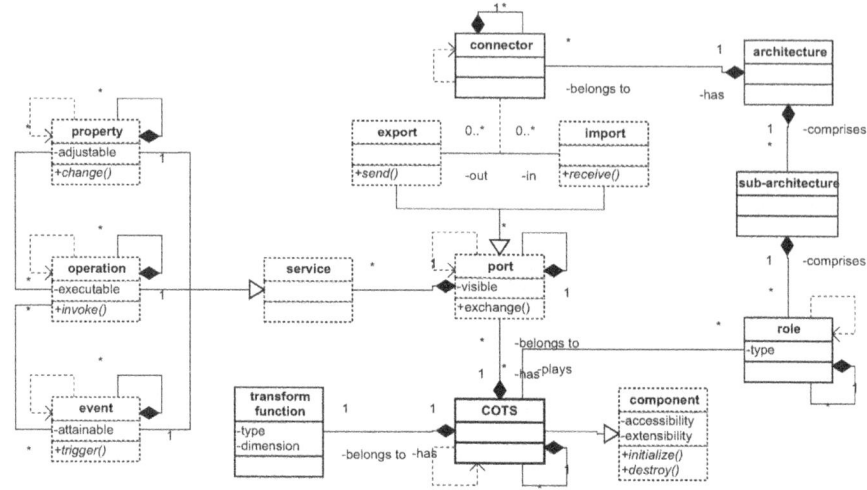

Fig. 4. Syntax meta-model for COTS/components

to have semantic information added in a reliable and precise way, we must have a testing, debugging, and certification process for COTS/components. Secondly, we also have to know if a combination of COTS and other software components has a certain meaning. For example, we have two sentences with the same structure and vocabulary "the cat kills the mouse" and "the mouse kills the cat" but their meanings are very different, and only the first sentence seems semantically rational in a normal situation. Therefore, the global meaning of the sentence cannot be deduced only from separate words but has to be determined in relation with other words under a specific context. Some ADLs define semantics but they do not properly study its connection with requirements [10].

The capabilities of a COTS component are represented under two forms: functionality (what the component can do) and non-functional properties (manner in which this functionality is performed). The overlapping of the three linguistic models reflects the logical interrelation between COTS components, system architecture and requirement in a COTS-based system. Based on these mutual relationships, we sketch a new method for requirements engineering in the next section.

4   Requirements Engineering for COTS-Based Systems

As mentioned earlier, there are two broad approaches when matching high-level requirements with low-level COTS capabilities: component-driven [4,5] and requirements-driven [7,8,9,14,15]. In the component-driven approach, we take COTS capabilities as a starting point, abstract them and then match them with system requirements to find the best fitting components. This process of

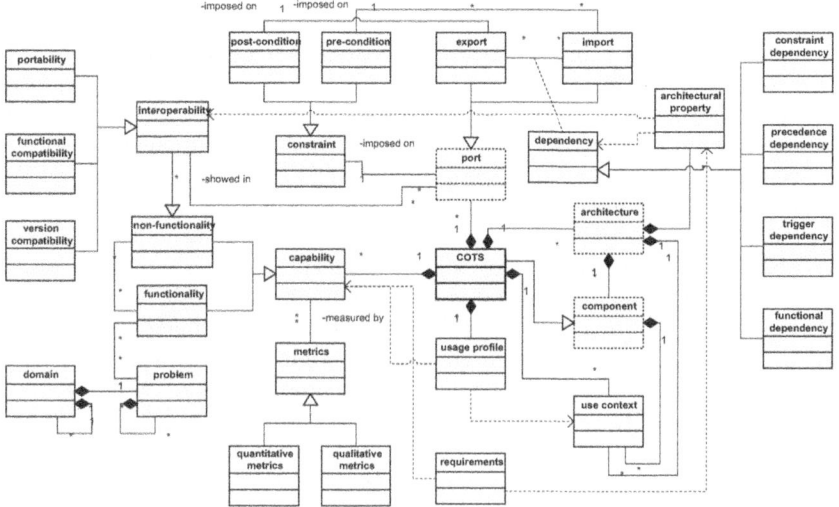

Fig. 5. Semantics meta-model for COTS/components

reverse engineering has some drawbacks in that certain functionalities (e.g. coordination, functional extension, resource sharing, etc.) as well as anomalies only emerge after system integration. When COTS components are evaluated in isolation, we may wrongly eliminate some promising components. This approach is only appropriate in the case when requirements definition is not so rigorous and provides only broad guidelines for COTS selection. In the requirements-driven approach, we rely on requirements at a highly detailed level and recursively break down into COTS components meeting these requirements. Furthermore, COTS capabilities have practically been shown to influence system requirements and business processes [2]. Thus this traditional top-down approach is applicable only when requirements are critical and must be strictly followed so as to decide whether to buy a fitting COTS product or to develop the component in-house. Both approaches are ad hoc for the reason that each one emphasizes either requirements or components as a starting point, reflecting only a special case of the COTS requirements tradeoffs process. [11,12] proposes an alternative method in which the COTS software selection and requirements definition are conducted concurrently. But this method does not analyze carefully the role of system architecture in requirements evolution and refinement. We believe that COTS requirements engineering does not only take place at the first phase of system development or evolution but has to cover all phases of the system lifecycle.

Based on linguistics viewpoint, how can we define a flexible requirements engineering method that takes advantage of the current methods? As argued previously, the meaning of a sentence depends not only on the meaning of constituent words but also on the grammatical structures and use contexts. Our opinion is that the requirements engineering process for COTS-based systems is not only driven by COTS components and system requirements but also by the system architecture. Each aspect is composed of several factors. PORE [12] acknowledges the need to make tradeoffs between these three aspects but does not support integration of the COTS software and components to explore emergent properties essential to test compliance with system requirements. As depicts Fig. 6, the requirements tradeoffs process is a central process that is influenced by the three linguistic aspects. These three aspects are mutually influenced. Available COTS components drive the requirements changes and affect the choice of other COTS components and the overall architecture. The adoption of an architecture and its underlying middleware technologies influences both the choice of COTS components and requirements definition and refinement. Finally, acquired requirements impact the choice of COTS components and architecture. In brief, the changes of factors in one aspect will trigger changes of others factors in the remaining aspects. Therefore we sketch our COTS-based requirements method as follows.

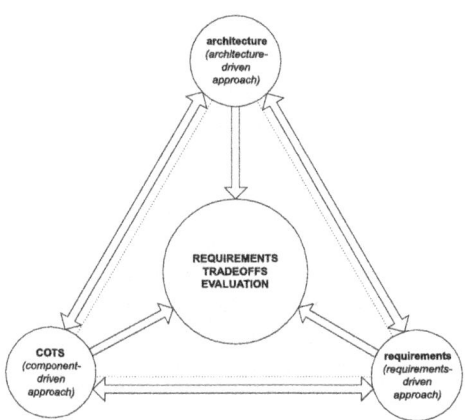

Fig. 6. COTS requirements tradeoffs evaluation process

First of all, we assume the hypothesis that the capabilities of COTS components are tested and certified. We will then select from the three linguistic groups the most critical factors for our system. For example, the requirements group has factors such as operational, functional, non-functional properties, etc. System architecture is characterized by topology, architectural styles, underlying middleware technologies, glue code, wrappers, etc. COTS components may have their proper technical factors such as functionality, non-functional properties as well as economic and legal factors, etc. We undertake this step in a recursive manner until the information collected from the three groups become clearly defined and stable. Thus the outcome is a set of different criteria for COTS components, system architecture, and requirements. Due to the conflicting nature of several criteria, we need to perform a tradeoffs evaluation process using multi-criteria decision-making techniques [7], for example, to determine the optimal configurations. Depending on the importance of selected factors, we may obtain many different configurations, each configuration is a collection of candidate COTS and other types of components, architectural styles, and system requirements. For each configuration, we select the prototypes that seem fitting best to our desired software system and then conduct an acceptance testing process using specific techniques as presented in [8,17]. The testing techniques complete our tradeoffs process, allowing us to determine which prototype is closest to our needs.

5   Conclusion

If software has been built from lines of code, componentware is now constructed from software components as its basic building blocks. Software components have to be treated in the same way as lines of code, that is to define what the basic constructs are, how to combine them together, and what meaning a combination conveys.

By analyzing the three linguistic models, it seems to us that the role of architecture within COTS requirements context has been neglected. As such, we have outlined a method to overcome this deficiency. Our linguistics-based method for COTS requirements engineering takes into account system architecture along with COTS capabilities and system requirements as the three important aspects of the requirements definition. It considers simultaneously these three aspects through a requirements tradeoffs evaluation process. We expect to be able to demonstrate our method in the time to come by carrying out some empirical case studies. Moreover, since the generated solution space may become very large, the method requires some heuristics to reduce this space and support tools using multi-criteria decision-making and component testing techniques to carry out the requirement engineering process.

Another perspective of this paper is to extend the COTS characterization in order to construct a multi-dimensional space for the classification of COTS/ components aiming at a common vocabulary for COTS software and other software components.

References

1. Allen, J.: Natural Language Understanding. 2nd edn, The Benjamin/Cummings Publishing Company Inc., CA (1995) 9-16.
2. Dean, J.C., Vigder, M.R.: System Implementation Using Off-the-shelf Software. In 9th Annual Software Technology Conference (1997).
3. Han, J.: An Approach to Software Component Specification. In Int. Workshop on Component-Based Software Engineering (1999).
4. Kontio, J.: A Case Study in Applying a Systematic Method for COTS Selection. In 18th Int. Conf. on Software Engineering, (1996) 201-209.

5. Kontio, J., Caldiera, G., Basili, V.R.: Defining Factors, Goals and Criteria for Reusable Component Evaluation. In Proceedings of CASCON (1996)17-28.
6. Le Moigne, J.-L.: La Théorie du Système Général, Théorie de la Modélisation. 4th edn, Presse Universitaire de France (1994) 63-64.
7. Lunga, S., Galoria, M.: Using COTS Components: Their Location, Qualification and Selection. In COTS Workshop - Extending COTS Software Research, Limerick, Ireland (2000).
8. Maiden, N., Ncube, C., Moore, A.: Lessons learned during the requirements acquisition for COTS systems. In Communications of the ACM (1997).
9. Maiden, N., Ncube, C.: Acquiring COTS Software Selection Requirements. IEEE Software (1998).
10. Medvidovic, N., Taylor, R. N.: A Classification and Comparison Framework for Software Architecture Description Languages. In IEEE Transactions on Software Engineering, vol. 26, no. 1, (2000) 70-93.
11. Ncube, C., Maiden, N.: Guiding Parallel Requirements Acquisition and COTS Software Selection. In Int. IEEE Conf. on Requirements Engineering, Limerick, Ireland (1999).
12. Ncube, C., Maiden, N.: COTS Software Selection: The Need to make Tradeoffs between System Requirements, Architectures and COTS/Components. In COTS Workshop - Extending COTS Software Research, Limerick, Ireland (2000).
13. Oberndorf, P., Brownsword, L., Morris, E., Sledge, C.: Workshop on COTS-Based Systems. SEI Special Report CMU/SEI-97-SR-019 (1997).
14. Rolland, C.: Intention Driven Component Reuse. Proceedings of the Workshop on Information Systems Engineering, Springer, S. Brinkkemper, E. Lindecrona, A. Solvberg (eds), Stockholm (2000) 197-208.
15. Rolland, C.: Requirements Engineering for COTS Based Systems. In Journal of Information and Software Technology, Elsevier, no 41, (1999) 985-990.
16. Voas, J.: Deriving Accurate Operational Profiles for Mass-Marketed Software. In COTS Workshop - Extending COTS Software Research, Limerick, Ireland (2000).
17. Voas, J.: Error Propagation Analysis For COTS. In Systems. Computing and Control Engineering Journal (1997).

Merging Integration Solutions for Architecture and Security Mismatch

Jamie Payton, Gerður Jónsdóttir, Daniel Flagg, and Rose Gamble*

Software Engineering & Architecture Team
Department of Mathematical and Computer Sciences
University of Tulsa, 600 S. College Ave., Tulsa, OK 74104
{payton,gogsi,flaggd,gamble}@utulsa.edu

Abstract. Integrating COTS products into a composite application can reduce development effort and associated costs. A major drawback comes from interoperability problems that hinder the seamless integration of components. Two types of problems are prominent: architecture mismatch and security mismatch. Because of their distinct properties, each problem is currently analyzed separately. The results are integration solutions that are constructed in isolation. Combining these solutions can yield another set of problems if their functionality is conflicting, duplicated, or overly complex. It is imperative to address these issues in component based software development. In this paper, we depict the architectural differences among components, their security access control policies, and the integration solutions that result from independent analysis. This is the first step toward including architectural interoperability issues and security conflicts in the design of an encompassing solution for an integrated application. We show a composition of the two solutions, highlighting redundancy and complexity.

1   Introduction

The business world is inundated with mergers, acquisitions, and various types of partnerships between corporations. Consequently, there is a demand to utilize resources that may span multiple business units within a company or even multiple companies beneath one corporate umbrella. For rapid development and cost effectiveness, it is usually the case that existing systems are integrated rather than replaced. This is in part due to advantages of component-based software engineering (CBSE) over system replacement, e.g., employees are already familiar with systems, time is not spent transferring data to new systems, etc. It is often practical to use commercial off-the-shelf (COTS) products because of their general availability and reliability to meet the needed functional requirements.

Managing and coordinating multiple security policies is also an intricate problem faced by companies integrating or sharing access to various information systems. This sharing is difficult when the involved systems use different access

---

* Contact author. This research is sponsored in part by AFOSR (F49620-98-1-0217) and NSF (CCR-9988320).

J. Dean and A. Gravel (Eds.): ICCBSS 2002, LNCS 2255, pp. 199–208, 2002.

control policies. Either the policies must be allowed to remain independent, and some mediation between them must occur, or a new, all-encompassing policy must be defined. The current belief is that "there is no single security policy and enforcement mechanism that is appropriate for all businesses" [1]. This makes the problem challenging since it is extremely difficult to handle heterogeneity at the policy level.

Separating concerns within a component-based software development project has proven to be invaluable to project completion. It allows developers to first focus on certain areas of functionality, such as architectural properties, evolution, reuse, communication, or security [2,3], without becoming entangled in other issues. However, when concerns are addressed separately, additional analysis is necessary to ensure a correct meld of the multiple solutions. Moreover, accurate composition requires that the solutions to each concern be developed at the same level of granularity.

In this paper, we illustrate that the separate interoperability analysis of the architectural properties and security issues of software components can produce redundant and overly complex integration solutions. This can lead to spaghetti code implementations that are inefficient and unreliable. A major problem is that the two solutions cannot even be compared unless they are expressed at the same level of abstraction. We normalize the analysis using *integration elements* and show how they may contain duplicate or overlapping functionality, and how they can be composed at the architectural level.

2   Background

Using COTS components within an integrated system reduces development time, cost, and complexity. However, their integration can be inherently difficult, and serious problems involving control and data exchange expectations and security risks [4,5,6] often occur as a side effect. Therefore, it is imperative that a wide range of interoperability problems be identified and mitigated.

We maintain that the level of abstraction offered by the software architecture of a component provides key information for interoperability assessment. The software architecture of a system is the blueprint of its computational elements, the means by which they interact, and the structural constraints on their interaction [7,8,9].

There are currently many different analysis methods to assess the software architecture of a system. Formal analysis methods include the chemical abstract machine (CHAM)[10], and Architecture Description Languages such as Wright [11] and Darwin [12]. Other methods, such as SAAM [13], ATAM [14], and SAEM [15] identify potential risks and verify that quality requirements have been meet. We rely on static property analysis methods that evaluate properties of the architecture to identify potential interoperability problems [16].

To resolve interoperability problems, the appropriate *integration architecture* must be designed. Integration architectures [17,18,19,20] describe the strategies and patterns that make up an integration solution for a particular application.

Integration architectures are constructed by composing sets of *integration elements*, minimal functional units that resolve architectural conflicts [17,18].

We use three types of integration elements: the translator, the controller, and the extender. The translator converts data and functions between component formats and performs semantic transformations. A translator performs functions such as filtering, composing, and converting. The controller coordinates the movement of information between components using predefined decision-making processes or strategies. Examples of controllers are mediators and gateways. The extender has a wide variety of functionalities to fill the gaps of an integration architecture in which translators and controllers cannot accommodate the full functional need. It performs various tasks such as buffering and opening or closing files.

To address security interoperability issues, we must identify those issues that are most important in the domain. Security is concerned with protecting a particular asset from intentional or unintentional unauthorized disclosure, modification or interruption. The four main goals of computer security are confidentiality, integrity, availability and accountability. The main security aspects that are employed to realize these goals are authentication, message protection, audit, and access control. In this paper, we focus on those interoperability problems related to access control.

Access control policies determine which operations a subject is allowed to perform on a particular object. With respect to access control, secure interoperability means that systems with different access control policies (e.g., Mandatory Access Control and Discretionary Access Control) are able to communicate and still provide the same level of security [21]. This often requires complicated policy management and coordination. Middleware products provide some low-level security functionality, but currently there is no support for high-level security policy management and coordination [22,23].

3   Architecture Interoperability Problems

In this section, we use a basic example to illustrate the separate integration solutions that respectively resolve architectural property and security interoperability problems. Consider a student who wants to enroll in the Graduate School at State University. Prior to enrollment, the Graduate School checks with the Business Office to determine if there are holds on the student's account. If there are no holds, the student is enrolled in the Graduate School. The Graduate School needs to let the Business Office know that the student is enrolled in certain classes so that the office can bill the student for the term. Also, the Graduate School needs to let the Office of Registration know what classes the student enrolls in so that office records and the student's transcript can be updated.

All of this communication is usually performed either via email, telephone, or campus mail correspondence. Moreover, each business unit uses independent COTS software with separate databases. Some of the databases contain overlapping information, such as the student's contact information and academic status.

The university now wants to streamline and automate its operations. In the subsequent sections, we examine the potential interoperability problems manifested during integration. We work with a typical integration architecture that meets the component communication expectations while satisfying the application requirements.

3.1   Architecture Interoperability Problems

When software components have different software architectures, it often indicates that problems with control and data exchange may arise [9,16]. The software used by the Business Office, referred to as BIZ, is multi-threaded (e.g., it can run payroll while allowing modification to a student's account). In contrast, the COTS products from the other departments are single-threaded. This architecture characteristic alone signals the potential for interoperability problems [16]. One problem is how control and data will be synchronized and passed to and from BIZ, requiring some coordination by the integration architecture.

Synchronization problems and the characteristics that influence them can also cause inconsistent data. For example, while BIZ is executing a task, another component may read the data before the BIZ process completes execution. Unknown to the receiving component, a "dirty read" may occur. Moreover, when components with different data formats communicate, invalid data may be exchanged.

Certain application requirements must be satisfied by the integration solution. The COTS products should still perform their original tasks reliably, but now share data. Location transparency is required to maximize this independence. Concurrent access to the data is also needed. In addition, the data across components is often redundant and consistency preservation is required to ensure its accuracy.

3.2   An Architectural Perspective

One integration solution that addresses these interoperability problems and satisfies the application requirements is the shared repository integration architecture [8,17,20,24]. This software architecture pattern yields an integration solution that allows for independent execution of components that must share data. It also minimizes the interfaces needed for communication. A shared repository architecture consists of a repository (which in this case comprises multiple databases), request/reply mediators, and an importer/exporter for each component involved in the integration (Fig. 1). The Repository (Fig. 2) logically encapsulates the shared data, though the data remains physically separated. The request/reply mediators (DBdeterminer and CPdeterminer in Fig. 2) respectively direct requests to the correct database in the Repository and responds to the correct translator. Each component's importer/exporter (INtranslator and OUTtranslator in Fig. 2) converts the data to and from a universal format used by the Repository.

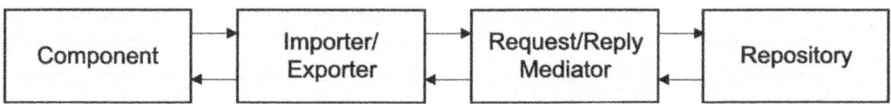

Fig. 1. Shared Repository Software Architecture Pattern

3.3   The Integration Architecture

In Fig. 2, INtranslator and OUTtranslator resolve differences in data representation by filtering parameters, transforming data representations, or otherwise preparing the requests and results between the components and the Repository. Once the INtranslator processes a request, some form of control is needed to determine the correct database within the Repository. The DBdeterminer facilitates location transparency since the component submitting the query is unaware of which database should receive it. Therefore, components can operate in a highly independent manner. In addition, the DBdeterminer facilitates concurrent access in the application. It can also preserve the consistency of redundant data. This works by including a static lookup table within the DBdeterminer that can hold entries reflecting the redundant data. The DBdeterminer can act upon these rules to update all databases with redundant information. The CPdeterminer is responsible for returning a response to the appropriate component.

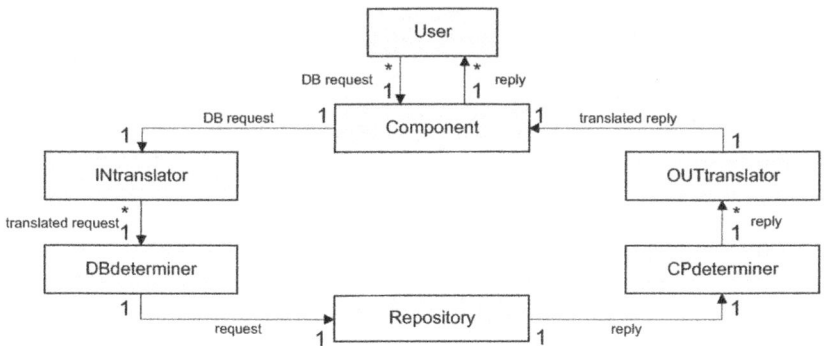

Fig. 2. Shared Repository Integration Architecture

4   Access Control Interoperability Problems

In Sect. 3, we discussed State University's need to streamline data communications and the architectural implications of the integration project. Recall that data was communicated between departments via telephone, email, and campus mail. These methods are obviously inadequate for communicating sensitive data, as the mediums are not secure and their use is not always documented. In addition, while the individual databases have security policies in place to govern use within the associated department, these policies are often circumvented when another department requests information via any of these mentioned mediums. In this section, we examine security issues and discuss a solution to the problems.

4.1   Mediating among Policies

Each database has its own access control policy. Thus, it is impossible for a subject (i.e., user, component process, etc.) in one department to access a database in another without some intervention. To gain appropriate access, integration functionality is needed to initialize the interaction. The overall integration solution must be capable of supporting several different types of access control policies. Its functionality must resolve differences between policies and must correctly determine if a subject should be granted access.

The Policy Mediation Architecture, as implemented by Galiasso [22] meets the original requirements set forth by the National Institute of Standards and Technology. This architecture allows for integration of databases with heterogeneous access control policies in a distributed environment. A *policy mediator* is associated with each database. Each policy mediator is responsible for receiving requests, determining if access should be granted, and returning responses. Thus, the Policy Mediation Architecture has the ability to represent multiple access control policies to ensure global consistency.

A single policy mediator is shown in Fig. 3. A request is made to access the database through the Query Channel Interface (QCI in Fig. 3), which is comprised of a Request Storage, QCIdeterminer, and Filter (Fig. 4). The query is stored and then forwarded to the Query Handler (QH), which processes the query and sends the request for access to the Policy Machine (PM).

The PM determines if the user should be granted access. If more information is needed to make the decision it contacts policy machines of other mediators through the Policy Channel Interface (PCI). After the PM reaches a decision, an authorization message is sent to the QH.

If the authorization message grants access, the QH contacts the Database Interface (DBI), which makes the connection. The QH receives the results of the query, performs some preprocessing, and sends the results to the QCI. The QCI then determines, based on its stored information, where to return the results.

4.2   Integration Architecture

In order to compare with the shared repository, we express the policy mediator at the same level of abstraction, using consistent terminology. Thus, we describe

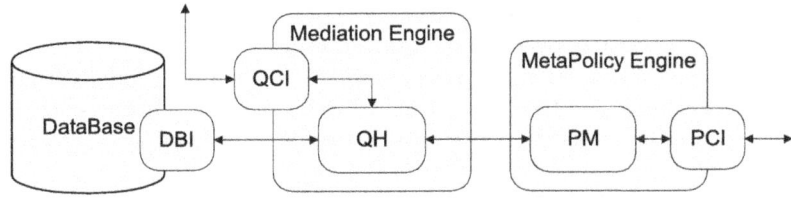

Fig. 3. Policy Mediator

its embedded functionality in Fig. 4 using integration elements (see Sect. 2 and [17,18]). For brevity, we discuss only the integration elements of the QCI. These elements are central to the communication between subjects and databases, and therefore, form the basis for the integration solution composition.

As described above, the QCI requires various extenders, controllers and translators to perform its function. An extender, called the Request Storage (Fig. 4), stores a copy of the information received from the user, as well as the information forwarded to the QH. The controller in the QCI, called the QCIdeterminer, decides to whom responses are sent. This decision is reached by analyzing the input received from the QH and the Request Storage. The QCIdeterminer always sends its output to one of several translators. Translators combine the data and discard unnecessary details. Each Filter translator in Fig. 4 is mapped to its associated subject.

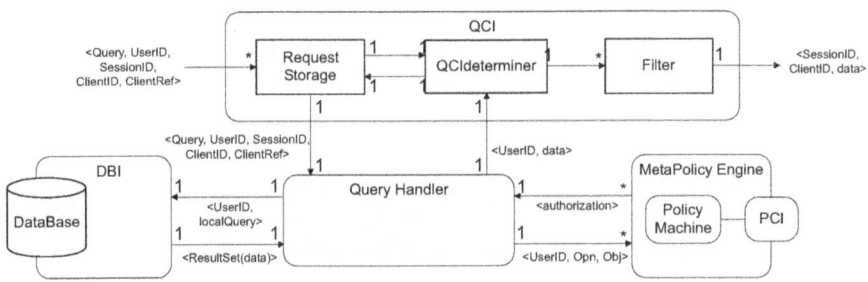

Fig. 4. Policy Mediator Integration Architecture

5   Forming a Unified Solution

Individually, established solutions fulfill the separate concerns of State University's integration requirements. When merged, the same requirements must be maintained. In fact, the composite integration architecture must retain the flavor of both solutions, with minimal modification. The goal is to identify points of intersection among the integration elements. This manifests duplication of effort and overlap within the integration functionality to decrease complexity while maintaining control over the integration solution.

The first intersection point occurs where the QCIdeterminer within the policy mediator duplicates the effort of the CPdeterminer within the shared repository integration architecture. Both return results to the subject that initiated the request.

In order to ascertain the placement of the single controller element, we check for special requirements of each integration architecture and of the overall application. In this instance, the policy mediator requires the QCIdeterminer to select the correct data recipient *before* the data leaves the QCI (refer to Sect. 4.2). Therefore, the controller should reside within the QCI. For this reason, we have chosen to eliminate the CPdeterminer and to keep the QCIdeterminer, as seen in Fig. 5.

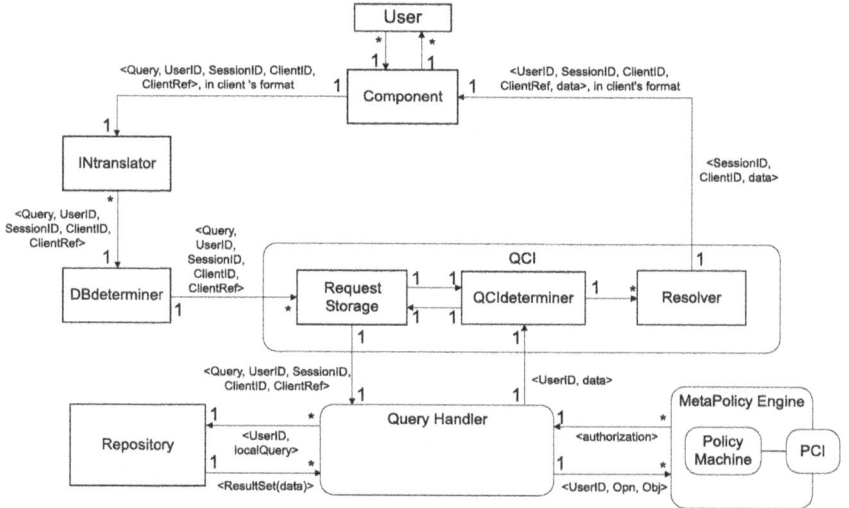

Fig. 5. Assembled Integration Elements

At first, the OUTtranslator and Filter seem to be duplicates. Their functionality has overlapping intent – returning correctly formatted data to the component. However, the translators perform different tasks. In the policy mediation architecture, a Filter transforms the data by removing extraneous parameters before sending a response from the QCI. In contrast, the OUTtranslator performs an actual change on the data format with respect to the receiving component. We create a unified translator to perform both the removal and format change. In the case of the translation functionality, it is simply a mathematical composition of the two relations.

Determining the placement of the new translator integration element depends on the fulfillment of the requirements of the individual architectures. It is required that the data leaving the QCI contain only certain parameters to be passed to a recipient, and that extraneous parameters be removed (refer to Sect. 4.2 and Fig. 4). Thus, a new translator, (Resolver in Fig. 5), is placed within the QCI.

Neither overlap nor duplication has been identified between any other elements within the individual architectures. Therefore, those integration elements remain the same in the composite integration architecture. The complete integration architecture addresses both the architectural interoperability problems of the components and the access control policies of the individual databases.

6   Conclusion

The integration of COTS products into a composite application can lead to architectural and security interoperability problems. In this paper, we study the effect of how separate analysis and solutions to those problems can lead to redundant and overly complex implementations. Using fine-grained integration elements in a uniform description, we examine the functionality of the shared repository integration architecture and the policy mediation architecture. By analyzing these solutions, it is possible to uncover potential problems during the composition of these integration architectures. If these problems are discovered early, a simpler, more robust solution can be constructed eliminating redundancy and unnecessary complexity. In the future, as this type of analysis matures, more complex problems can be discovered and reconciled at this step.

References

1. OMG: CORBA Security Services Specification. (2001).
2. Rouvellou, I., Sutton, S., Tai, S.: Multidimensional Separation of Concerns in Middleware. In, Workshop on Multi-Dimensional Separation of Concerns, (2000).
3. Viega, J., Evans, D.: Separation of Concerns for Security. In, ICSE Workshop on Multidimensional Separation of Concerns in Software Engineering, (2000).
4. Lindqvist, U., Jonsson, E.: A map of Security Risks Associated with Using COTS. In Computer,Vol. 31(6), (1998), 60-66.
5. Zhong, Q., Edwards, N.: Security Control for COTS Components. In Computer, Vol. 31(6), (1998), 67-73.
6. Profeta, J., et al.: Safety-Critical Systems Built with COTS. In Computer, Vol. 29(11), (1996), 54-60.
7. Perry, D., Wolf, A.: Foundations for the Study of Software Architecture. In ACM SIGSOFT, Vol. 17(4), (1992), 40-52.
8. Shaw, M., Garlan, D.: Software Architecture: Perspectives on an Emerging Discipline. Prentice Hall, Englewood Cliffs, NJ, (1996).
9. Garlan, D., Allen, A., Ockerbloom, J.: Architectural Mismatch, or Why it is hard to build systems out of existing parts. In, 17th International Conference on Software Engineering, Seattle, WA, (1995).
10. Compare, D., Inverardi, P., Wolf, A.: Uncovering Architectural Mismatch in Component Behavior. Science of Computer Programming, Vol. 33(2), (1999), 101-31.

11. Allen, R., Garlan, D.: A Formal Basis for Architectural Connection. ACM Transactions on Software Engineering and Methodologies, Vol. 6(3), (1997), 213-49.
12. Magee, J., Dulay, N., Eisenbach, S., Kramer, J.: Specifying Distributed Software Architectures. In, The 5th European Software Engineering Conference, Barcelona, Spain, (1995).
13. Kazman, P., Bass, L., Abowd, G. and Webb, S.M.: SAAM: A Method for Analyzing the Properties of Software Architectures. In Proceedings of the International Conference on Software Engineering, (1994), 81-90.
14. Kazman, R., Klein, M., Barbacci, M., Lipson, H., Longstaff, T., Carriere, S.: The Architecture Tradeoff Analysis Method. In International Conference on Engineering of Complex Computer Systems, Monterey, CA, (1998).
15. Duenas, J., Oliveira, W., Puente, J.: A Software Architecture Evaluation Model. In, ESPRIT ARES Workhop, Las Palmas: Springer Verlag, (1995), 148-57.
16. Davis, L., Gamble, R., Payton, J., Jonsdottir, G., Underwood, D.: A Notation for Problematic Architecture Interactions. In, Proceeding of European Software Engineering Conference/Foundations of Software Engineering, Vienna, Austria (2001).
17. Keshav, R.: Architecture Integration Elements: Connectors that Form Middleware. M.S. Thesis, Department of Mathematical and Computer Sciences: University of Tulsa, (1999).
18. Keshav, R., Gamble, R.: Towards a Taxonomy of Architecture Integration Strategies. 3rd International Software Architecture Workshop, (1998).
19. Sitaraman, R.: Integration of Software Systems at an Abstract Architectural Level. M.S. Thesis, Department of Mathematical and Computer Sciences: University of Tulsa, (1997).
20. Mularz, D.: Pattern-Based Integration Architectures. In Pattern Language of Programming, (1994).
21. Gong, L., Qian, X.: Computational Issues in Secure Interoperation. In, IEEE Transactions on Software Engineering, Vol. 22(1), (1996), 43-52.
22. Galiasso, P.: A Policy Mediation Architecture for Multi-Enterprise Environments Ph.D. Dissertation, Department of Mathematical and Computer Sciences: University of Tulsa, (2001).
23. Lang, U., Schreiner, R.: Flexibility and Interoperability in CORBA. Electronic Notes in Theoretical Computer Science, (2000).
24. Payton, J., Gamble, R., Kimsen, S., Davis, L.: The Opportunity for Formal Models of Integration. In, 2nd Int'l Conference on Information Reuse and Integration, (2000).

The Integration of COTS/GOTS within NASA's HST Command and Control System

Thomas Pfarr[1] and James E. Reis[2]

[1] Computer Sciences Corporation
Space Telescope Science Institute
Baltimore, Maryland, 21218, USA
pfarr@stsci.edu
[2] National Aeronautics and Space Administration
Goddard Space Flight Center
Greenbelt, Maryland, 20771, USA
jreis@hst.nasa.gov

Abstract. NASA's mission critical Hubble Space Telescope (HST) command and control system has been re-engineered with commercial-off-the-shelf/government-off-the-shelf (COTS/GOTS) and minimal custom code. This paper focuses on the design of this new HST Control Center System (CCS) and the lessons learned throughout its development. CCS currently utilizes more than 30 COTS/GOTS products with an additional $\frac{1}{2}$ million lines of custom glueware code; the new CCS exceeds the capabilities of the original system while significantly reducing the lines of custom code by more than 50%. The lifecycle of COTS/GOTS products will be examined including the package selection process, evaluation process, and integration process. The advantages, disadvantages, issues, concerns, and lessons learned for integrating COTS/GOTS into the NASA's mission critical HST CCS will be examined in detail. This paper will reveal the many hidden costs of COTS/GOTS solutions when compared to traditional custom code development efforts.

1 Introduction

The Hubble Space Telescope (HST) is NASA's flagship astronomical observatory. HST was originally designed in the 1970s and was launched on April 24, 1990 from Space Shuttle Discovery (STS-31). HST continues to be a state-of-the-art telescope due to on-orbit service calls by Space Shuttle astronauts. The telescope is designed to be modular which allows the astronauts to take it apart, replace worn out equipment, and upgrade instruments. These periodic service calls make sure that HST produces first-class science using cutting-edge technology.

The HST is a low Earth orbiting (LEO) satellite. It is located 320 nautical miles above the surface of the Earth. Each day, HST archives between 3 to 5 gigabytes of data and delivers between 10 and 15 gigabytes to astronomers around the world. HST has a resolving power calculated to be 10 times better than any Earth-based telescope. The telescope has taken more than 330,000

J. Dean and A. Gravel (Eds.): ICCBSS 2002, LNCS 2255, pp. 209–221, 2002.
© Springer-Verlag Berlin Heidelberg 2002

separate observations and has observed more than 25,000 astronomical targets. The telescope has created a data archive more than 7.3 terabytes. HST circles the Earth once every 95 minutes and has traveled more than 1.5 billion miles. Approximately 11,000 telemetry parameters are received from the telescope for 82 minutes of each Earth orbit. HST has received more than 93 hours of on-orbit improvements within three successful servicing missions.

2   Vision 2000 Project

HST has been producing extraordinary scientific results since its launch in 1990. In the mid-1990s, the life of HST mission was extended to 2010. HST Project staff recognized that significant improvements to spacecraft operations and ground system maintenance were needed to maintain the quality of science return and to ensure health and safety of the spacecraft. In 1995, HST Project staff instituted the Vision 2000 Project to reengineer the ground-based control system for HST. The main purpose of the Vision 2000 Project was to significantly reduce the costs of operating the telescope for the life of the mission without impacting ongoing scientific observations. The Vision 2000 Project is organized into four Product Development Teams (PDTs) including Planning and Scheduling (P&S), Science Data Processing System (SDP), Flight Software (FSW), and Control Center System (CCS). This paper focuses on the design of this new HST Control Center System and the lessons learned throughout its development.

The CCS Product Development Team was chartered to create the new Control Center System. The CCS Product Development Team successfully utilized new government practices by using government and contractor personnel within a badgeless and co-located facility. The success of the PDT approach was due, in part, to the integration of domain and technology experts within a cohesive team dedicated to a common goal. These domain and technology experts included end users, developers, testers, network administrators, security engineers, and system engineers. Major challenges facing the CCS Product Development Team were to incorporate new technology into the control center, to integrate commercial-off-the-shelf (COTS) products with legacy software, and to provide worldwide access from any remote location. In addition, the new Control Center System had to be modular and scalable such as to support single-server configurations for standard test facilities as well as to support multi-server configurations ($\sim$20 machines) for mission-control operational configurations.

3   CCS Overview

The Control Center System is the new command and control system for the HST. The CCS provides a unified architecture for commanding, engineering data processing, data archiving, data analysis, spacecraft and ground system monitoring, and simulation. The CCS is currently installed on 4 operational control center multi-server strings, 25 operational test facility single-server strings, and 4 development multi-server strings. The new Control Center System for HST's

Space Telescope Operations Control Center (STOCC) is operated at the Space Telescope Science Institute (STScI) in Baltimore, Maryland.

The Control Center System is a data-driven scalable architecture. The Control Center System is partitioned into six major subsystems including the Graphical User Interface (GUI), Command Processing, Front End Processing (FEP), System Monitoring, Data Management, and CCS Management. See Fig. 1, CCS Functional Architecture. A critical Middleware layer is also utilized for interprocess communication. The CCS Middleware layer provides a suite of services for message and data transport between application and COTS/GOTS products while executing on a variety of hardware platforms.

The Control Center System is segmented into secure network levels that accommodate remote engineering data access while protecting the command and control system. See Fig. 2, CCS System Architecture. Network and security functions have been integrated into the CCS to provide worldwide access from any remote location. The Control Center System receives spacecraft events from P&S at STScI based on the upcoming science observations. The CCS receives and processes engineering telemetry data. This telemetry is provided real-time to client workstations as well as stored in a life-of-mission long-term archive. The engineering telemetry is also provided to the SDP for use in calibration and analysis of science observations. CCS interacts with the FSW facility to validate and uplink the content of the spacecraft's onboard computer programs.

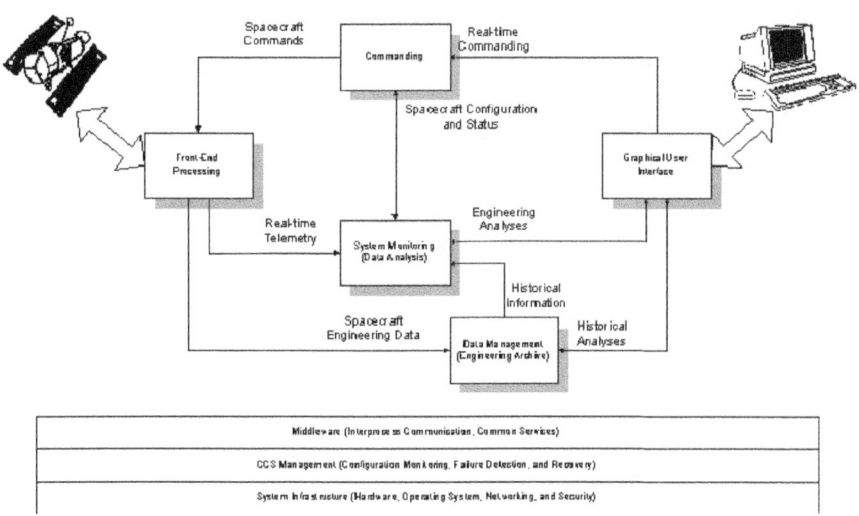

Fig. 1. CCS Functional Architecture

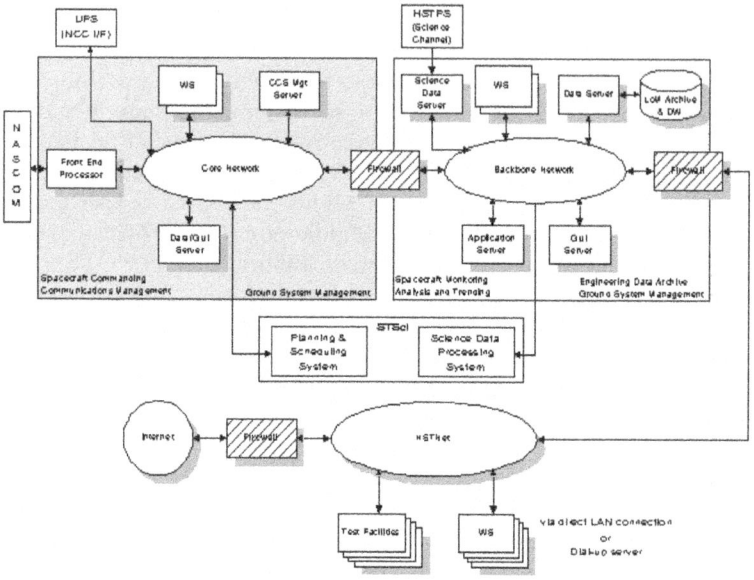

Fig. 2. CCS System Architecture

3.1 Graphical User Interface

The CCS GUI is implemented in the Java programming language. Java is a viable, highly productive, platform-independent software technology. The CCS vision to use Java applications running in web browsers was established as our GUI in 1995. All CCS tools and functions are available from a user's PC. To the user, the CCS is yet another tool that coexists with e-mail, web browsers, office applications, etc. The Control Center System software can be executed from any location that has an Internet connection (office, home, road, etc.). The original concept to run the Java applets under a web browser proved to be unrealistic considering the complexity of the applications. For reliability and performance it was necessary to be able to run separate virtual machines for each application. Browsers do not support this so the decision was made to run the applets as applications with a custom built class loader and packager. Netscape was abandoned as the primary browser due to continuing bugs and lack of support. Internet explorer and the Microsoft VM have proved to be the best in class. The concept of using java applications running in a browser is a good example of the hidden cost aspect of COTS integration. Since the user interface was crucial to the entire operation of the system we were committed to the technology and assumed that the COTS vendors were also serious about committing support to the browser products. Funding for consultant support directly from the vendor was obtained and a list of problems were developed and plans to fix the problems were put in place. The result of this high cost approach to fixing the problems was the announcement from the vendor that the product was no longer going to be supported and the fixes were not going to be made. The cost of trying to use a product, which cannot be fixed, is high and the risk is even higher. The risk was managed by having fallback plans in place. The browser was replaced by running java applications and a small custom class loader was written to replace the browser functionality in that area. The fallback approach was prototyped and plans were made to change the development focus in that direction if the original plans did not pan out. In the end that's exactly what happened.

3.2   Command Processing

The CCS spacecraft commanding is the most critical function of the ground system. The security requirements were very strict and the software is written specifically for HST. Typically a custom scripting language forms the core of these types of systems. For CCS the Tool Command Language (TCL) was chosen as the core scripting language with custom extensions used to integrate legacy applications. TCL has proved its worth in providing a modern interface while maintaining a backward compatible interface for existing scripts. A one-time translation of the legacy scripts to TCL was performed and validated in an automated test facility. The CCS Product Development Team also identified and integrated a database oriented GOTS product to manage the spacecraft event data and mission timeline; the Mission Operations Planning and Scheduling System (MOPSS) is developed and supported by many missions at the Goddard Space Flight Center (GSFC). The TCL language proved to be an excellent choice for a "glueware" application. Since the commanding functions for HST are unique to the space environment and vehicle the underlying code that performs most of the commanding functions was a port of Fortran code written almost 15 years ago. What we wanted to upgrade with TCL was the user interface aspects of the system and the unique capabilities of the scripting language itself. In this case we got the best of both worlds – reuse of a lot of old code that still worked and a brand new more flexible interface to that code.

3.3   Front End Processing

The Front End Processor (FEP) is the communications interface for telemetry, command, and external communications management. A COTS hardware/ software product, VEDA Omega series, processes the incoming telemetry data including removing communications protocol artifacts, time-tagging, de-commutation, and conversion of the raw data into engineering units. The FEP distributes the telemetry to the archive and publishes the telemetry for real-time GUI displays. A GOTS product is used for real-time telemetry data distribution; the Information Sharing Protocol (ISP) is developed by the Johnson Space Center. ISP servers exchange telemetry on a demand basis for changes-only data at one-half second intervals. The FEP functions are obviously a critical area of the system and another source of hidden costs during the development. Many features had to be added on an hourly charge basis to the base product to make it compatible with the HST requirements. This feature development and maintenance was over a 4 year period and included the move from an original VME hardware platform to a purely software platform over that period. Changes in the product and hardware requirements resulted in ripple cost effects throughout the system. Despite these costs however the product did replace about 250,000 lines of previous custom code at lower cost than the previous systems.

3.4 System Monitoring

The System Monitoring subsystem provides engineering data analysis tools for general plotting, trending, reporting, and analysis. The automated real-time monitoring component performs fault detection and isolation. COTS products have been used for spacecraft monitoring via an expert system, RTWorks, and for data analysis and plotting, PVWave. System Monitoring subsystem also provides the infrastructure to report and distribute CCS system level event messages. These event messages are used for analysis of spacecraft and ground system anomalies. The System Monitoring subsystem also provides spacecraft sensor analysis tools that perform attitude determination, sensor bias and calibration comparisons, and sensor data analysis algorithms. These functions are provided by legacy Fortran software that has been integrated into the CCS architecture.

3.5 Data Management

The Data Management subsystem provides data storage, cataloging, retrieval, and database services. The engineering data archive was designed with three major components: a short-term all-points online archive, a long-term offline all-points archive, and a changes-only online data warehouse. COTS products were selected for system database requirements, Oracle, and for data warehousing capability, Redbrick. Redbrick supports rapid complex query support of telemetry and spacecraft event data. The CCS data warehouse will contain over 15TB of information that is fully indexed and searchable. The selection of Red Brick was preceded by the most formal prototype effort of the project. The focus of the effort was to prove that the large volume of data could be efficiently retrieved. It was shown early on that getting data into the warehouse was fast and efficient. However it took several years of custom development to be able to generate effective queries on the data and to efficiently retrieve the data. The commercial query packages tested were not able to handle the volume of returned data. In addition none of the query engines could handle caching of data to prevent duplicate retrieval of data in the same effective query "job".

3.6 CCS Management

The CCS Management subsystem manages the overall ground system by providing system configuration, startup/shutdown control, monitoring, and failover capabilities. Several COTS products were integrated with a custom central server.

The Control Center System monitors itself at the network, hardware, and software application levels to determine its state and to aid in the detection/resolution of problems. Custom software and COTS products such as Patrol are used to monitor hardware and software. A knowledge-based COTS product, Tivoli T/EC, is used to collect this hardware and software monitoring information. Tivoli has been configured to interpret the events and determine the appropriate action (e.g., restart a process, failover to another node, notify a system administrator, etc.). This application area had a number of problems that covered the gamut of COTS integration issues. The original product selection looked very promising but the vendor never was able to deliver on a product that ran on our primary Unix platform. No other product at that time seemed viable so custom development was begun to implement the process control functions. That development was replaced at a later date by another COTS product that had expanded its functionality over the years into exactly the product that we originally wanted to have. In this case even during our development phase we continued to evaluate COTS alternatives to eliminate custom development where at all possible.

4   COTS/GOTS Products

The CCS Product Development Team has integrated over 30 commercial-off-the-shelf/government-off-the-shelf (COTS/GOTS) products. Even with that the project required over $\frac{1}{2}$ million lines of new custom code along with the reuse of almost a million lines of existing code to meet all the project requirements. As a point of comparison the systems that were replaced by CCS contained at most 1 or 2 COTS products and totaled over 3 million lines of code. The new CCS exceeds the capabilities of the original system while significantly reducing the lines of custom code by more than 50%. CCS staff has delivered 10 major releases in 48 months with a total of $1\frac{1}{2}$ million lines of code; each release has been deployed to approximately 4 operational multi-server strings, 25 operational test facility single-server strings, and 4 development multi-server strings.

From the outset NASA proposed a true reengineering of the system and started by using commercial best practices to develop a vision, reengineer the processes and commit to a COTS/GOTS development approach using cyclic development methodologies and just in time training to accomplish the tasks.

Due to the new development concepts being used an approach to quickly show progress was adopted. A proof of concept system was built in 3 months to show end-to-end data flow, concepts and user interface ideas. This effort allowed management to commit fully to the project by demonstrating real world capabilities that the COTS/GOTS products were capable of. The first production release of the system was demonstrated 1 year after the conception of the project in actual flight support conditions. It quickly showed the ability of the new architecture to do things the prior system could never do.

The CCS Product Development Team established and used an 80-20 rule as the basis for COTS/GOTS product selection. This rule states that if a COTS/

GOTS product meets 80 percent of the total requirements for a function this product would be acceptable pending final approval from HST Project staff to defer implementation of the remaining requirements. This 80-20 rule approach reduced the amount of time and effort needed to perform COTS/GOTS trade studies. CCS development staff was trained with the selected COTS/GOTS products and technologies using rapid just-in-time training sessions. The quick COTS/GOTS product selection process and rapid just-in-time COTS/GOTS training allowed the CCS Product Development Team to meet aggressive schedules. In certain critical areas onsite support with dedicated consultants was used to efficiently transfer knowledge from experts to the staff. This technique was used primarily to support object oriented design and implementation areas for the custom code development. Working directly with the experts on a day-to-day basis quickly trained the development personnel in all aspects of system development. The staff quickly translated their extensive domain knowledge of spacecraft ground systems into leading edge distributed, networked application implementations.

Significantly one of the primary reasons for the rejection of a COTS/GOTS product from consideration was issues related to security; particularly the ability to work through commercial firewall products. In some cases this was not possible, in other cases custom interfaces were developed to circumvent port issues at the firewall. To this date few commercial products are designed with firewalls in mind. One particular area where custom development was required was the movement of data files to/from one security area to another in a transparent manner. A distributed file transportation system was developed which automatically moves data without applications needing to know where files are from a security point of view.

The overall system design employed the concept of interface design and encapsulation of the COTS/GOTS products. The functions provided by the products were clearly delineated using object-oriented design and all access to the products was performed by abstract interfaces to the applications. This single design feature allowed for the redesign and re-implementation of many parts of the system to accommodate problems and changes in the COTS/GOTS products with little or no changes to the applications themselves after the initial implementation. Interface development and insulation of the applications from the "black boxes" is an essential tool in developing any system of this complexity.

The CCS operational COTS/GOTS software refers to the software that runs within the Control Center System (multi-server or single-server) on a daily basis. CCS administrative COTS software refers to the software that is used by system, security, network, or database administrators to keep CCS working but is not part of the day-to-day operational system. CCS development COTS software refers to the software used by developers to enhance the operational system software. See Table 1 for a list of major operational COTS products in use by CCS. See Table 2 for a list of major operational GOTS products in use by CCS. See Table 3 for a list of major development and system administration products in use by CCS staff. In addition to the COTS/GOTS products listed below, CCS

uses a large number of freeware, shareware, or low-cost COTS products including
gnu-compilers, gnu-make, gnu-ftp, gnu-zip, tcl, tk, ntp, snmp, Netscape browser,
Internet Explorer browser, Apache Server, Adobe Acrobat, and GhostScript.

Table 1. Operational COTS Software

Vendor	Product	Subsystem	Copies	Yr cost
SGI	Irix	operating system	many	$415k
Hewlett-Packard	HP-UX	operating system	site	$22k
Compaq	Open VMS	operating system	site	$13k
Sun	Solaris	operating system	25	$500
Roguewave	Rogue Wave	Middleware	4	$13k
Microsoft	Java VM	GUI	many	free
Microsoft	Java RTE	GUI	many	free
Veridian	ITAS	FEP	many	$112k
Visual Numerics	PVWave	System Monitoring	47	$100k
Talarian	RTWorks	System Monitoring	15	$40k
Acceler8 Technology	Transl8	System Monitoring	site	$14k
Oracle	Oracle, SQLplus	Data Management	site	$94k
Informix	Redbrick Warehouse	Data Management	4	$60k
ADIC	AMASS	Data Management	36	$24k
Checkpoint Software	Checkpoint/1	CCS Management	many	$75k
IBM	Tivoli/TEC	CCS Management	3	$75k
BMC	Patrol Agent	CCS Management	84	$14k
DataFellows	SSH	CCS Management	275	$11k
Telemon	Telalert	CCS Management	4	$2k

Table 2. Operational GOTS Software

Vendor	Product	Subsystem	Copies	Yr cost
GSFC	MOPSS	Command	6	1 FTE
JSC	ISP	FEP	many	free

The majority of the operational COTS/GOTS products listed in Table 1 and
Table 2 are critical to the success of Control Center System. Some COTS/GOTS
products have been integrated with minimal effort while others have required
substantial resources. Some COTS/GOTS products selected have met all of
our requirements while others have met only a portion. A smaller number of
COTS/GOTS products selected have required substantial resources to integrate
or have required a reselection. Examples of products that meet our requirements
and have worked well include Java, ISP, Rogue Wave, and Patrol. Examples
of products that only meet a portion of our requirements and have required

Table 3. Development/Administrative COTS Software

Vendor	Product	Subsystem	Copies	Yr cost
Legato	Networker Client	System Admin	24	$14k
Bud Tools	Bud Tools	System Admin	1	free
McCabe	TruChange	Development	1	$33k
McCabe	Purify	Development	site	$13k
Mercury Interactive	WinRunner	Development	13	$9k

substantial resources to successfully integrate include TCL, Oracle, Redbrick, PVWave, and RTWorks. Other examples of products that have met the requirements but had not integrated well and eventually required a reselection include the Netscape browser and a suite of Tivoli tools that were never delivered by the vendor.

A recent review of the COTS/GOTS software products in use by CCS reported that many of the products in use are still quite adequate for operation of the system but that some products should be reevaluated. The review concluded that in many cases where better products are available today, the cost to procure and effort to modify the existing system architecture generally exceeds the benefits of these new products. There are some COTS products currently in use by CCS that are prime candidates for replacement based on an increasing lack of support and responsiveness from the vendor. Current COTS products that have been identified to be re-assessed include Tivoli/TEC, TruChange, Checkpoint/1, and Networker. Alternatives selections for these COTS products still need additional research and formal recommendations need to be made with respect to their replacement.

Java: The Java COTS product was selected in 1995. This product is successfully integrated within the Control Center System. The CCS GUI is written completely using Java. The Java product would be very difficult to replace but the Java code itself is very easy to maintain.

ISP: The Information Sharing Protocol (ISP) GOTS product was select early in the CCS development phase and is also successfully integrated within the Control Center System. The ISP product is tightly coupled in the CCS architecture and replacing it with another product would be infeasible. JSC owns the ISP product but if needed we could maintain our own baseline; the source code for ISP is available and ISP code itself is easy to maintain. The ISP product meets all of the CCS requirements.

Rogue Wave: The Rogue Wave COTS product was selected early in the CCS development phase and is successfully integrated within the Control Center System. This product is used throughout the CCS architecture and replacing this product would be very difficult. Other COTS products are now available that would most-like be better selections if our decision were made today. The source code for Rogue Wave is available and is easy to maintain.

Oracle: The Oracle product was selected early in the CCS development phase and is successfully integrated within the Control Center System. The Oracle product required substantial resources to properly integrate this product with CCS applications. A large number of resources were used to write and maintain an Oracle Application Programmer Interface (API). In addition, the Oracle product has shown itself to be problematic over the last few years when running on the SGI platform. Technical support for this product has not been highly responsive to problems because of the SGI/Irix hosting. However, our recent COTS review concluded that it would not be cost-effective to replace the Oracle product with another product unless it's cost were to increase significantly in the near future.

Redbrick: The Redbrick product was selected to store spacecraft telemetry and orbital events data online for immediate retrieval. The Redbrick product required substantial resources to properly integrate this product within the CCS architecture. Training of development and system administration staff was expensive and keeping in-house experts is difficult. New hardware and software technologies will continue challenge the Redbrick product selection. Although the Redbrick product meets the requirements, the long-term sustaining costs may drive a re-assessment of this COTS selection.

PVWave: The PVWave product is a programmable data-visualization tool used to present spacecraft engineering data using plots and graphs. Other products of this type exist; however, PVWave has been sufficiently integrated into the CCS architecture as to make it very costly to replace. PVWave is a fine product that meets all of the CCS requirements.

RTWorks: The RTWorks product provides a rule-based environment for the specification and execution of spacecraft monitoring functions within CCS. There are other products that can provide this functionality, but few are as tailored to support real-time processing. RTWorks is also a fine product that meets all of the CCS requirements. CCS only uses a small portion of the RTWorks product capabilities and the RTWorks capabilities could be rewritten using custom code. Although the RTWorks product meets the requirements, the long-term sustaining costs may drive a re-assessment of this COTS selection.

Netscape: The Netscape browser product was selected early in the CCS development phase to drive the CCS GUI. The Netscape browser product was problematic running on the SGI and Windows NT platforms and vendor was not responsive to problems.. The Netscape browser is used in conjunction with CCS for standard web browsing function but was dropped for it's original purpose to run CCS. The stand-alone Java application replaced the Netscape browser product for executing the CCS application. Internet Explorer and the Microsoft VM have proved to be very reliable and efficient.

TruChange: The TruChange product provides configuration management functions for the CCS source code and related products. Over the last year, the vendor has become considerably less responsive to problems and issues regarding the product. Other comparable configuration management products exist that could be used by CCS staff. It has been recommended that a more detailed assessment be performed to determine the long-term cost effectiveness of migrating from TruChange to another product.

Checkpoint/1: The Checkpoint/1 product is used to provide security firewall functionality across all development, operational, and various test facility CCS configurations. Since the original selection of the Checkpoint/1 product, numerous other respectable firewalls have become available. In addition, over the last year, the vendor has become increasingly less responsive to requests for information. It has been recommended that alternate systems be reviewed to replace the existing firewalls.

Networker: CCS system administrators use the Networker product to backup the operational system data across the CCS strings. The product meets our current needs but occasionally has problems that require system administration staff support to recover. It has been recommended that a periodic review of similar products be assessed to determine if a more stable product can be found to replace the Networker product. Procedures for activating, transferring, and maintaining licenses are difficult and also support justification for product replacement.

5   Conclusion

NASA's Vision 2000 Project has successfully reengineered the Hubble Space Telescope ground-based command and control system. The new Control Center System utilizes more than 30 COTS/GOTS products with an additional $\frac{1}{2}$ million lines of custom code. The CCS Product Development Team successfully incorporated new technology into the control center by integrating commercial-off-the-shelf products with legacy software. The success of the new Control Center System is due in part to the careful selection of COTS/GOTS products. The CCS Product Development Team was able to meet their aggressive schedules by developing successful processes to quickly select and provide training for COTS/GOTS products. Once selected, each COTS/GOTS product has an individual life cycle; some products have been successful from their initial selection, some products have been failures, and a larger number of products fall somewhere in between these two extremes. As a part of the CCS maintenance activities, the long-term success of the Control Center System will depend on periodic re-assessments and re-evaluations the COTS/GOTS product selections.

Important lessons learned include:

Establish a clear design philosophy towards the use of COTS/GOTS products and the methods to insulate those products from the true domain applications.

Constantly reevaluate the implementation at each release and change out the products if they are not performing.

Early in the development process get on-site experts in new technology areas to train your personnel in day-by-day implementation and design issues.

Make COTS selections with a clear set of criteria but without time consuming processes. The sooner you actually use a product in real conditions the sooner you really know if it is going to work (or not).

The architecture of a system is the key to its success, not the individual components that implement that architecture. Components should always be replaceable and upgradeable without destroying the system.

References

1. Barrett, L., Lehtonen, K.: Culture Management on the NASA Hubble Space Tele-scope Control Center Reengineering Project. (1999).
2. Barrett, L., Speigel, D.: Vision 2000: Radical Reengineering of the Hubble Space Telescope Control Center System.
3. Dougherty, A., Garvis, M., Whittier, W.: Re-engineering of the Hubble Space Tele-scope to Reduce Operational Costs.
4. Friedman, B.: Deploying the Control Center System into Hubble Space Telescope Test Facilities.
5. http://hubble.gsfc.nasa.gov.

Replaceable Components and the Service Provider Interface

Robert C. Seacord

Software Engineering Institute, Carnegie Mellon University*
Pittsburgh, PA 15213
rcs@sei.cmu.edu

Abstract. A highly touted property of components and component-based software engineering is the ability to treat components as fully replaceable units. Commercially successful component models such as EJB, COM and JavaBeans have not yet produced a marketplace of replaceable components while Sun's service provider interface (SPI) has produced replaceable components in several technology areas. This paper considers both the meaning of, and motivation for, replaceable components and evaluates the properties of commercially successful component models and the SPI approach that effect their ability to support replaceable components.

1 Introduction

A highly touted property of components and component-based software engineering is the ability to treat components as fully replaceable units. Philippe Krutchen of Rational Software, for example, has defined a software component as a nontrivial, nearly independent, and replaceable part of a system that fulfills a clear function in the context of a well-defined architecture.

Beyond eliminating some forms of architectural mismatch, commercially successful component models such as JavaBeans, Enterprise JavaBeans, and COM do little to support or encourage components as replaceable units. Consequently, replaceable components that implement these component models have not materialized in the marketplace. Sun's service provider interface (SPI), on the other hand, has been considerably more successful in this regards – encouraging the creation of replaceable components in a handful of technology areas including cryptographic service providers, naming and directory services, and data base connectivity. Additional SPIs are also being developed (or matured) for printing services, XML parsing and other technologies.

This paper examines the characteristics of Java's SPI, analyses why SPIs has generated a market of reusable components while standard component models have not, and what (if any) value these other component models hold over the use of SPIs.

---

* Special permission to use the "Replaceable Components and the Service Provider Interface" (c) 2001 by Carnegie Mellon University, in *The Proceedings of ICCBSS* is granted by the Software Engineering Institute.

J. Dean and A. Gravel (Eds.): ICCBSS 2002, LNCS 2255, pp. 222–233, 2002.
© Springer-Verlag Berlin Heidelberg 2002

2   Replaceable Components

A replaceable component is one for which another component can be substituted without substantial modification to the new component or the existing system.[1] In considering a component model for replaceable components it is necessary to first understand the motivations for supporting replaceable components. This understanding is necessary before a replaceable component model can be defined or recognized. For example, in a replaceable component model:

- Is it necessary or useful to re-install a component that has already been replaced?
- Should components be replaceable by the end-user of the system? By the system administrator or by the system developer or maintainer?
- Do components need to be replaceable at run-time?

In the following sections we draw parallels between physical systems and software systems in an attempt to expose the motivations for supporting replaceable components.

2.1   Physical Systems

The idea of replaceable components has obvious physical system parallels. Consumer products such as automobiles, vacuum cleaners, stoves, and refrigerators all contain replaceable components. For the most part, these products are engineered with replaceable components because:

- It is costly to replace the overall system.
- Some system components tend to wear and break before other components.
- It is economical to replace failing parts rather than to replace the entire system.

Electronic products such as cameras, stereos, and computers use replaceable parts not only because these components can fail but also to modify or enhance the functionality of these systems. For example, a photographer may wish to replace a 50mm camera lens with a telephoto or wide-angle lens. Similarly, a computer user may decide to upgrade to a higher resolution monitor.

Another reason many consumer products have replaceable components is for flexibility in manufacturing. Systems with replaceable components can be easily reconfigured for different price points by selecting components of varying functionality, quality (and cost). Manufacturers can also incorporate different components when a principal supplier is not able to meet a need.

In summary, the reasons for replacing components in hardware systems include:

---

[1] A degenerate case exists when the new component is a modified version of the original component. Typically, this case is considered an upgrade and not a replacement. To be considered fully replaceable, substitute components should be available from a vendor other than the developer of the original component.

- Replacing failing components.
- Enhancing or modifying system functionality.
- Providing manufacturing flexibility.

2.2 Software Systems

While it is interesting to explore physical system parallels, it is often dangerous to draw analogies between software and hardware components since each class of component has significantly different qualities. As a result it is necessary to consider each reason in turn to determine if the analogy holds.

The first reason, to replace failing components, immediately appears to break the physical systems analogy. Unlike fan belts in automobiles, software components are not subject to failure from wear and tear. However, fielded components may eventually become obsolete, as their environment changes around them. Platform, operating system, and middleware upgrades (as well as upgrades to other components of the system) may make it necessary to replace an existing component. The motivation for replacing the software component is often the same as the motivation for replacing a failing part – simply to maintain the existing system's functionality.

The principal drivers in replacing a "failing" software component are cost and transparency. In particular, replacing the component should not cause the redevelopment of a significant amount of code in the existing system, or require the new component to be modified in any way. This is typically accomplished by obtaining a more recent version of the product from the vendor, either through a maintenance contract or a new purchase. In this case, support for replaceable components exceeds our requirements – it is sufficient for the vendor to provide an upgrade path. There are occasions, however, in which the component vendor is no longer developing new versions of the product. In these cases a replaceable component is a decisive benefit.

The second reason given for replacing a component is to enhance or modify the functionality of a system. In the case of a camera, different lenses may be attached to a camera for different purposes. All share a standard interface with the camera, and can communicate information such as the **f**-stop and shutter speed. There are tradeoffs involved, however, in the selection of a lens. A telephoto lens may provide for greater magnification but require additional lighting. As a result, no single lens provides the optimal set of qualities for all situations.

From a user perspective, being able to replace the lens has the advantage of changing the functionality of the camera without significantly changing the size or weight. If size and weight were not an issue, for example, wouldn't it be better to have several lenses attached to the camera and simply rotate a wheel to use a different lens? This would allow all of the lenses to be available all of the time.

An often provided example of a software component is a dictionary. Different dictionary components may provide the same functionality, but vary in the lists of terms supplied based on language or domain (for example, medical terms vs. legal terms). So why would we want to replace these components rather than simply add new ones? Again the reason must be size, in memory, and on disk. If size were not an issue, a software solution such as "add-ins" or "plug-ins" may be more appropriate – allowing us to extend, rather than replace, the capabilities of an existing tool or product. There are also situations in which an organization or user simply has no need for multiple options, but needs to select an option that is compatible with existing systems or corporate policy. Replaceable components are well suited to each of these situations.

The third reason provided for supporting replaceable software components is flexibility in manufacturing. Software, of course, is not manufactured in the same sense as hardware components yet some similarities with software development remain. In particular, manufacturers may turn to an alternate supplier to reduce cost, incorporate a higher quality component or because the original supplier could not supply the component in sufficient quantity. Unlike hardware components, it is extremely simple to replicate software and having a sufficient supply is never an issue. However, software component suppliers may discontinue a component or go out of business. In this case, the continuing supply of new *versions* of the software is threatened. Without this continuing supply of new component versions the long-term maintainability of the system becomes threatened, requiring the replacement of the original component.

The use of replaceable components to provide flexibility in manufacturing also has some interesting parallels in software product lines [6]. Support for replaceable components may lead to the development of applications that can be more quickly customized to a particular application.

2.3   Component Model Properties

Having identified the principal motivations for replaceable components it is possible to answer the questions posed earlier concerning the properties of a replaceable component model.

The first question is "Is it necessary or useful to re-install a component that has al-ready been replaced?" The answer depends at least in part by what we mean by "replaced". In maintaining a system that uses multiple components, the replacement of a component or a tool (such as a compiler) is always treated as a major risk to the reliability, functionality and performance and other qualities of the system. Normally, a configuration branch is created in which the new component is introduced and any necessary work to integrate the replacement component is performed. Once the integration is completed, significant effort is exerted to revalidate the operation of the overall system. Eventually, the configuration management board will examine the evidence to determine if the component replacement has been successful, and if so, promote the configuration branch containing the replacement component. In answering this first question, it is assumed that the component is not considered replaced until this promotion occurs.

None of our motivations for replaceable components suggest that re-installing a replaced component is a requirement of a replaceable component model.[2] Ob-

---

[2] The exception to this is add-ins. Since there are reasons for preferring replaceable components, the motivations for using add-ins are not considered further in this paper.

solete components or components with diminished functionality are unlikely to be re-installed. Product lines normally start with a base system that is then customized in a particular direction. Each customization represents a separate evolutionary branch, so while one component may be installed in one branch while a different component installed in a different branch, it is unlikely that an already replaced component would be reinstalled in the same product line branch.

The second question is "Should components be replaceable by the end-user of the system, by the system administrator or by the system developer or maintainer?" and the third question is "Do components need to be replaceable at run-time?" None of our motivations for replacing components requires that either the system administrator or end-user of the system would need to replace components. In all cases, these changes could be made by system developer and pushed out to the end-users of the system. Similarly, there is no real requirement for components to be replaced at run-time. Of course, a component model that allowed end-users to replace components at runtime would be preferable to one that did not, but this should not be considered a necessary condition of a component model that supported replaceable components.

While there is no requirement for end-users to replace components at runtime, there is a requirement that replaceable components share a similar, if not identical set of interfaces. Unless this is true, modifications will need to be made to the existing system or the new component to resolve the mismatch, preventing simple replacement. It is often permissible for the new component to add interfaces, as long as the legacy interfaces are fully supported. It is also important to realize that non-functional "interfaces" such as memory usage and latency may need to be maintained for the system to continue to function properly after the replacement component has been installed.

3   Component Models

Component models such as Enterprise JavaBeans, JavaBeans and COM have not stimulated a marketplace of replaceable components. For the most part, this is because these component models are designed to be general and support the development of a broad range of components. In this section we provide some background on Enterprise JavaBeans, JavaBeans and COM and describe what these component models do (or do not do) to support the development of replaceable components.

3.1   Enterprise JavaBeans

Enterprise JavaBeans provides a component model for server-side components that are typically transactional and often need to be secure. As a result, the component model integrates transactions and security services into the framework, allowing these capabilities to be easily supported by the system.

Enterprise beans are required to provide certain interfaces, but these interfaces exist largely to support life-cycle management. The bean provider defines the functional API exported by the enterprise bean. The functionality supported by an enterprise bean is not constrained by the EJB specification, and not restricted by the EJB server.

There exists the possibility that independently developed specifications define APIs for replaceable enterprise beans, but these fall outside of the EJB specification. Beyond eliminating the potential for architectural mismatch between enterprise beans (and enterprise beans and EJB servers) the EJB component model does little to support the development of replaceable components.

3.2   JavaBeans

The JavaBeans component model is primarily used for developing graphical user interface (GUI) components and controls. The three most important features of a JavaBean are the set of properties it exposes, the set of methods it allows other components to call, and the set of events it fires [3].

Properties are named attributes associated with a bean that can be read or written by calling appropriate methods on the bean. The methods a JavaBean exports are simply Java class methods that can be called from other components or from a scripting environment. Events provide a way for one component to notify other components that something interesting has happened. Under the event model an event listener object can be registered with an event source. When the event source detects that something interesting happens it calls an appropriate method on the event listener object.

The JavaBeans specification imposes no interface restrictions on individual JavaBeans, but simply defines a mechanism for integrating JavaBeans, and for accessing their properties, methods and events from integration tools (such as a GUI builder). Because of this, JavaBeans does not impose sufficient interface constraints to support a replaceable component.

3.3   COM

COM is a binary compatibility specification and associated implementation that allows clients to invoke services provided by COM-compliant components (COM objects). Services implemented by COM objects are exposed through a set of interfaces that represent the only point of contact between clients and the object.

COM defines a binary structure for the interface between the client and the object. This binary structure provides the basis for interoperability between software components written in arbitrary languages. As long as a compiler can reduce language structures down to this binary representation, the implementation language for clients and COM objects does not matter – the point of contact is the run-time binary representation. Thus, COM objects and clients can be coded in any language that supports Microsoft's COM binary structure [4].

Similar to EJB and JavaBeans, COM is a general component model and makes no attempts to define specific functional interfaces that can be used to build replaceable components.

4   Service Provider Interfaces

The service provider interface (SPI) mechanism is used in the development of Java class libraries and standard extensions to the Java programming language. SPIs have not been promoted by Sun as a component model, but exhibit some interesting properties that support the development of replaceable components. SPIs have been used by Sun in the development of cryptographic service providers, naming and directory services, and data base connectivity. The Java API for XML Parsing (JAXP) also includes a "plugability" layer that, while not described as a SPI, provides a similar capability. Characteristics of the JNDI and JAXP SPIs that support replaceable components are examined in the following section.

4.1   Java Naming and Directory Interface

The Java Naming and Directory Interface (JNDI) is a standard extension to the Java platform, providing Java applications with a single interface to heterogeneous enterprise naming and directory services.

The JNDI architecture consists of an API and a SPI. Java applications use the JNDI API to access a variety of naming and directory services. The SPI enables a variety of naming and directory services to be "plugged in", allowing the Java application using the JNDI API to access their services as shown in Fig. 1.

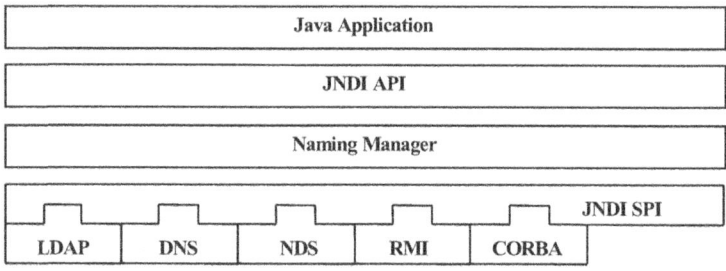

Fig. 1. The JDNI architecture consists of both an API and SPI

To use the JNDI, you must have the JNDI classes and one or more *service providers*. A service provider is software that maps the JNDI API to actual calls to the naming or directory server. The Java 2 SDK, v1.3 includes three service providers for the following naming/directory services:

- Lightweight Directory Access Protocol (LDAP)
- Common Object Request Broker Architecture (CORBA) Common Object Services (COS) name service
- Java Remote Method Invocation (RMI) Registry

Service providers exist for other naming and directory services as well. But how does the SPI support replaceable components?

4.1.1 Replaceable Components.

The implementation of the JNDI (and other) SPIs is based on Java interfaces. The Java Naming SPI, for example, contains a number of interfaces that must be implemented by the service provider. Variables in the end user application are declared using the interface data type. These variables can then reference any object implementing that interface, and any methods defined in the interface can be accessed. For example, a variable of type `Context` can be used to invoke any methods defined by the `Context` interface on any object, provided by any service provider, that implements the interface. This use of interfaces allows the Java program to invoke methods on a object whose type is not known until run-time.

Before performing any operation on a naming or directory service, an initial context must be acquired to serve as the starting point into a namespace. The LDAP service must be able to determine which service provider to use to create the initial context. This is accomplished by putting the name of the class into the initial context factory environment variable before creating the initial context. A different service provider (component) can be installed by simply specifying a different class as the initial context factory – supporting replaceable components that can be replaced dynamically at run-time.

4.1.2 Federation.

In addition to supporting replaceable components, JNDI also has a capability that more closely resembles the add-ins discussed earlier in this paper. Multiple service providers can be used by a single application in conjunction to support *composite namespaces* that incorporate multiple naming systems. Figure 2 shows a composite namespace where DNS is used as the global naming system. This name space is then split divided between NDS and LDAP.

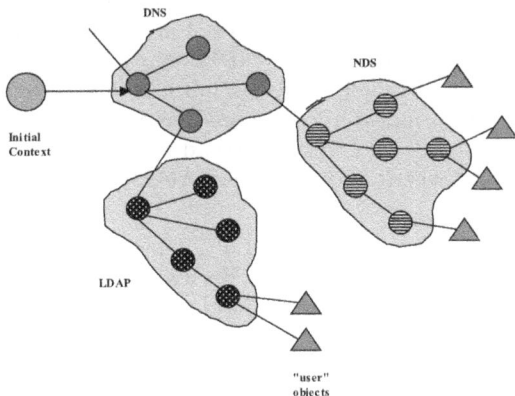

Fig. 2. Composite namespace

A composite name may span multiple namespaces, or it may have only a single compound name component that belongs to a single namespace. The context implementation determines which part of the name is resolved in its context and passes the rest onto the next context. This may be done syntactically by examining the name, or dynamically by resolving the name. The resolution of a (multi-component) composite name proceeds from one naming system to the next, with the resolution of the components that span each naming system handled by a corresponding context implementation. From a context implementation's point of view, it passes the components for which it is not responsible to the context implementation of the next naming system.

There are several ways in which the context implementation for the next naming system may be located. It may be located explicitly through the use of a junction, where a name in one naming system is bound to a context in the next naming system. For example, with the composite name `cn=fs,ou=eng/lib/xyz.zip`, the LDAP name `cn=fs,ou=eng` might resolve to a file system context in which the name `lib/xyz.zip` could then be resolved.

Alternately, the next naming system may be located implicitly. For example, a context implementation may choose the next naming system based upon service-specific knowledge of the object that it has resolved. For example, with the composite name `ldap.sei.cmu.edu/cn=fs,ou=eng`, the DNS name `sei.cmu. edu` might name a DNS entry. To get the next naming system beyond DNS, the DNS context implementation might construct a context using location of services resource records found in that entry, which in this case, happens to name an LDAP context. When the next naming system is located in this fashion, JNDI composite name separator is used to denote the boundary from one naming system to the next, and is referred to as the implicit next naming system pointer. However the next naming system is located, the remaining portion of the composite name is handed to the context implementation to resolve.

4.1.3   Locating Service Providers. Each service provider implements a context factory object that supports JNDI operations with a name space. An initial context can be established using the initial context constructor. Names spaces can be federated, using composite names and a variety of mechanisms for locating the next context. The only outstanding question, is how does JNDI know how to locate the service providers that provide the context within which a name can be resolved?

The answer is relatively simple. Each deployable component is responsible for listing the factories that it exports. Each service provider can create a resource file that contains properties specific to that provider. JNDI locates all application resource files in the class path. These files are searched for lists of JNDI factories, which are then used at runtime to implement JNDI API requests.

4.2   Java API for XML Processing

The Java API for XML[3] Processing (JAXP) provides basic support for parsing and manipulating XML documents through a standardized set of Java Platform APIs. JAXP does not explicitly claim to provide a SPI, but nonetheless, the interface provides a similar (if not identical) capability.

JAXP defines plugability interfaces for SAX[4], DOM[5], and XLST[6]. The plugability interfaces to SAX and DOM allow access to the functionality defined in the SAX 2.0 API[7] and DOM Level 2 specification[8] respectively, while allowing the choice of the implementation of the parser [5]. Depending on the needs of the application, JAXP provides developers the flexibility to swap between XML processors (such as high performance vs. memory conservative parsers) without making application code changes. The plugability interface for XLST allows an application programmer to obtain a transformer object that is based on a specific XSLT stylesheet.

All three JAXP plugability interfaces are implemented in a similar fashion, so any one of them is representative of the plugability interface. The SAX Plugability interface is as good an example as any to consider.

4.2.1   SAX Plugability. The SAX plugability classes allow an application programmer to provide an implementation of the default handler API to a SAX parser implementation to parse XML documents. As the parser processes the XML document, it calls methods on the provided default handler.

To obtain a SAX parser instance, an application programmer first obtains an instance of a SAX parser factory. The SAX parser factory instance is obtained via the static new instance method of the SAX parser factory class. The new instance method searches system properties and JAR files to determine the SAX Parser Factory implementation class to load:

---

[3] The eXtensible Markup Language (XML) is a meta-language defined by the World Wide Web Consortium (W3C) used to describe a broad range of hierarchical mark up languages. It is a set of rules, guidelines, and conventions for describing structured data in a plain text format.

[4] The Simple API for XML (SAX) is a public domain API that provides an event-driven interface for XML document processing. SAX provides a callback mechanism for notifying the application as the parser recognizes XML syntactic constructions in the document.

[5] The Document Object Model (DOM) is a set of interfaces defined by the W3C DOM Working Group. DOM provides a programmatic representation of a parsed XML document.

[6] The XSL Transformations (XSLT) describes a language for transforming XML documents into other XML documents or other text output defined by the W3C XSL Working group.

[7] The SAX 2.0 API is located at `http://www.megginson.com/SAX/index.html`.

[8] The DOM Level 2 Core Recommendation is located at
`http://www.w3.org/TR/2000/REC-DOM-Level-2-Core-20001113/`.

5   SPI-Component Model Comparison

Although only two SPI implementations were examined in this paper, there are similarities and differences in capabilities that can be noted.[9] Both the JNDI SPI and JAXP meet the minimal conditions for supporting a replaceable component model outlined earlier in this paper. In addition, both support runtime replacement of components by the end user of the system through modification of system properties to install a different service provider. The JNDI SPI is also interesting in that it goes beyond replaceable components to support an add-in capability. In other words, multiple service providers can be installed simultaneously with the correct service provider being invoked based on the composite name and other factors described in this paper. JAXP has no need to provide this capability (and does not) since a single XML parser should be sufficient in almost any case.

Component models such as Enterprise JavaBeans, JavaBeans and COM do little to support the development of replaceable components. These component models impose interfaces on components that allow them to be manipulated in a standard fashion by component frameworks. However, these component models do not impose any kind of functional interfaces on components that conform to the model, making it impossible to replace these components without modification to the remaining system.

In many ways the service provider interface is a more effective mechanism for supporting replaceable components than any of the standard component models. This is because each SPI is focused on a particular functional area, and defines a common API that can support that functional area while still allowing for variations in *how* the functionality is implemented. Standard component models are meant to be more general and do not provide this level of functional interface specification. This is not a criticism of these component models. In fact, the major point of this paper may be that expecting these general component models to generate a marketplace of replaceable components is unreasonable.

References

1. Szyperski, C. & Vernik, R.: Establishing System-Wide Properties of Component-Based Systems. Proceedings of OMG-DARPA-MCC Workshop on Compositional Software Architecture, Monterey, Ca., Jan. (1998).
2. Szyperski, C.: Component Software Beyond Object-Oriented Programming. Boston, Ma.: Addison-Wesley and ACM Press, (1998).
3. Long, F., Seacord, R.C.: A Comparison of Component Integration Between JavaBeans and PCTE. In Proceedings of the 1998 International Workshop on Component-Based Software Engineering Kyoto, Japan.
4. Santiago Comella-Dorda: Component Object Model (COM), DCOM, and Related Capabilities. URL: http://www.sei.cmu.edu/str/descriptions/com_body.html.

---

[9] These differences are certain to exist and should not be considered a criticism, given that the SPI is not a standardized component model, but more of a generic mechanism that has been used on multiple occasions by Sun developers.

5. Rajiv Mordani, James Duncan Davidson, Scott Boag: Java API for XML Processing Version 1.1 Final Release. Sun MicroSystems, February (2001).
6. Paul Clements, Linda Northrop: Software Product Lines. Addison-Wesley, July (2001).
7. Kurt Wallnau, Scott Hissam, Robert Seacord: Building Systems from Commercial Components. Addison-Wesley, July (2001), ISBN: 0201700646.

The Standard Autonomous File Server, a Customized, Off-The-Shelf Success Story

Susan K. Semancik and Annette M. Conger

NASA Goddard Space Flight Center's Wallops Flight Facility
Wallops Island, Virginia, USA
{Susan.K.Semancik.1, Annette.M.Conger.1}@gsfc.nasa.gov
http://www.wff.nasa.gov/~websafs/

Abstract. The Standard Autonomous File Server (SAFS), which includes both off-the-shelf hardware and software, uses an improved automated file transfer process to provide a quicker, more reliable, prioritized file distribution for customers of near real-time data without interfering with the assets involved in the acquisition and processing of the data. It operates as a stand-alone solution, monitoring itself, and providing an automated fail-over process to enhance reliability.

This paper describes the unique problems and lessons learned both during the COTS selection and integration into SAFS, and the system's first year of operation in support of NASA's satellite ground network.

COTS was the key factor in allowing the two-person development team to deploy systems in less than a year, meeting the required launch schedule. The SAFS system has been so successful; it is becoming a NASA standard resource, leading to its nomination for NASA's Software of the Year Award in 1999.

1   Introduction

Deciding to use a commercial off-the-shelf (COTS) product as the basis or cornerstone of your system software design is a risky business. Among the strongest fears is the "unknown" component either of the product or the vendor. High among concerns using COTS products are the following:

- What if the vendor goes out of business or drops the product you've chosen?
- What if future versions of the product change or eliminate features you were depending on or around which you built your application?
- What if the product does not operate/function as advertised (and you don't discover this until you are deep into your development/schedule)?
- What if the product has errors/bugs that the vendor won't/can't correct, or is willing to correct, but not in time to meet your schedule?
- What if future versions won't operate on your platform, or version of the operating system, or become incompatible with your hardware components or drivers? (And these new versions contain bug fixes or features you need?)

J. Dean and A. Gravel (Eds.): ICCBSS 2002, LNCS 2255, pp. 234–244, 2002.

All of these questions are even more critical if you are considering a new COTS product or version and you perform all of your initial investigation with a demo or pre-release version of the product. Just replace the words "future version/product" with "the new release" for equally troubling COTS concerns.

2   Project

This was the situation in which we found ourselves in the summer of 1997, when the assignment was given to design, develop, deploy, and field-test an autonomous file server (Standard Autonomous File Server – SAFS) at National Aeronautics and Space Administration (NASA) ground stations in time to support the Quick Scatterometer (QuikSCAT) satellite launch planned in less than one year. This system had to manage distribution of satellite files to customers of near real-time data without interfering with the assets involved in the acquisition of the data at the ground stations, and the processing of the data by the customers. By the Fall of 1997, the SAFS team of two had budgeted the timeline as shown in Fig. 1.

This gave us roughly five months for design and prototyping, three months for procurement and development, and three months for shipping and personally installing systems at NASA Goddard Space Flight Center in Greenbelt, Maryland; NASA Wallops Flight Facility (WFF) at Wallops Island, Virginia; Poker Flat Research Range in Fairbanks, Alaska; and the new satellite tracking station in Svalbard, Norway.

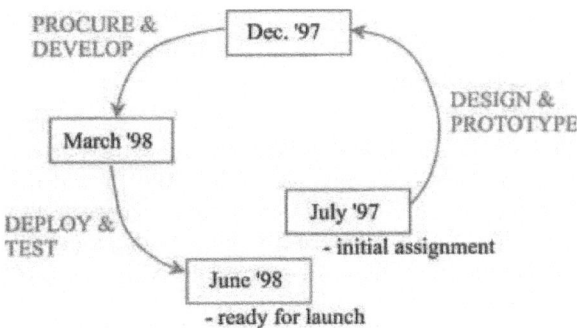

Fig. 1. SAFS Project Timeline for QuikSCAT

3   Design

We designed a system that would allow the SAFS to operate as a stand-alone solution, monitoring itself, and providing an automated fail-over process for enhanced reliability. Soon after the initial assignment, we began a search and evaluation process for COTS products, not only to help meet the schedule, but also because it is NASA's policy to use COTS software and hardware products wherever possible to save time and money, as well as to re-use government-developed products in the most efficient manner. With our aggressive schedule, we desperately needed a COTS software product that would provide the reliable, guaranteed file delivery part of our design, and COTS hardware for speed, reliability, and redundant, hot-swappable storage.

We were able to pattern part of our software design for automated file handling and messaging on a system developed at WFF, and concentrated our COTS software search for a product that would provide a quicker, more reliable, prioritized file distribution.

We created a prioritized list of features desired in the COTS software product to help us better evaluate available products:

- Reliable, guaranteed file delivery
- Recovery from point of failure
- Multi-platform support
- Stop-resume transmission control
- Auto-detection of incoming files
- Processing flexibility:

  • Multiple distribution points
  • Pre-/post- processing capability
  • Alternative actions on failed transfers

- File transfer security
- Programmable bandwidth

4   COTS Research

We searched the Internet and talked with local experts having experience in similar areas. But while the Internet was helpful, it did not yield a comprehensive list. During peer and preliminary design reviews, especially those including people from other NASA Centers, we gained additional insights and sources to consider. This is actually how we were pointed in the direction of the product we eventually chose.

The Internet is very useful in gaining detailed information about the products and vendors under consideration during a COTS search, and in some cases, even getting demonstration versions of products. It is imperative to obtain demo versions of the COTS software or loaner COTS hardware whenever possible to be sure features are as advertised and that the learning curve to use the product will meet your timeline. It is also important to get references from vendors of the customers that are using their hardware or software in similar situations. By contacting these sources, you may be able to find out if they had product or vendor problems and if so, how easily were they resolved, and if there are any configuration/use limitations with the product before actually committing any of your resources.

5 COTS Software

At the end of our COTS software product investigation, we had a list of several products with features similar to those contained in our list. Some had only a few of our desired features, and others had more capabilities, such as multicasting, which were not part of our project's requirements. A "lesson learned" that worked very much in our favor was to select a product appropriately sized for our application, and a vendor whose size did not inhibit a working relationship with us. This way we did not pay for more features than we needed. In general, a product with a smaller feature set is more likely to be less complex for the vendor to maintain, thus giving faster responses to bug fixes. Also, if the product is closely aligned with your project's requirements, the enhancements you suggest may fit into the vendor's development plan, also resulting in faster upgrades.

Our development process started with a demo copy of the COTS software product that best matched our requirements. We followed on-line vendor tutorials and documentation to gain a good foundation in the use of the product. By this simple approach (which some developers skip to save time, but which usually results in lost time due to false starts and lack of overall understanding of the product's capabilities), we gained insight about how to best incorporate the product into our design. During this initial period, we developed a working relationship with the vendor as he responded to our inquiries for clarifications about more complex procedures, especially involving fail-over strategies. The vendor's willingness to assist us and to extend our trial period while we determined how well the product fit with our requirements, were both good indicators of the level of support we could expect after purchasing the product.

During this trial period, we were able to demonstrate the ease of integration of the COTS software product with the re-used software scripts and the COTS software processing flexibility. We purchased different hardware versions of the COTS software product in order to simulate in a lab how the product would work on various customer's platforms, as well as to model the field operational environment. What we learned from this prototyping was passed on to project customers, helping them to reduce their learning curve with the product, and making them a more willing partner in our development effort. We also encouraged them to purchase vendor support as we did, because of the time and sanity it could save.

To accommodate those customers who decide not to use this COTS software for file transfer with the SAFS system, we built in an alternative option to use File Transfer Protocol (FTP) for their file acquisition from the SAFS. Most of our projects' customers choose to use the COTS software because of the added security, reliability, and guaranteed delivery that it provides through our system.

6 COTS Hardware

The COTS hardware search concentrated on servers and redundant array of independent disks (RAID) components that would be robust, reliable, and expandable, meet our speed requirement, and be maintainable in remote locations.

At the time, our investigations found the fastest server and RAID drive systems were not available from the same vendor. This led us to a dilemma: we could either get all components from the same vendor and not meet all our performance requirements, or get the best components from multiple vendors, and possibly have configuration or compatibility problems later. After much discussion in peer and pre-design reviews, we were able to convince any opponents that the latter decision was the best. While this approach is likely to be more expensive, it gave the results we needed to meet our aggressive schedule. We did have a few instances in our early development where it was more difficult to track hardware/configuration problems to the specific component because of the multiple vendors, but the performance aspects of the system far out-weighed this difficulty.

The expansion capability of any COTS hardware system and the level of vendor support needed, both during development and deployment, can heavily influence the product you choose. The RAID vendor we selected had the fastest and easiest system to expand, and also used an external personal computer (PC) in their design to free the server from the RAID monitoring and configuration tasks. With their worldwide network of support personnel, they could provide a field engineer to accompany us during field installations to optimally configure our systems, which greatly helped us in remote locations such as the satellite tracking station in Svalbard, Norway. The integration of COTS software with the configuration of COTS hardware from different vendors can be a significant effort. Whenever possible, it is important for the design/development team to personally perform on-site installation of their systems. It gives the team concrete knowledge about field configuration of the system, an appreciation for the operating environment, and an opportunity to develop a rapport with the staff for future problem resolution.

7   Vendor Support

We found it was crucial to have support/maintenance contracts from both COTS hardware and software vendors through our development, deployment, and first year of operation in order to have quick resolution to problems, and to assist in optimally integrating and configuring the systems. The first year of operation is normally a "shake-down" period that tests your system to the limit in situations not always possible to predict or duplicate in a prototyping environment. Under normal conditions, no operator involvement is needed for the SAFS. Our biggest problem during operations came from an unexpected source – the operators of an external system that normally sends data to the SAFS through an automatic process. While we designed the system well to handle automated processing, the ever-changing operational environment at the ground stations (both commercial and NASA) led to occasional operator errors when they needed to perform manual transfers from their systems to the SAFS. This put us in the mode of training new personnel in correct procedures to follow to avoid problems with options we are using within the automation part of the COTS software product.

We developed an early warning system that will alert us when such errors are occurring so we can manually correct them before it causes a system problem while we explore options for an automated solution.

8 Prototyping

It is important to prototype your system's hardware and software in a lab setting as similar to the field environment as possible. Testing should be ongoing while your design matures in order to improve the design and to identify any problems while you are still in the development stage, rather than in field-testing, at which stage it may be too costly or impossible to retrofit a solution. Utilities created to help validate and verify development efforts should be considered as tools useful for operational assessments as well. For example, while developing in the lab, we created a display that visually indicates the file transfers and message interactions of the systems as they occur. This not only helped us in our development effort, but also was especially helpful in our project readiness demonstration. It was so indispensable, that it eventually led to the creation of an automated web site that continually reports on the operational file transfers and message interactions at both the ground station and customer levels so all users can track the SAFS performance.

9 Development

Using an iterative waterfall methodology, we developed the prototype in stages in the lab environment, with ongoing integration and testing through the design's maturity. The initial phase was critical, since we not only learned how to master the intricacies of the products, but also were successful in prototyping a system to handle file transfers for single project support. This was the first version released to support the QuikSCAT project, with Fig. 2 illustrating our software configuration.

After QuikSCAT launched, we had to maintain our operational systems in the field while we continued working on Phase 2, multiple project support. This involved analysis of both feedback from our end users and expanded requirements to handle more projects desiring to use the SAFS. Additional projects meant new deployments at the satellite tracking station in McMurdo, Antarctica; and at the University of Alaska in Fairbanks, AK; and the need for COTS hardware, operating system, and software upgrades and enhancements. The second phase of our design needed a more robust, generic system, with a customizable priority scheme to handle multiple projects. After discussing the possible techniques for accomplishing this with the COTS software vendor, he enhanced his product by implementing a file priority parameter that would allow files of equal priority to transfer using shared bandwidth, and files of lower priority to suspend transfers until higher priority transfers completed.

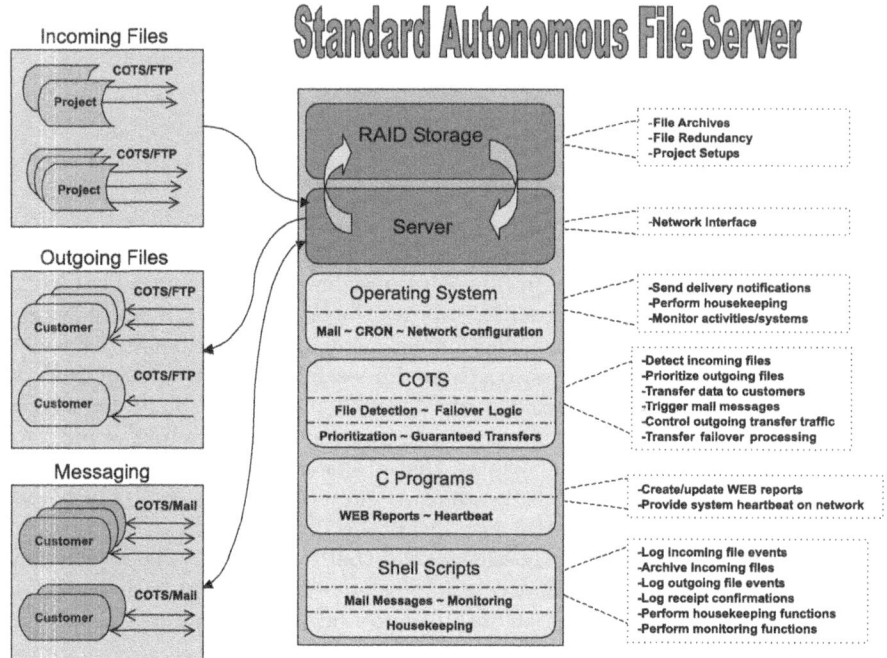

Fig. 2. SAFS Component Design

10   Enhancements

What helped us immensely in being able to handle everything in a timely fashion was keeping a prototype system in our lab. We used it to test enhancements to the system, and to configure the COTS hardware upgrades before field installation. Problems discovered in the lab were easier to resolve because resources were more accessible and operational systems did not have to be disrupted. Both of the COTS hardware vendors had the desirable feature of also being able to remotely access their components for debug/problem resolutions in the field. One desirable feature in a COTS software product is its ability to perform internal logging. Since the internal operations of a COTS software product are often hidden from the user, this feature may be the only way to trace errors or define the point within the product at which they occur, thereby getting speedier resolution to problems during either the development or operational periods. Though this can also be a possible source of some problems. For instance, one problem did not show up until the systems had been running for about a year. In that time, the quantity of file activity had generated so many logging files that it was causing system errors and poorer performance. It was at this point that we learned there were COTS software housekeeping functions we needed to perform on a regular basis to keep the system operating optimally.

As a system matures and expands, it is important not to approve all requests for additional options by customers or new projects that come on line. We tried not to make concessions that would compromise the performance of the system or would make the design less generic and more difficult to maintain. We did have to make some adjustments to handle project file names as well as the SAFS naming scheme initially developed for QuikSCAT support. These changes were accomplished in a reasonably short period because our design was flexible and modular in nature.

11 Lessons Learned

Table 1 illustrates the lessons we have learned with the SAFS project and how these lessons impacted our design, development and maintenance efforts.

Table 1. SAFS Lessons Learned

LESSON	IMPACT
RESEARCH: — Consider use of COTS products and re-use of previously developed internal products. — Create a prioritized list of desired COTS features. — Talk with local experts having experience in similar areas.	— Shortens development time. — Focuses the COTS evaluation effort for a better decision. — Helps to identify additional resources to explore or re-use; improves the design.
EVALUATE: — Obtain demonstration versions of COTS products. — Obtain customer references from vendors. — Use vendor tutorials, documentation, and vendor contacts during COTS evaluation period.	— Assures features are as advertised; determines if product learning curve will fit into project timeline; helps identify configuration/use limitations. — Helps identify previous product, configuration, or vendor problems, and how easily they were resolved. — Results in time saved by gaining insight into how best to incorporate the product into your design; provides baseline for level of vendor support to expect after purchase.

LESSON	IMPACT
— Consider the expansion capability of any COTS product. — Determine if the vendors support is adequate for your requirements.	— Ensures ease of future integration without redesign. — Enables worldwide on-site personnel for hardware support in remote sites.
DESIGN: — Conduct frequent peer and design reviews. — Accommodate your customers, where possible, by building in alternative options.	— Improves the design; provides early identification of changes to either the project requirements or operational environment. — Provides flexibility and modularity to the design, making the system more robust and generic.
SELECT: — Select a product appropriately sized for your application. — Choose a product closely aligned with your project's requirements. — Select a vendor whose size will permit a working relationship. — Select the best COTS components for product performance even if they are from multiple vendors. — Select COTS products with the ability to do internal logging.	— Reduces cost, design complexity, and maintenance of product. — Results in vendor being more likely to incorporate requested enhancements into the product, resulting in faster upgrades. — Improves vendor response time for requests for clarifications and help with advanced applications. — Promotes product performance in lieu of design simplicity. — Helps trace errors or define the point within the COTS product in which they occur; produces speedier resolution to problems.

LESSON	IMPACT
DEVELOP: — Prototype your systems hardware and software in a lab setting as similar to the field environment as possible; simulate how the product will work on various customer platforms; model the field operations; develop in stages with ongoing integration and testing. — Pass pertinent information on to your customers. — Create visual representations of system interactions where possible.	— Helps to identify problems while still in the development stage, not in operations when it may be disruptive or not possible to retrofit a solution; provides a more mature design resulting in fewer problems in the field. — Helps to reduce their learning curve with the COTS product, and makes them a more willing partner in the development effort. — Helps during development effort, in demonstrations of the project's readiness, and provides a prototype for an operational utility.
DEPLOY: — Personally perform on-site installations whenever possible.	— Gives the team concrete knowledge about the system's field configuration, an appreciation for the operating environment, and an opportunity to develop a rapport with the field staff.
MAINTAIN: — Have support/maintenance contracts for hardware and software through development, deployment, and first year of operation. — Obtain feedback from end users. — Maintain the prototype system after deployment. — Don't approve all requests for additional options by customers or new projects that come on line.	— Saves time and your sanity; use support to optimally configure and integrate the COTS product into your system. — Helps to identify problems early; provides a more flexible design; gives an indication of system performance during operations. — Provides a non-operational test-bed for enhancements and for configuring upgrades. — Avoids compromising the performance of your system, making it less generic or more difficult to maintain.

12   Summary

In summary, we were able to mitigate some of the risks/concerns we had with using COTS products by considering a vendor's history and reputation through their customer's feedback, our success with trial versions on multiple platforms, vendor support during evaluation periods, modular design, prototyping, maintenance and support contracts, frequent contacts with vendors and customers, peer and design reviews, constant testing, on-site spares for operational backups, and re-use of successful operational software. We found the addition of an operation's contractor assigned to operational system administration and maintenance responsibility helped greatly in allowing the team to complete development of Phase 2. For those desiring more details about the SAFS design, development, and deployment phases, please see the paper at the following link: http://www.wff.nasa.gov/~websafs/iafpaper.pdf.

The SAFS project was successfully transitioned to an operations contract this year, January 2001, which was made easier by the success and reliability already proven by the SAFS system in support of QuikSCAT and Earth Observing-1 (EO-1) satellite missions. Our successful integration of COTS products into the SAFS system has been key to its becoming accepted as a NASA standard resource for file distribution, and leading to its nomination for NASA's Software of the Year Award in 1999.

Implementing Large-Scale COTS Reengineering within the United States Department of Defense

James D. Smith II[1] and Duane Hybertson[2]

[1] Carnegie Mellon Software Engineering Institute [***]
4301 Wilson Blvd., Suite 902, Arlington, VA 22203-4191, USA
jds@sei.cmu.edu
[2] The MITRE Corporation
7515 Colshire Drive, McLean, VA 22102, USA
dhyberts@mitre.org

Abstract. This paper reports on empirical research into the organizational and process changes necessary to implement large-scale reengineering using COTS. The research goal is to identify how these changes can be effected within the context of the existing United States Department of Defense acquisition management, requirements management, and planning, programming, and budgeting systems. While this effort is still in its early stages, initial results indicate that there are significant challenges in developing and defending budget inputs to support an evolutionary COTS-oriented acquisition model. At the same time, recent changes in acquisition constraints and other mitigating circumstances are being exploited to improve the likelihood of success.

1 Introduction

The dismal state of software-intensive systems acquisition within the United States Department of Defense (DoD) is well known. Over the past 14 years, several commissions, "blue ribbon" panels, and the like have conducted studies on DoD software development and acquisition; their reports have been consistent in describing a system in crisis [1]. Numerous remedies have been proposed, and in some cases mandated, by senior DoD leadership (e.g., "Acquisition Reform", process improvement, earned value management, etc.), but few-if any-have been fully implemented. While many of these measures showed initial promise, all have failed to achieve any lasting improvements as measured by the success rates for DoD software acquisition efforts. What, then, are the root causes for these repeated failures in software development and acquisition, and how can they be overcome?

This paper reports on our efforts, working with a DoD organization, to uncover and mitigate some of these causes in the context of a large, multi-year

[***] Special permission to use the "Implementing Large-Scale COTS Reengineering Within the United States Department of Defense" (c) 2001 by Carnegie Mellon University, in *The Proceedings of ICCBSS* is granted by the Software Engineering Institute.

J. Dean and A. Gravel (Eds.): ICCBSS 2002, LNCS 2255, pp. 245–255, 2002.
© Springer-Verlag Berlin Heidelberg 2002

reengineering and modernization effort for a complex family-of-systems. We examine the role of DoD acquisition regulations and organizational culture in these problems. The increasing emphasis within DoD in general, and in the subject organization in particular, on the use of commercial-off-the-shelf (COTS), Government-off-the-shelf (GOTS), and non-developmental items (NDI) solutions and commercial practices is at odds with both traditional acquisition practice and organizational culture. We also discuss our attempt to incorporate innovative solutions and practices into this context to overcome the procedural and organizational barriers to success.

2   DoD Acquisition Environment

To understand how the "traditional" DoD acquisition system organization and processes impede, rather than enhance, the successful acquisition of software-intensive systems – especially COTS-based systems – some review is required. The Defense Acquisition System is defined by DoD Directive 5000.1, which "[p]rovides policies and principles for all DoD acquisition programs" [2]. These policies and principles are broken out into five major categories:

1. Achieving interoperability
2. Rapid and effective transition from Science and Technology to Products
3. Rapid and effective transition from Acquisition to Deployment and Fielding
4. Integrated and effective operational support
5. Effective management

Operation of the Defense Acquisition System is defined by DoD Instruction 5000.2, which establishes a "simple and flexible" framework for translating validated mission requirements and technological opportunities into acquisition programs [3]. Key enablers for successful DoD acquisitions include the Department's principal decision support systems: the Requirements Generation System, the Defense Acquisition System, and the Planning, Programming and Budgeting System. Additionally, the Clinger-Cohen Act (CCA) of 1996 (formerly the Information Technology Management Reform Act (ITMRA) of 1996) amends and updates a suite of statutory guidance to which a program manager must adhere [4].

2.1   Requirements Generation System

The Requirements Generation System "... produces information for decision makers on the projected mission needs of the warfighter" [5]. These broadly-defined mission needs are captured in the Mission Needs Statement (MNS). Validation of the MNS certifies that no non-material solution (e.g., operational work-around, revised tactics, etc.) exists; these validated requirements are further refined into a Capstone Requirements Document (CRD) (if required) or

Operational Requirements Documents (ORDs). ORDs translate the MNS and CRD requirements into detailed operational performance capabilities and characteristics of the desired system. These performance capabilities and characteristics establish the requirements base for the Acquisition Management System and Planning, Programming, and Budgeting System for any subsequent DoD acquisition programs and are to be reviewed, and revised as necessary, before each acquisition milestone.

2.2   Defense Acquisition System

As mentioned above, the Defense Acquisition System provides a process to translate user needs and technological opportunities into "reliable and sustainable systems" which provide operational capability to the warfighter. The Defense Acquisition System comprises a continuum of three phases, or general areas of activity:

1. Pre-system acquisition, where technologies are researched, developed, and demonstrated (concept and technology development).
2. Systems acquisition, where systems are developed, demonstrated, produced or procured, and deployed.
3. Post-systems acquisition, where deployed systems are supported throughout their operational life, until disposed.

There are multiple entry and exit points for each of these phases. In fact, for all but the most trivial of DoD acquisition programs, it is common for a program to be in all three of these phases simultaneously – especially with COTS-based software intensive systems. DoD Regulation 5000.2-R establishes mandatory procedures for Major Defense Acquisition Programs (MDAPs) and Major Automated Information Systems (MAIS) acquisition programs, which further define specific phase entry and exit points [6].

2.3   Planning, Programming, and Budgeting System

The Planning, Programming, and Budgeting System (PPBS) is the resource management system for the DoD. The objective of the PPBS is to provide "... the optimal mix of forces, equipment, and support, which can be achieved within fiscal constraints" [7]. Under the guidance of the PPBS, DoD Components develop their plans, establish programs to implement these plans, and price these programs. Component price figures (Budget Estimate Submissions, or BESs) are rolled-up into the DoD budget request (documented in the Program Budget Decisions, or PBDs), where they become part of the President's Budget (PB), which is then submitted to Congress. Since fiscal year 1988, DoD has developed budgets on a two-year cycle; Congress has not, however, fully accepted biennial budgeting and only appropriates funds for the first (i.e., the even-numbered) fiscal year. As a consequence, DoD Components must develop and submit an

Amended BES (ABES) in the odd-numbered years. The adjudication of the
ABESs, by the Secretary of Defense, results in an amended PB, which is submitted to Congress in January or February of the even-numbered years. The
time from documenting a new funding requirement in a BES, and receiving the
authority to obligate funds for that purpose, is at least three years.

2.4   Clinger-Cohen Act (CCA)

The CCA was enacted to address long-standing Government weaknesses in information resources management. The CCA directed DoD to implement modern
management practices where senior executives are directly responsible for information resource decisions [4]. The DoD implementing directive [8] identified four
imperatives critical to DoD's successful implementation of the CCA:

1. Orient information technology investments towards a strategic business and
   mission focus
2. Manage information resource investments based on performance and results
3. Mandate performance measurements for all information technology, including National Security Systems
4. Use business process reengineering prior to information system acquisitions

2.5   Putting It All Together

The Defense Acquisition System is very complex, with innumerable checkpoints
to ensure that appropriated funds are only spent against validated requirements,
and to ensure accountability, back to Congress, for the efficient expenditure of
these funds. The sequential, lock-step nature of these decision support systems
is at odds with many of the practices better suited for COTS-based systems and
spiral, or evolutionary, software development and acquisition [9,10,11].

   Despite the constraints of the DoD acquisition regulations described above,
the Department does in fact recognize the need to change the traditional acquisition culture, and has been updating the regulations accordingly. The inconsis-
tencies in the various regulations reflect the challenge of achieving this cultural
change in a coherent manner, but the changes that are appearing provide an
opportunity for DoD organizations to begin moving in the right direction. More
specifically, recent changes to DoD acquisition regulations such as the latest update of DoD 5000.2-R provide more latitude for moving away from the long-term
fixed goal approach to a more evolutionary approach. The revised requirements
generation system permits time-phased requirements. One major goal is to reduce the time needed to field some operational capability by splitting the overall
acquisition into evolutionary cycles or 'blocks', where each block is a manageable part of the overall system. Furthermore, a spiral development process is
encouraged within each evolutionary block [12]. These changes are targeted to
the acquisition phase, but not to the concept and technology development (pre-
acquisition) phase.

The rest of this paper will discuss the subject organization's reengineering efforts, and what steps are being taken to mitigate the difficulties posed by DoD acquisition constraints.

3   Current Research

The subject organization is in the early stages of a large reengineering and modernization effort. This section describes the context and goals of this effort and the two research phases. Section 3.1 describes the context elements, which consist of the current subject system, the subject organization culture, the reengineering vision, and reengineering status. Section 3.2 describes the first research phase, in which we analyze factors that we think affect the success of the reengineering effort, and define an approach that we think will achieve maximum probability of success. Section 3.3 briefly describes the second research phase, in which we apply the approach and record the results.

3.1   Reengineering Context

3.1.1   The Current System.   We are supporting a government organization that provides an information service in a specific application domain to the DoD community. The current effort is an extensive modernization of the large family-of-systems (we will refer to it as "the subject system" in this paper) that provides the service. Data is received in "raw" form, undergoes extensive analysis to turn it into information, and the information is made available to users. The current database consists almost exclusively of government-collected data; the information is available primarily as predefined products. The application domain is one in which increasing amounts of information are available from commercial sources, as well as COTS software to manage the information. Although commercial information does not – and probably never will – completely satisfy the needs of the government, it is becoming a more important contributor. In addition, a significant number of COTS products are already part of the subject system, but it is not conceived of specifically as a COTS-based system.

3.1.2   The Organizational Culture.   Since the subject organization is in DoD, major upgrades to the subject system have followed the traditional DoD acquisition process, i.e., the multi-year requirements-driven waterfall process as described in Sect. 2. It often takes two or three years or more to define all the requirements and reach agreement among stakeholders. Although COTS products are already part of the subject system, and the cultural clash with the traditional process is already being felt, the subject organization has not performed an overall reengineering of business processes or engineering processes to address the implications of a COTS-based system. Some parts of the organization have begun experimenting with other processes, but this has not been an organization-wide effort. These characteristics are not unique to the subject organization, but are, in fact, reflective of many DoD organizations.

3.1.3 The Reengineering Vision and its Implications. The vision for the subject system is to move to a flexible, responsive online system that provides customers ready access to the information, and does not restrict them to a predefined set of product types. The vision also emphasizes standards-based COTS solutions and commercial practices, including an "e-business" approach.

This vision has several far-reaching implications for the subject system and for the organization. The operational or business processes must be reengineered from a production orientation to an online information services organization. The implications for the acquisition and engineering processes are discussed in Sect. 4.

3.1.4 Reengineering Status. The modernization activity that is the subject of this paper is currently in a "pre-acquisition" phase that we will refer to as long-term planning. A team responsible for the long-term future has been established, and is becoming the focal point in the organization for the future system. The authors are part of this team. The starting point for this activity was the standard DoD acquisition process. The team has been coming to grips with the difficulties of achieving the vision within the DoD acquisition constraints. The result is the approach described in the next section.

3.2 Phase 1 Research

3.2.1 Large System Factors. Most large information systems today are not new "from scratch" acquisition or development efforts. The size of the investment in a large system generally results in a long system life span. As a consequence, the environment of a large system changes during its lifetime, and the system must change to remain useful. Changes that affect the system over time include requirements, technology, and business processes. A large system therefore undergoes changes ranging from routine changes to major upgrades. In other words, the system is obliged to evolve. These characteristics are true of the subject system.

3.2.2 COTS Factors. The inclusion of significant amounts of COTS software and hardware in a system has a number of effects on the system and how it is built and changed. There is less development work, because more of the system is "bought" rather than "built". There is more integration work, because COTS software products are from multiple vendors and are not (typically) built to interact with each other. Generally, no single wiring or component standard is used (especially in large systems), a situation that complicates integration and interoperability. The user community for a vendor product is a change force, and the vendor wants to improve its product to increase market share. The cumulative impact of multiple COTS products is another factor. The schedules of product updates are independent of each other, with the result that something is always changing. In a large COTS-based system, a "final" or goal system cannot be defined; instead, the system continues to evolve.

These forces cause COTS-based systems to differ from traditional systems in three ways. First, they change more frequently. Second, the force for change is more externally based: changes in a traditional system are driven primarily by users of that system, whereas changes in a COTS-based system are driven more by the market. Third, more effort is required to achieve and maintain integration and interoperability. All of these differences have implications for the engineering process.

3.2.3 Needed Elements of an Approach.

Some synergism exists between the large-system factors and COTS factors, namely, both require an approach that supports change and evolution. COTS products in a system simply increase the rate of change that must be supported.

The system acquisition and engineering processes must be reengineered from the traditional sequential requirements-driven approach to an agile approach that balances market forces with user requirements and evolves with the COTS market. The traditional acquisition approach virtually guarantees obsolescence before fielding. A 5-10 year time to market is inconsistent with today's commercial technology refresh rates. Technology assessment is a continuing need throughout the life of the system.

The maintenance process must also be reexamined and incorporated into the evolutionary engineering process. Exploiting COTS products affects maintenance as well as development processes [13]. In fact, development and maintenance need to be combined into one continuing evolutionary process.

Finally, an ongoing capability for integration, test, and experimentation is needed. The continually changing COTS products require continual assessment of upgrades and re-integration to maintain a working system as it evolves.

3.2.4 Assessing Current Context versus Needed Elements.

Both the DoD acquisition environment and the organizational culture are moving toward recognition and support of the necessary approach as described above, but neither is fully supportive yet. The evolutionary blocks and time-phased requirements of the updated acquisition regulations provide some support, but the separation of the technology development phase from evolution, which is allowed only in the acquisition phase, is inconsistent with the need to have continuing technology assessment throughout the life of the system. The part of the organization responsible for the current major upgrade understands the culture change necessary, but the rest of the organization will need to understand and support it as well. Labs and integration facilities are available in the organization, but they are somewhat fragmented. What is needed is a facility (or perhaps multiple integrated facilities) with an overall systems integration mission and a focus on continual COTS product evaluation, experimentation, and risk reduction.

3.2.5 Resulting Approach.

Elements of our approach were developed from the foregoing analysis. The defined plan is intended to accomplish four goals:

1. Provide a process that supports change and evolution
2. Incorporate integration, evaluation, and risk reduction
3. Help the overall organization move from the traditional acquisition process to the new process
4. Provide an approach for reconciling DoD acquisition directives with the needs described in above.

Corresponding to these four goals, our methodology will now be described respectively in terms of evolutionary process, integration and evaluation testbed and prototyping, organizational coordination, and addressing DoD acquisition constraints.

3.2.5.1 Evolutionary Process. We are endeavoring to move the discussion away from the goal of "define the requirements and architecture for 10 years from now" to a goal of "define the process of evolving the system, requirements, and the architecture, and begin the evolution now". Part of the plan involves adopting key elements of the SEI's Information Technology Solutions Evolution Process (ITSEP) [14]. Although ITSEP is new, it is based on more than 10 years experience with COTS-based systems, and reflects a tailoring of the Rational Unified Process [15] for use in composing COTS-based solutions. The basic approach is summarized in Fig. 1.

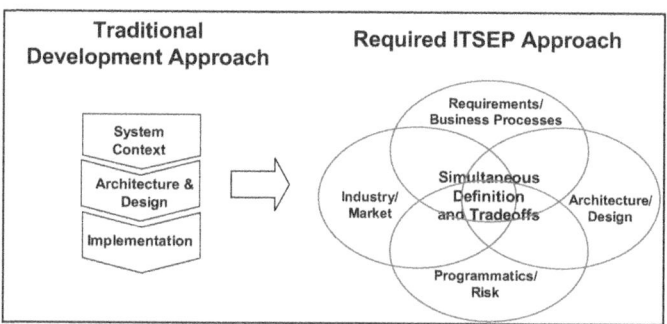

Fig. 1. ITSEP Fundamental Approach

The traditional approach proceeds from requirements to architecture and design to implementation. In contrast, ITSEP emphasizes simultaneous and balanced consideration of four spheres of influence: market, requirements and business processes, architecture/design, and programmatics/risks. This emphasis reflects the reality that in a COTS-based system, the market has significantly more influence than in a custom-built system. COTS products each have a certain defined functionality, and embody specific assumptions about their intended use and context. If an architecture is defined without consideration of this COTS alignment of functionality, the COTS products will likely not fit the architecture. Even at the requirements level, COTS products present tradeoff decisions: If a requirement is not, or cannot be satisfied by a COTS solution, is the requirement sufficiently important to build a custom solution?

The four spheres present different and sometimes conflicting views of what the system should be, and these conflicts must be negotiated. ITSEP provides for iteratively converging decisions based on tradeoffs among the four spheres. As the process refines the understanding of the solution, the trade space shrinks until the conflicts are sufficiently resolved. This spiral process is repeated in each evolutionary cycle.

3.2.5.2   Testbed and Prototyping.   A testbed environment for evaluation and integration of COTS products is being set up. The evolving system will be installed, and new updates of COTS products will be tested as well as their integration into the system. As risks are identified, prototyping and other risk reduction activities will be supported as well.

3.2.5.3   Coordination.   The long-term planning team is cognizant of the need for broad organizational support of the process if this ambitious modernization goal is to succeed. The planning team must therefore coordinate and communicate with the other parts of the organization and with the stakeholders to develop this support.

The strategy for achieving this is to invite participation of other parts of the organization in the long-term planning activities, and to share plans that are being developed. An example of this is a planned series of workshops that is designed to bring together representatives of all stakeholders to define common goals, work toward agreement on top priority requirements, develop common high level agreement on business processes, and promote an evolutionary engineering process. A positive factor is that certain parts of the organization are already moving toward processes that are more COTS-compatible.

3.2.5.4   Addressing DoD Acquisition Regulations.   We are taking advantage of the evolutionary acquisition process as defined in DoD 5000.2-R. This process allows acquisition to proceed in steps or "blocks", and the acquisition requirements apply to each block rather than the entire system. The evolution of the commercial marketplace can influence the architecture and the planning and budgeting of later blocks. This means that technology assessment will be part of each evolutionary cycle, not a one-time up front activity.

3.3   Phase 2 Research

The approach described above is applied in Phase 2 of the research. As this approach is used, some modifications may be necessary. The results and lessons learned from this approach will be observed and recorded.

4   Research Status and Conclusions

Phase 1 of the research has been completed, and the approach has been documented and agreed to by organization management. The team is in the early stages of Phase 2. Collaboration with other parts of the organization is underway, and early reactions have ranged from "wait-and-see" to positive. Plans for experimentation and COTS testbeds are progressing well. At a more global level, we believe external forces – such as users, the commercial world, and even DoD goals – will be supportive of the vision and processes we are promoting.

It is important to emphasize, however, that the effort to reconcile acquisition constraints with the needs of a COTS-based system, and to achieve adoption of the new process throughout the organization, is still a daunting task. The Phase 2 results will not be known for some time.

At this stage in the process, we have two general conclusions:

1. DoD acquisition directives are becoming less inimical to COTS-based systems, but the changes are new and somewhat experimental, and the directives are not yet uniformly COTS-compatible.
2. The subject organization is willing to take on the challenge of attempting a major COTS modernization within the problematic constraints of these acquisition directives.

Phase 2 will see the implementation and tracking of this effort as it proceeds over the next few years. We will be recording the progress of our approach as we pursue reengineering of the system and the engineering process. We expect to develop suggestions to DoD for further changes to the acquisition regulations to achieve better alignment with COTS-based systems.

References

1. Office of the Under Secretary of Defense for Acquisition and Technology: Report of the Defense Science Board Task Force on Defense Software [online]. Available: http://www.acq.osd.mil/dsb/defensesoftware.pdf, (2000).
2. U.S. Department of Defense: The Defense Acquisition System (DoD Directive 5000.1) [online]. Available: http://www.dtic.mil/whs/directives/corres/html/50001.htm, (2000).
3. U.S. Department of Defense: Operation of the Defense Acquisition system (DoD Instruction 5000.2) [online]. Available: http://www.dtic.mil/whs/directives/corres/html/50002.html, (2001).
4. Public Law 104-106, Section 5123: The Clinger-Cohen Act (CCA) of 1996 [online]. Available: http://frwebgate.access.gpo.gov/cgi-bin/getdoc.cgi?dbname=104_cong_bills&docid=f:s1124enr.txt.pdf, (1996).
5. Chairman of the Joint Chiefs of Staff: Requirements Generation System (CJCSI 3170.01B) [online]. Available: http://www.dtic.mil/doctrine/jel/cjcsi/3170_01b.pdf, (2001).

6. Office of the Secretary of Defense: Mandatory Procedures for Major Defense Acquisition Programs (MDAPs) and Major Automated Information System (MAIS) Acquisition Programs (DOD 5000.2-R) [online]. Available: `http://www.acq.osd.mil/ar/docs/dodd5000-2-r-memo-061001.doc`, (2001).
7. Air Force Material Command: Financial Management Handbook [online]. Available: `http://web2.deskbook.osd.mil/scripts/rwisapi.dll/e_search.env?CQ_PROCESS_LOGIN=YES&CQ_LOGIN=YES&CQ_USER_NAME=guest&CQ_PASSWORD=guest&CQ_SAVE[ORG]=&CQ_SAVE[SearchText]=PPBS&CQ_SAVE[file_name]=DAF\028GZ\003\028GZ003DOC.HTM&CQ_SAVE[docid]=DskBkRef294&CQ_SAVE[CQlibs]=DskBkRef#FIRSTHIT`, (2001).
8. Assistant Secretary of Defense (Command, Control, Communications, and Intelligence) Memorandum: Information Technology Management Reform Act of 1996 Implementation. Washington D.C. (1997).
9. Goldenson, D., Fisher, M.: Improving the Acquisition of Software Intensive Systems (CMU/SEI-2000-TR-003 [online]. Available: `http://www.sei.cmu.edu/publications/documents/00.reports/00tr003.html`, (2000).
10. U.S. Department of Transportation: The Road to Successful ITS Software Acquisition [online]. Available: `http://wwwcf.fhwa.dot.gov/tfhrc/safety/pubs/its/architecture/rdsuccessvol1.pdf`, (1998).
11. Adams, R., Eslinger, S.: Lessons Learned From Using COTS Software on Space Systems [online]. Available:
   `http://www.stsc.hill.af.mil/CrossTalk/2001/jun/adams.asp`, (2001).
12. Hansen, W. et al.: Spiral Development and Evolutionary Acquisition. The SEI-CSE Workshop, September (2000), Special Report, CMU/SEI-2001-SR-005 [online]. Available: `http://www.sei.cmu.edu/publications/documents/01.reports/01sr005.html`, (2001).
13. Hybertson, D., Ta, A., Thomas, W.: Maintenance of COTS-intensive Software Systems. Software Maintenance: Research and Practice, Vol. 9., (1997) 203-216.
14. Albert, C., Brownsword, L.: The Information Technology Solutions Evolution Process. To be published by Carnegie Mellon Software Engineering Institute, Pittsburgh.
15. Kruchten, P.: The Rational Unified Process: An Introduction. 2nd edn, Addison-Wesley, Boston (2000).

Author Index

Lecture Notes in Computer Science

For information about Vols. 1–2179
please contact your bookseller or Springer-Verlag

Vol. 2180: J. Welch (Ed.), Distributed Computing. Proceedings, 2001. X, 343 pages. 2001.

Vol. 2181: C. Y. Westort (Ed.), Digital Earth Moving. Proceedings, 2001. XII, 117 pages. 2001.

Vol. 2182: M. Klusch, F. Zambonelli (Eds.), Cooperative Information Agents V. Proceedings, 2001. XII, 288 pages. 2001. (Subseries LNAI).

Vol. 2183: R. Kahle, P. Schroeder-Heister, R. Stärk (Eds.), Proof Theory in Computer Science. Proceedings, 2001. IX, 239 pages. 2001.

Vol. 2184: M. Tucci (Ed.), Multimedia Databases and Image Communication. Proceedings, 2001. X, 225 pages. 2001.

Vol. 2185: M. Gogolla, C. Kobryn (Eds.), «UML» 2001 – The Unified Modeling Language. Proceedings, 2001. XIV, 510 pages. 2001.

Vol. 2186: J. Bosch (Ed.), Generative and Component-Based Software Engineering. Proceedings, 2001. VIII, 177 pages. 2001.

Vol. 2187: U. Voges (Ed.), Computer Safety, Reliability and Security. Proceedings, 2001. XVI, 249 pages. 2001.

Vol. 2188: F. Bomarius, S. Komi-Sirviö (Eds.), Product Focused Software Process Improvement. Proceedings, 2001. XI, 382 pages. 2001.

Vol. 2189: F. Hoffmann, D.J. Hand, N. Adams, D. Fisher, G. Guimaraes (Eds.), Advances in Intelligent Data Analysis. Proceedings, 2001. XII, 384 pages. 2001.

Vol. 2190: A. de Antonio, R. Aylett, D. Ballin (Eds.), Intelligent Virtual Agents. Proceedings, 2001. VIII, 245 pages. 2001. (Subseries LNAI).

Vol. 2191: B. Radig, S. Florczyk (Eds.), Pattern Recognition. Proceedings, 2001. XVI, 452 pages. 2001.

Vol. 2192: A. Yonezawa, S. Matsuoka (Eds.), Metalevel Architectures and Separation of Crosscutting Concerns. Proceedings, 2001. XI, 283 pages. 2001.

Vol. 2193: F. Casati, D. Georgakopoulos, M.-C. Shan (Eds.), Technologies for E-Services. Proceedings, 2001. X, 213 pages. 2001.

Vol. 2194: A.K. Datta, T. Herman (Eds.), Self-Stabilizing Systems. Proceedings, 2001. VII, 229 pages. 2001.

Vol. 2195: H.-Y. Shum, M. Liao, S.-F. Chang (Eds.), Advances in Multimedia Information Processing – PCM 2001. Proceedings, 2001. XX, 1149 pages. 2001.

Vol. 2196: W. Taha (Ed.), Semantics, Applications, and Implementation of Program Generation. Proceedings, 2001. X, 219 pages. 2001.

Vol. 2197: O. Balet, G. Subsol, P. Torguet (Eds.), Virtual Storytelling. Proceedings, 2001. XI, 213 pages. 2001.

Vol. 2198: N. Zhong, Y. Yao, J. Liu, S. Ohsuga (Eds.), Web Intelligence: Research and Development. Proceedings, 2001. XVI, 615 pages. 2001. (Subseries LNAI).

Vol. 2199: J. Crespo, V. Maojo, F. Martin (Eds.), Medical Data Analysis. Proceedings, 2001. X, 311 pages. 2001.

Vol. 2200: G.I. Davida, Y. Frankel (Eds.), Information Security. Proceedings, 2001. XIII, 554 pages. 2001.

Vol. 2201: G.D. Abowd, B. Brumitt, S. Shafer (Eds.), Ubicomp 2001: Ubiquitous Computing. Proceedings, 2001. XIII, 372 pages. 2001.

Vol. 2202: A. Restivo, S. Ronchi Della Rocca, L. Roversi (Eds.), Theoretical Computer Science. Proceedings, 2001. XI, 440 pages. 2001.

Vol. 2203: A. Omicini, P. Petta, R. Tolksdorf (Eds.), Engineering Societies in the Agents World II. Proceedings, 2001. XI, 195 pages. 2001. (Subseries LNAI).

Vol. 2204: A. Brandstädt, V.B. Le (Eds.), Graph-Theoretic Concepts in Computer Science. Proceedings, 2001. X, 329 pages. 2001.

Vol. 2205: D.R. Montello (Ed.), Spatial Information Theory. Proceedings, 2001. XIV, 503 pages. 2001.

Vol. 2206: B. Reusch (Ed.), Computational Intelligence. Proceedings, 2001. XVII, 1003 pages. 2001.

Vol. 2207: I.W. Marshall, S. Nettles, N. Wakamiya (Eds.), Active Networks. Proceedings, 2001. IX, 165 pages. 2001.

Vol. 2208: W.J. Niessen, M.A. Viergever (Eds.), Medical Image Computing and Computer-Assisted Intervention – MICCAI 2001. Proceedings, 2001. XXXV, 1446 pages. 2001.

Vol. 2209: W. Jonker (Ed.), Databases in Telecommunications II. Proceedings, 2001. VII, 179 pages. 2001.

Vol. 2210: Y. Liu, K. Tanaka, M. Iwata, T. Higuchi, M. Yasunaga (Eds.), Evolvable Systems: From Biology to Hardware. Proceedings, 2001. XI, 341 pages. 2001.

Vol. 2211: T.A. Henzinger, C.M. Kirsch (Eds.), Embedded Software. Proceedings, 2001. IX, 504 pages. 2001.

Vol. 2212: W. Lee, L. Mé, A. Wespi (Eds.), Recent Advances in Intrusion Detection. Proceedings, 2001. X, 205 pages. 2001.

Vol. 2213: M.J. van Sinderen, L.J.M. Nieuwenhuis (Eds.), Protocols for Multimedia Systems. Proceedings, 2001. XII, 239 pages. 2001.

Vol. 2214: O. Boldt, H. Jürgensen (Eds.), Automata Implementation. Proceedings, 1999. VIII, 183 pages. 2001.

Vol. 2215: N. Kobayashi, B.C. Pierce (Eds.), Theoretical Aspects of Computer Software. Proceedings, 2001. XV, 561 pages. 2001.

Vol. 2216: E.S. Al-Shaer, G. Pacifici (Eds.), Management of Multimedia on the Internet. Proceedings, 2001. XIV, 373 pages. 2001.

Vol. 2217: T. Gomi (Ed.), Evolutionary Robotics. Proceedings, 2001. XI, 139 pages. 2001.

Vol. 2218: R. Guerraoui (Ed.), Middleware 2001. Proceedings, 2001. XIII, 395 pages. 2001.

Vol. 2219: S.T. Taft, R.A. Duff, R.L. Brukardt, E. Ploedereder (Eds.), Consolidated Ada Reference Manual. XXV, 560 pages. 2001.

Vol. 2220: C. Johnson (Ed.), Interactive Systems. Proceedings, 2001. XII, 219 pages. 2001.

Vol. 2221: D.G. Feitelson, L. Rudolph (Eds.), Job Scheduling Strategies for Parallel Processing. Proceedings, 2001. VII, 207 pages. 2001.

Vol. 2223: P. Eades, T. Takaoka (Eds.), Algorithms and Computation. Proceedings, 2001. XIV, 780 pages. 2001.

Vol. 2224: H.S. Kunii, S. Jajodia, A. Sølvberg (Eds.), Conceptual Modeling – ER 2001. Proceedings, 2001. XIX, 614 pages. 2001.

Vol. 2225: N. Abe, R. Khardon, T. Zeugmann (Eds.), Algorithmic Learning Theory. Proceedings, 2001. XI, 379 pages. 2001. (Subseries LNAI).

Vol. 2226: K.P. Jantke, A. Shinohara (Eds.), Discovery Science. Proceedings. 2001. XII, 494 pages. 2001. (Subseries LNAI).

Vol. 2227: S. Boztaş, I.E. Shparlinski (Eds.), Applied Algebra, Algebraic Algorithms and Error-Correcting Codes. Proceedings, 2001. XII, 398 pages. 2001.

Vol. 2228: B. Monien, V.K. Prasanna, S. Vajapeyam (Eds.), High Performance Computing – HiPC 2001. Proceedings, 2001. XVIII, 438 pages. 2001.

Vol. 2229: S. Qing, T. Okamoto, J. Zhou (Eds.), Information and Communications Security. Proceedings, 2001. XIV, 504 pages. 2001.

Vol. 2230: T. Katila, I.E. Magnin, P. Clarysse, J. Montagnat, J. Nenonen (Eds.), Functional Imaging and Modeling of the Heart. Proceedings, 2001. XI, 158 pages. 2001.

Vol. 2232: L. Fiege, G. Mühl, U. Wilhelm (Eds.), Electronic Commerce. Proceedings, 2001. X, 233 pages. 2001.

Vol. 2233: J. Crowcroft, M. Hofmann (Eds.), Networked Group Communication. Proceedings, 2001. X, 205 pages. 2001.

Vol. 2234: L. Pacholski, P. Ružička (Eds.), SOFSEM 2001: Theory and Practice of Informatics. Proceedings, 2001. XI, 347 pages. 2001.

Vol. 2235: C.S. Calude, G. Păun, G. Rozenberg, A. Salomaa (Eds.), Multiset Processing. VIII, 359 pages. 2001.

Vol. 2236: K. Drira, A. Martelli, T. Villemur (Eds.), Cooperative Environments for Distributed Systems Engineering. IX, 281 pages. 2001.

Vol. 2237: P. Codognet (Ed.), Logic Programming. Proceedings, 2001. XI, 365 pages. 2001.

Vol. 2239: T. Walsh (Ed.), Principles and Practice of Constraint Programming – CP 2001. Proceedings, 2001. XIV, 788 pages. 2001.

Vol. 2240: G.P. Picco (Ed.), Mobile Agents. Proceedings, 2001. XIII, 277 pages. 2001.

Vol. 2241: M. Jünger, D. Naddef (Eds.), Computational Combinatorial Optimization. IX, 305 pages. 2001.

Vol. 2242: C.A. Lee (Ed.), Grid Computing – GRID 2001. Proceedings, 2001. XII, 185 pages. 2001.

Vol. 2243: G. Bertrand, A. Imiya, R. Klette (Eds.), Digital and Image Geometry. VII, 455 pages. 2001.

Vol. 2244: D. Bjørner, M. Broy, A.V. Zamulin (Eds.), Perspectives of System Informatics. Proceedings, 2001. XIII, 548 pages. 2001.

Vol. 2245: R. Hariharan, M. Mukund, V. Vinay (Eds.), FST TCS 2001: Foundations of Software Technology and Theoretical Computer Science. Proceedings, 2001. XI, 347 pages. 2001.

Vol. 2246: R. Falcone, M. Singh, Y.-H. Tan (Eds.), Trust in Cyber-societies. VIII, 195 pages. 2001. (Subseries LNAI).

Vol. 2247: C. P. Rangan, C. Ding (Eds.), Progress in Cryptology – INDOCRYPT 2001. Proceedings, 2001. XIII, 351 pages. 2001.

Vol. 2248: C. Boyd (Ed.), Advances in Cryptology – ASIACRYPT 2001. Proceedings, 2001. XI, 603 pages. 2001.

Vol. 2249: K. Nagi, Transactional Agents. XVI, 205 pages. 2001.

Vol. 2250: R. Nieuwenhuis, A. Voronkov (Eds.), Logic for Programming, Artificial Intelligence, and Reasoning. Proceedings, 2001. XV, 738 pages. 2001. (Subseries LNAI).

Vol. 2251: Y.Y. Tang, V. Wickerhauser, P.C. Yuen, C.Li (Eds.), Wavelet Analysis and Its Applications. Proceedings, 2001. XIII, 450 pages. 2001.

Vol. 2252: J. Liu, P.C. Yuen, C. Li, J. Ng, T. Ishida (Eds.), Active Media Technology. Proceedings, 2001. XII, 402 pages. 2001.

Vol. 2253: T. Terano, T. Nishida, A. Namatame, S. Tsumoto, Y. Ohsawa, T. Washio (Eds.), New Frontiers in Artificial Intelligence. Proceedings, 2001. XXVII, 553 pages. 2001. (Subseries LNAI).

Vol. 2254: M.R. Little, L. Nigay (Eds.), Engineering for Human-Computer Interaction. Proceedings, 2001. XI, 359 pages. 2001.

Vol. 2255: J. Dean, A. Gravel (Eds.), COTS-Based Software Systems. Proceedings, 2002. XIV, 257 pages. 2002.

Vol. 2256: M. Stumptner, D. Corbett, M. Brooks (Eds.), AI 2001: Advances in Artificial Intelligence. Proceedings, 2001. XII, 666 pages. 2001. (Subseries LNAI).

Vol. 2257: S. Krishnamurthi, C.R. Ramakrishnan (Eds.), Practical Aspects of Declarative Languages. Proceedings, 2002. VIII, 351 pages. 2002.

Vol. 2258: P. Brazdil, A. Jorge (Eds.), Progress in Artificial Intelligence. Proceedings, 2001. XII, 418 pages. 2001. (Subseries LNAI).

Vol. 2259: S. Vaudenay, A.M. Youssef (Eds.), Selected Areas in Cryptography. Proceedings, 2001. XI, 359 pages. 2001.

Vol. 2260: B. Honary (Ed.), Cryptography and Coding. Proceedings, 2001. IX, 416 pages. 2001.

Vol. 2264: K. Steinhöfel (Ed.), Stochastic Algorithms: Foundations and Applications. Proceedings, 2001. VIII, 203 pages. 2001.